GROUNDS
FOR
LIVING

Solid Foundations
for Sure Footing
in Growth and Grace

Jack W. Hayford

Sovereign World

Sovereign World Ltd
PO Box 777
Tonbridge
Kent TN11 0ZS
England

ISBN 1 85240 289 X paperback edition

ISBN 1 85240 297 0 hardback edition

The publishers aim to produce books which will help to extend and build up the Kingdom of God. We do not necessarily agree with every view expressed by the author, or with every interpretation of Scripture expressed. We expect each reader to make his/her judgement in the light of their own understanding of God's Word and in an attitude of Christian love and fellowship.

Typeset by CRB Associates, Reepham, Norfolk.
Printed in the United States of America.

Pleased and Honored
... but with
One Concern!

Introductory remarks by the author, Pastor Jack W. Hayford

I was a 17-year-old college student when I sat under my first professor in a class pursuing theological studies. Two textbooks were involved, each with a radically different style and purpose; the first, Augustus Strong's *Systematic Theology*, the second, Pardington's *Studies in Christian Doctrine*. The first was a towering tome of over 1000 pages, exceeding fine print, and with elaborate development of classic theology written for the scholarly community. The second was less than 300 pages, brief, warmly accessible and popular in approach. The first was to provide for exhaustive study as a scholar's necessity or depth of pursuit required it; the second was to provide an overview of basic truth for the common man.

It is exactly 50 years later as I write these words, with appreciation for the trust and encouragement of Sovereign World to release the present volume for publication in the form offered here. They have invited me to allow their preparation of a resource much like the second one mentioned above. I have been pleased and honored, and gladly consented to do this, but I have felt one concern. That's why I have recalled the distinction between the above two books I used those many years ago, for it serves my desire for the reader's understanding as you take *Grounds for Living* in hand. It is unlike any book of mine – in two regards:

First, due to my inability to schedule "by-my-own-hand" writing time (as with most of my more than thirty books) I have been graciously assisted by the publisher's editorial team. They have taken a 24 cassette teaching series of mine (by the same title) and have diligently distilled those messages into the present printed form. They have beautifully maintained the mood and delivery-form of the *spoken* teachings, mostly presented in Sunday evening and midweek services to our congregation at *The Church On The Way*. The fruit of their labors will, I trust, be acceptable to you. To say I am pleased and honored by their willingness to prepare and publish these teachings is hardly descriptive of my feelings. Far more, I am both heart-warmed and humbled.

Second, this approach, however, inescapably introduces the risk of an author being misread, when gesture, intonation and chalkboard content are unseen by the reader. Thus, I invite the generosity of any who might wonder about the "pulpit delivery" literary style present in this work. Further, with this "popular" approach, I want to distinguish these discussions of Bible doctrine from appearing to any to be an effort at a scholarly theological textbook. Rather, the target here is the average, day-to-day Christian whose hunger for the *essence* of Bible doctrine is focused on *living* it – not critiquing it. For every reader coming with that quest, I hope you find what I've sought to provide: **practical** *understanding* **of** *biblical* **truth** *for* **personal** *use in* **life and service**.

I think pastors and other Bible students will find value here, but they will note that structural precision in style has been sacrificed to retain the practical, personal, congregational teaching approach in the original recorded sessions. Thus, this book is more of a conversation than it is a treatise. Though 24 cassettes barely open the full dimensions of any of these themes (our ministry's tape library contains over 2500 teachings, our catalog over 1000), I believe the divine "heartbeat" of each of these truths is present here. My hope and prayer is that the pulse of these messages will thus warm each reader's heart as he or she feels the Father's heart within each theme.

Again, let me affirm my gratitude for the publisher's belief that multitudes of dedicated Christians and Church workers will be spiritually stimulated and gain practical profit hereby. My sincere thanks to Chris Mungeam and his team for their zeal for dispensing living truth into the hands and hearts of believers around the world. Also, my deepest gratitude and respect for Tim Pettingale whose extensive labor in producing the written text from the taped resources, so abundantly assisted my final work on this book. It's a joy to offer this resource to fellow-servants of our dear Savior who will seek *more* than personal benefit – **to all who seek solid grounds for living that they may serve others with the life, love and Kingdom power of our Lord Jesus – daily.**

Unto Him be glory in the Church!

Jack W. Hayford
Pastor/Chancellor

The Church On The Way
The King's College and Seminary
Van Nuys, California

Contents

PART 9
Heaven: The Ultimate Reward of God's Grace;
Hell: The Ultimate Cost of Rejecting God

PART 10
Tithes and Offerings: The Cycle of Abundance

PART 11
Divine Healing: A Covenant for Life and Strength

✑ PART 1 ✑

The Holy Scriptures: The Fountainhead of Truth

The Holy Scriptures:
The Fountainhead of Truth

Theme Text

"But you have carefully followed my doctrine, manner of life,
purpose, faith, longsuffering, love, perseverance . . .
and that from childhood you have known the Holy Scriptures
which are able to make you wise for salvation . . .
in Christ Jesus.
All Scripture is given by inspiration of God . . .
that the man of God may be complete,
thoroughly equipped for every good work . . .
for the time will come when they will not endure sound doctrine . . .
but you be watchful."

(II Timothy 3:10, 15–17; 4:3, 5)

Solid Ground for Beginning!

To begin the pursuit of truth that we can build a life on, we open to the Holy Scriptures. This is where solid ground for beginning can be found – because it is there that Christ is found.

As believers in the Lord Jesus Christ, we declare that our lives stand firm on one Foundation alone: *Him!* It is there – in Christ alone – that confidence can be found and secured, establishing certainty about who we are, what we are destined to become, and what God has called us to do.

How can we speak with such certainty in such an uncertain world? The reason is simply yet unshakably founded in the *truth* of these statements which, along with many others, have been revealed to humankind through the Bible – the Word of God. This is the divinely given record of divinely directed history. The truth we study has been worked out in the crucible of life circumstances. The Bible is not a textbook of high ideals alone, it is a handbook of those truths being experienced by real people – and recorded for our benefit.

> *"For whatever things were written before were written for our learning, that we through the patience and comfort of the Scriptures might have hope."* (Romans 15:4)

Our theme text observes of Timothy, "You've known these things from childhood" by which Paul is affirming the practical, life-establishing benefit and power of the Scriptures to "make life work." The truth in the Holy Scriptures has been *transmitted* to us by the Holy Spirit, who breathed the words onto the pages through the pens of men whom He moved and inspired. So our confidence in receiving and believing them, and our belief they will "work" in practical living, is not based on the arrogance of a humanly contrived system. This is more than an observation of mere religious sincerity, it is a conviction rooted in divine revelation. The *inner-knowledge* that grips us with confidence is rooted in the *absolutes of the objective truth revealed in God's Word – the Holy Bible.*

The Holy Spirit "gave" us the Scriptures by revelation, and both history and personal experience attest to Their life-giving power. We embrace the Bible therefore, not as if It were some good-luck charm, and certainly not as an idol, but recognizing It for what It is: the only historically verified, categorically authoritative textbook on the ultimate issues of life – the only sure foundation on which to build our lives.

Those who are skeptical of such claims try to erode the authenticity of the Bible by saying it is unreliable, contradictory, or simply a collection of "quaint mythical stories". But, as we shall see, such accusations are totally without substance.

People who have investigated the "holy books" of other religions have found the Bible to be without peer among religious literature – chiefly for its historic authenticity and its consistent transmission throughout the centuries. The more you look at the teachings presented in these other holy books, however sincere or interesting their content, the more you are drawn back to the Bible. It stands unique, alone, in the library of spiritual resource. See the beauty of Its balance; the wholesomeness of Its message; the life-giving power It brings in liberating, transforming and energizing human experience! That is why, time and again, objective, academic analysts of the Bible have so often come to faith in Christ – simply by reading the Scriptures, simply discovering the radical difference in this Book. It is one like no other.

How the Bible is viewed

How the Bible is viewed and how it is used, determines everything about the thought and texture of life within any grouping in the Christian community. The mindset and the manner, the viewpoint and the use of the Bible, is radically different in at least three major circles of nominal Christian faith. I use the word "nominal" here, simply because we are talking about the very broad field of Christian tradition – a realm that encompasses numerous traits and variations of belief. The third category we will examine is especially, by definition "liberal", in which some would conjecture there might be no "real Christians" at all. But there are, no doubt, people within every tradition who – notwithstanding the faith, practice or unbelief of others in their group – still put their faith in the Savior above all. So, in looking at these *general* distinctives, we attack none who love Christ.

The Evangelical view

The Evangelical view holds an approach to the Scriptures that sees the Bible as a source of *life*. This view can be described as virile and vital – even victorious, if you will, for the texture of the life of those holding it is made increasingly vibrant through the Bible. This Book is a *fountain* of life to them, because "living faith" flows to and through them as they open themselves to It. Generally, this category of Christian believer is called "evangelical" – because they focus on the good news of the gospel (evangel) and the mission of world evangelism. It includes hosts of denominational and independent fellowships, pentecostals, charismatics and other Christians.

Central to this group's view of the Bible is that it is the authoritative Word of God and that *every word* of Scripture, as originally given, is inspired by the Holy Spirit and intended for our benefit:

> *"All Scripture is given by inspiration of God, and is profitable for doctrine, for reproof, for correction, for instruction in righteousness."*
> (II Timothy 3:16)

They also believe that the Bible is presently applicable to our lives – the belief that the life and truth of the Word of God is for practical, daily growth and development, powerful to effect personal transformation, useful and instructive, giving wisdom and insight for living.

"You have carefully followed my doctrine, manner of life ... from childhood you have known the Holy Scriptures, which are able to make you wise for salvation through faith which is in Christ Jesus ... I charge you therefore ... Preach the word! ... convince, rebuke, exhort, with all longsuffering and teaching."

(II Timothy 3:10–4:2)

The Apostle Paul modeled true Christian faith and doctrine to his protégé, Timothy. He urged Timothy to "live out" that which he had learned and to teach it to others. Evangelical Christians accept the charge to do as Timothy did, even though it may stand in stark contrast to a culture that embraces their other ideas about the Bible, supposedly clever, innovative, philosophical notions that reject the life-giving, substantial message of truth that alone will endure.

The Orthodox view

I am making a distinct use of the term *orthodox, not* as a reference to that large segment of Christian tradition embracing the Orthodox Church. Rather, I use the word for its strictest definition, literally meaning, "the bones are set straight", that is, "orthodox" in the sense that nothing is allowed to go "crooked". (Greek *orthos*, straight, erect, upright; *orthopodeo*, straight feet, to walk in a straight course.) So, I describe the people who hold a second Christian perspective of the Bible.

There is a sizeable segment of the Body of Christ comprising people with this texture of life: they are solid, stable, and secure in their convictions about the trustworthiness of the great truths of the Bible. They believe that the Bible is an historically accurate document giving account of the truths about the Living God. But the Bible, rather than being a book of life to them, is viewed more in terms of a reference book – it is the place where they derive the source of their beliefs. They see the Bible as accurate, as God's Word, and the rulebook for correct faith and moral behavior. But the present dynamic possibilities of appropriating God's Word to present-moment realities is not generally a focus in this circle. Biblical truth is, in this view, a body of convictions about God that should be embraced and never allowed to be lost, but about which one need not necessarily *do anything* further, other than simply *believing* in the truths. For example, to passionately propagate the truths of Scripture, or to presently apply its promises as Paul encouraged Timothy to do, would not be a characteristic of this group.

This does not mean that orthodox Christians do not possess deeply held beliefs. They would, in many cases, *believe* the same truths as the evangelical Christian and be deeply committed to them. But there would be an absence of the expectation that the Holy Spirit who gave the Word, would presently bring that Word alive in them today. Nor does it mean that Evangelicals are in any position to look scornfully upon such a group. In fact, because of the academic nature of the orthodox approach, this section of the Body of Christ has provided some of the finest learning resources available to the Christian community. They have sustained a base for earnest scholarship concerning the foundational doctrines of the Bible. We are wisely humble to be grateful for this, and while I do not imply a deficiency of scholarship in the evangelical community, we feel the Lord has not given us His Word for study and scholarly pursuit alone. He desires that our theology be *outworked* in our lives, resulting in an active and dynamic faith by the power of the Holy Spirit.

The Liberal view

This third category is somewhat difficult to define because its borders are often blurred and indistinct. An "anything goes" relativist mind-set characterizes some members of this group. A highly selective "Believe whatever you want, wherever it fits" mentality abounds.

While this term describes a group that contains people of nominal Christian persuasion, who would refer to the Bible at times, and may see it as a source of great comfort, perhaps in times of need or distress, its authority and decisive truth is not final to their view. They may refer to the Bible, but their "liberal" attitude disregards the ultimacy and finality of Jesus Christ as the world's Savior, and the certainty of the truth of all the Bible's content. They would generally see the Bible as a book containing faith-inspiring stories, legends and myths that only carry weight in relation to each person's subjective interpretation. Other religion's scriptures would be seen as equally "inspired by God," – even great poetry, novels or other literature as similarly inspired.

People in this group, though acknowledging "something unique and special" about Jesus, would resist, or at least be very hesitant to affirm such crucial issues as: He was the Christ, the only begotten Son of God; that He was born of the Virgin Mary, completely sinless; that He bore the sins of the world through His death on the Cross; that His blood was atoning for our salvation; that He literally and physically rose from the dead and ascended to the right hand of God in heaven, from where He will literally and physically come again.

Members of this group, when discussing such specific truths as mentioned above, will often prefer not to take a definite stance. They may say, without being critical of the beliefs of others, "These things seem too mysterious for me to understand and I don't want to be opinionated about them." However, one often finds this benign "being non-opinionated" changes when they reference the first group – the Evangelicals – whom they would say *are opinionated*. Thus, their opinion is that no *final opinion* should ever be held on the Bible, God, Jesus, or anything else. The philosophies of humanism and relativism establish the mood of the liberal. The Evangelical's viewpoint would appear to them to be extremely narrow-minded.

Four ways we squarely stand upon the Bible

The larger circle of denominations and church groups to which my own congregation and denomination belongs, holds to the evangelical view of Scripture. We embrace the Bible as the sourcebook and grounds for authority with our doctrine and as the guiding light for our daily lives. We stand solid, bold and forthright – the classic meaning of the word *"foursquare"* – recognizing the living Word of God as the only sure and eternal foundation for *any* church, denomination, group or individual to stand upon. Let us examine four ways in which we can squarely – solidly – stand in regard to the Word of God: trusting its **accuracy**, believing its **history**, coming under its **authority**, and receiving its **prophecy**.

1. We trust its accuracy –

▶ *The Bible is antiquity's most trustworthy document.*

Knowing that the Bible is accurate and trustworthy is an essential and logical starting point for any thinking person – all the more so considering that we are affirming it as the foundational guiding document for our lives. But, how do we know that it is what it claims to be?

People will regularly raise questions about the trustworthiness of the Bible, simply because it is an ancient book. They argue that the Bible has been re-translated and copied so many times, that one can't be confident that the version we have today is the same as the original Scriptures. They sometime propose a "lack of reliability" of the ancient manuscripts that form the basis for all modern translations of the Bible.

However, those who are committed enough to study, and to seek to verify them, can go back to the literary resources from which our modern Bibles originate, and they will discover the undeniable fact: what we read in our Bibles today *is* what was originally written. Volumes exist which explain the research and findings of scholars regarding the Bible's trustworthiness, but for our purpose in this one, we must focus just a few of their findings.

The accuracy of the Bible is:

- **Evidenced by the number of existent manuscripts**. Many of the most well known works of antiquity, such as the writings of Plato and Aristotle, are known from only 25–40 manuscripts – that is 25–40 copies of their writings made by *others* and dating to within a few hundred years of the author's writing, but not the original writings of the men themselves. In contrast, there are more than 6000 manuscripts or parts of the New Testament, many from within the first two centuries AD, that are available for us to compare. This large number, from scattered locations, from early yet varied dates, provides a base for comparison that would give every reason to expect a high degree of variance between manuscripts. Yet notably, although not surprisingly if the Bible really is the Word of God, there is an incredibly high level of consistency and continuity between them.

- **Evidenced in the reliability of the text**. Because of the fact that manuscripts were hand-copied, one might well assume that errors and mistakes could easily creep in. The *Iliad* by Homer, for instance, contains 15,600 lines of which literary scholars question the accuracy of 746 lines (due to errors or omissions). According to literary scholars (and it is important to stress here that these are not necessarily Christian believers, but people pursing the New Testament solely as an historical Greek manuscript) there are 20,000 lines, only 40 lines of which have given their most critical eye any reason to question the accuracy. Even more profoundly, and significant to every believer in the Bible, even among these few contested "lines", *not one* relates to a major doctrinal issue.

- **Evidenced by the discovery of the Dead Sea Scrolls**. Before the Dead Sea Scrolls were discovered, the oldest Old Testament manuscripts dated to the tenth century AD (known as the Masoretic text). Given that the book of Malachi is estimated to have been written around the fourth century before Christ, and the Masoretic text is dated around the tenth century after Christ, there existed a hiatus of about 1400 years between the time of the last writer in the OT and the oldest existing copy of the Hebrew Scriptures. Then – the discovery of The Dead Sea Scrolls in 1948! This find has been categorically described as the greatest archeological discovery of the entire 20th century! Significant for us is that, for example, a scroll of the complete text of the book of Isaiah was found – a copy dated to 125 BC, almost one thousand years earlier than the Masoretic text! With a millennium having transpired between the two, scholars expected to find that many changes and mistakes had been introduced into the Masoretic text when comparing them to the Scrolls. But they found almost none – the integrity of the text was remarkably well preserved, a full thousand years' passage giving evidence for our believing the Bible we have in hand today is indeed what was written long ago.

- **Evidenced by the testimony of scholars**. Frederick Kenyon, a leading authority in the field of New Testament textual criticism, said,

"One word of warning already referred to must be emphasized in conclusion: no fundamental doctrine of Christian faith rests on any disputed reading in any of the manuscripts. Constant references to mistakes and divergences of readings, such as the plan of this book necessitates, might give rise to the doubt whether the substance, as well as the language of the Bible, is not open to question. It cannot be too strongly asserted that in substance, the text of the Bible is certain. Especially is this the case with the New Testament. The number of manuscripts of the New Testament, of early translations from it, of quotations from it in the oldest writers of the Church, is so large that it is practically certain that the true reading of every doubtful passage is preserved in some one or other of these ancient authorities. This can be said of no other ancient book in the world. Scholars are satisfied they possess substantially the true text of the principal Greek and Roman writers whose works have come down to us: of Sophocles, of Thucydides, of Cicero, of Virgil, yet our knowledge of their writings depends on a mere handful of manuscripts, whereas the manuscripts of the New Testament are counted by hundreds and even thousands."

We can therefore say with certainty, that when we come to the Scriptures, we rightly trust in their accuracy. Further evidence we haven't time to elaborate also exists within the broader field of middle eastern archeology, but suffice to say regarding the literary text of Bible alone – in it, we come to a book not only *given* by God's Holy Spirit, but also *sovereignly protected* by Him through the centuries.

2. We believe its history –

▶ *The Bible is unique regarding primary issues of history.*

There are two primary issues that the Bible addresses concerning the history of earth and Man. First, *Creation* – the Bible is unique in its disclosure of the origin of all things regarding earth and humankind; how Man came into being; his environment, and the purpose of humankind here. Second, *Redemption* – how Man, created in the image of God, fell from grace, and how God in *His grace* provided a plan to bring about his recovery. It is important that we examine what the Bible has to say regarding these two issues, if we are to present a reasoned argument to any who ask, as we seek to communicate the Gospel to others.

With regard to creation

- We believe that God created all things – the earth, the seas, the heavens, the whole universe. We believe that the transcendent God made them and that He exists beyond and beside nature. God is not infused in His creation; He is not part of nature as humanistic philosophy suggests; rather He is external to it and sustains it (see John 1:1–3; Colossians 1:17; Hebrews 1:3, 11:3).

- The Bible does not provide us with a conclusive schedule regarding the timing of the events of creation. Genesis 1 describes a series of "days" during which a "restructuring" took place after a great chaos had come into an already-existent creation. The "days" of Genesis 1 are not necessarily 24-hour days. The Hebrew word used to describe these "periods" could mean literal "days" or could refer to geological ages. We cannot conclusively verify one or the other from the text of Scripture, but the Bible does not require that we hold a particular belief about the *schedule* of creation. The Scriptures simply identify God as the Creator of all things and call us to acknowledge and pledge our allegiance to Him.

- The Bible tells us about the origins of life on earth. The "kinds" which God created and the "species" which man has subsequently defined are not necessarily the same categories. There is widespread evidence of *mutation* within species – that is, the transforming of one species into a distinct and different variety. For example, God created dogs. He created the dog as a "kind" of animal. The Bible does not insist that we believe God created *all variations* of dog at one time. It is possible, through cross-breeding over a period of time, that a variety of dog that did not appear before comes into existence. There can be mutation within species (not *trans*mutation), and this in no way attempts to remove or reduce the fact that God created that species.

- Humankind, "Man" of Adam's race, is a special creation. Adam's race is now the only race of man on the planet. However, the Bible record does not preempt the possibility that beings existed on our planet prior to the creation of Adam's race. Biblical evidence is thin, but some scholars believe that a man-like race of beings did live on earth before Adam. The primary issue is, however, the uniqueness of the human race as we know it today is due to God's uniquely and specially *creating* us, and in His sovereignly unique purposes for doing so.

With regard to redemption

- God promised a Redeemer because He loves Man and He has a high destiny for us all. When Man sinned, God could have obliterated His original creation of humankind in the Garden of Eden and started over. But because of the uniquely purposed destiny He has in mind for our race, He instituted the processes of redemption. From the moment of the Fall, through His dealings through the Jewish nation, after His call upon Abraham's life, in the fullness of time, through that people, God introduced to the world His own Son, begotten of the Virgin Mary – God incarnate in our midst. Through Jesus, the Father taught us what kind of God He was and how redemption was to happen. Jesus lived sinlessly and with purpose, and He died to bear the penalty for the sins of all mankind. We will study God's plan of redemption fully in later chapters.

3. We come under its authority –

▶ *The Bible calls to faithful, sensible obedience.*

Paul instructed Timothy: *"Continue in the things you have learned and been assured of."* He emphasized the importance of *steadfastly responding and obeying* the Word of God (II Timothy 3:14). From childhood he had been taught the way of the Lord (II Timothy 1:5), and here he is called to live it out, having been "assured" of its truth and authority.

Peter also wrote profoundly, calling to a life lived in obedience to the truth and authority of the Holy Scriptures – "precious promises" by which we grow, become fruitful and finally enter "the everlasting kingdom" (II Peter 1:4, 11). The grounds for the authority he invokes is the inspiration of Scripture: *"Prophecy never came by the will of man, but holy men of God spoke as they were moved by the Holy Spirit"* (II Peter 1:21).

Here, Peter is citing the fact that the Bible not only has life-giving power, but life-governing authority, because its human authors were agents through which the Holy Spirit breathed the Word. To grasp the seriousness of this issue in his view, note one of the most pivotal statements in all the Bible about the importance of Scripture. It is presented in the way he contrasts *what the Bible says* (its authority as being conclusive and ultimate) with *what human experience suggests* (even at its highest and best). Notice:

- Peter first describes his experience as one of the three disciples present at Christ's transfiguration, saying, *"...we were eye-witnesses of His majesty."* He gives details of how they were on the mountain with Jesus when this event occurred, even including, *"And we heard this voice which came from heaven..."*

- Peter concludes his report of this experience by saying, *"And so we have the prophetic word confirmed."* In other words, (1) he saw Jesus transformed, (2) he even heard the voice of God speaking from heaven, but (3) *beyond all of that* he seeks to draw our attention to the *weight and authority of the Scriptures* that had prophesied the coming of Christ in the first place. It is a profound demonstration from apostolic experience: God's inspired Word of the Holy Scriptures, not personal experience, is the authority upon which we found our life and our faith in Christ.

In contemporary culture we see a constant sliding away from the authoritative directives of the Word. Each generation of Man makes its statements regarding what it sees as the "outmoded nature of religious requirements" – such as the Ten Commandments. They say that the ways of God are "traditions" that will not work in our modern society. However, the result of not obeying the authoritative truth, objectively stated and supernaturally revealed in God's Word, will always prove futile in life and fatal in eternity. God's instruction in His Word is timeless. We heed it, not to verify ourselves as religious bigots or mindless drones, but simply because we've found His life-principles *work*.

4. We receive its prophecies –

▶ *The Bible speaks clearly about the future.*

There are extensive and elaborate passages of Scripture which relate to prophecy – both those regarding future events and many regarding the continually present circumstances of humankind. We stand squarely upon God's Word because we see the evidence of past prophecies having been fulfilled, prophecies regarding the future being fulfilled, and every reason to believe others will yet be fulfilled.

Prophecy relating to the present

- Prophecy includes the Word speaking to us daily as we read and meditate upon it. *"This Book of the Law shall not depart from your mouth, but you shall meditate in it day and night, that you may observe to do according to all that is written in it. For then you will make your way prosperous, and then you will have good success"* (Joshua 1:8). We should spend time in the Word daily, meditating on it and allowing it to distill in us. As we do this, the Holy Spirit can literally "speak" to us. It is *present prophecy* as He guides us and speaks into our life.

- Prophecy includes the preaching of the Word, and its impact upon our lives as the Spirit brings the Word alive. *"The letter kills, but the Spirit gives life"* (II Corinthians 3:6).

- Prophecy includes public utterance by the gift of the Holy Spirit (I Corinthians 12:7; 14:3) and the private, inner voice of the Holy Spirit to one's own heart (John 16:13). These prophecies are always to be subject to, and judged by, the Word of God. It alone is the plumb line and the measuring rod of truth. The private "word" of the Holy Spirit will *never* contradict the final revelation of the written Word of God.

Prophecies relating to the future

- **Regarding the Second Coming of Christ**. The Bible reveals that Jesus Christ, the Son of God will descend again from heaven and return to earth. We are shown this both as it applies to the hope of the Church, as well as to the fate of all of mankind.

    i. As it applies to the Church: *"For the Lord Himself shall descend from heaven with a shout, with the voice of an archangel, and with the trumpet of God ... Then we who are alive and remain shall be caught up together with them..."* (I Thessalonians 4:16–17).

    ii. As it applies to all people: *"All who are in the graves will hear His voice and come forth – those who have done good, to the resurrection of life, and those who have done evil, to the resurrection of condemnation"* (John 5:28–29).

- **Regarding Heaven and Hell**.

    i. Hell cannot be defined by the shallow human depictions of a God having an angry tantrum, or by medieval caricatures of people boiling in bubbling vats of liquid fire. No, hell is worse than that. Without minimizing the fact that impending fiery judgment is a reality Jesus described Himself (Matthew 18:19; Mark 9:42–48), and the Lake of Fire is a biblical truth (Revelation 20:7–15), the horror of hell is in its endless, pointless, relentless extension into eternity of the life a person chooses now. It is the revealed, logical projection, unto eternity, of the result of setting oneself against God. It is the self-imposed consequence of eternal separation from the God whose loving purpose and plan of redemption was either ignored or unwanted and refused. The worst thing about hell will be the realization it was not assigned, it was *chosen* – either by decision or default. We take it seriously, and it contributes to the believer's passion for evangelism (II Corinthians 5:11–15; Jude 20–23). It is against God's will that any of humankind should be destined to hell (II Peter 3:9), but even the will of God cannot preempt the choice of the human soul that wills to resist His will. It is warned of in the Scripture, and to be avoided by seizing today on the offer of divine grace and eternal life.

    ii. Heaven, likewise, is more grand and glorious than the equally shallow notions depicting scenes where syrupy music accompanies the oo-ing and ah-ing of winged singers, whose countenances seem painted with semi-mindless smiles arched beneath ethereal, drippy-eyed gazes. The pitifully small idea of heaven as an endless party on a cloud, as an eternal vacation, or as a playful sexual romp, cater to the secular mindset that spiritual reality – if it exists

– is either irrelevant, boring or self-serving. In contrast, the Bible shows heaven as a place *prepared* (John 14:1–6) – indicating there is a *plan*, not only to its architecture, but a plan with eternal purpose for all who go there. It will be an endless, unfolding discovery of God's great destiny for us (Ephesians 2:7); the joyous reward – not for any human achievement, but for the simple wisdom of choosing to receive His love and life. It will be eternal "oneness" in the Spirit, with our Father God and our Savior Jesus Christ; joined forever to discover what our Creator has destined to be our role in serving Him throughout the cosmos (Romans 8:18–22). Purpose and fulfillment – joy untainted by sorrow – characterize the Bible's description of heaven (Revelation 22:1–5). It is God's promise, to be believed and anticipated with hope.

Thus, the revelation of God's Word in the Scriptures of the Holy Bible, given in the sixty-six books of the Old and New Testaments, constitute the conclusive and final authority for our lives. With this "Ground" to stand upon, let us proceed to study – to *know God, and to know His Word.*

"Let us know, let us pursue the knowledge of the Lord.
His going forth is established as the morning;
He will come to us like the rain,
like the latter and former rain to the earth."

(Hosea 6:3)

PART 2

The Eternal Godhead: The Glory of the Trinity

THE ETERNAL GODHEAD (PART 1): BEGINNING TO KNOW THE TRINITY

THEME TEXT

"The grace of the Lord Jesus Christ, and the love of God, and the communion of the Holy Spirit be with you all. Amen."
(II Corinthians 13:14)

In the light of God's Word, and the beauty of His self-revelation through creation's glory and redemption's grace, let us begin a study of the eternal Godhead – Father, Son and Holy Spirit. Our theme text above is one of many NT passages that refer to the Trinity, and evidence the truth of the Persons constituting the Godhead.

We say "persons" because, as we shall later discuss, we are forced to use human terminology in our attempt to describe the marvel and mystery of the *God above all* and *Creator of all*. That there are *three-in-one* is clearly taught, and that they are entirely *one-in-three* is as well. That it is so mysterious a revelation should not surprise us. That the very essence of God's being itself would exceed our full capacity to understand is as logical as any proposition imaginable. Nonetheless, He has disclosed enough about the wonder of His being and person, so it is also clear He welcomes our thoughtful inquiry into this mystery.

The self-revelation of God to humankind has been a progressive unfolding, initiated from His side to ours. If He had not, there is no way we could even begin to know or understand Him. But He has revealed Himself, and it clearly is His heart to invite us to open to, and explore, the wonder of His Person and Being.

When the first human was *created* and first stood upright in the garden, he was immediately introduced to the One who had created him. God introduced Himself to Adam; gave him instructions about life and how it could be lived, and showed him how his intended destiny could be fulfilled (Genesis 2:1–20). He was equally clear in His assignment to both the first couple, regarding their intended purpose (Genesis 1:28–30) and their relationship to each other (Genesis 2:21–25).

Every aspect of God's heart and personal interest is unfolded in the story of Eden, as we see Him designing a paradise for a creature without any knowledge of sin or sickness; without anything other than the high destiny and purpose God intended. Sadly, however, God's purposes were violated by the Fall of Man, through sin – the disaster of disobedience that removed everything in our world outside God's originally created order and purpose. As a result, God's mercy set into motion a plan of redemption that would eventually bring a Savior to earth. The purpose would be to ultimately bring humankind back into relationship with God, and thereby return to them the possibilities intended in God's original plan for each one – personally and collectively.

Originally, Man was created with a rich and full revelation of God – a Person-to-person communion with Him on a daily basis. But so much was lost through the Fall – blinding man to God's glory, goodness and purposes – that God virtually had to start again in His communications with mankind. Despite the fact that Man had previously had a full awareness of God, and walked in a constant companionship and communication with Him, now – like trans- mission cables torn by a storm – the lines of contact were down. From that point, the flow of the Bible's narrative is a record of God's process of seeking Man – to help him know *God* – that is, to know His nature, His heart, His love, His grace, His will, His salvation and His personal purpose for each of His creatures. From then until now, He has been relentlessly, mercifully reaching to a world of creatures – all broken, bound and blinded by sin. In doing so, little by little through the ages, He unfolded more and more of His will, His Word and His way to human understanding, until finally presenting us with Himself – His Son Jesus, God incarnate.

As we walk through the Scriptures we see a *growing revelation* of God's heart toward us and His purpose for Man. At each encounter with Man, God is seeking to reveal more of Himself, and the purpose of His revelation is that humankind may once more *know Him*. *Knowing God* is the primary purpose of Man – to know Him intimately; to know His heart; to know how He thinks; to know His personal interest in us; to know the economy of His dealings – how He relates.

The Bible unfolds so much regarding God's character, His nature, and His disposition of love toward Man, nobody should ever need to experience anything less than a full and intimate relationship with Him. Imagine knowing God's heart, mind and presence in the same way Adam enjoyed in the beginning. That is the objective God has when He calls us to personally come to His Son, turn from our own ways, and give our life over to Jesus Christ – God-come-to-redeem us. Being "redeemed" – purchased from loss, reconditioned with new life and restored to new hope – is possible for every one of us. The price of Jesus' blood and death on the Cross is the payment that unchains fallen Man from the impact of his Fall. Intimate relationship with God can be found with the Father once again. The grounds and basis for such a relationship as Adam had with God has been *re-established* for you – for each of us. [1]

However, having a relationship with the Father through the Lord Jesus Christ, and coming to know Him intimately and personally, requires more than your just having been *saved*. It means allowing the Holy Spirit to teach you "who God is" from the Scriptures. It means allowing Him, through the passage of time and experience, to integrate the life-giving power of the Word into your life, so that the dynamic of "knowing Him" becomes real and active in your heart.

How can we know God?

God wants to reveal Himself to you. He does not want to remain mysterious or unknowable. He wants us to experience His strength, His grace, the provision of His goodness, His faithfulness. He wants us to ever-increasingly *know Him* in a continually deepening way. But to do so calls us to answer a pre-requisite: we must come with open, ready, teachable, hungry hearts. Jeremiah 29:13 tells us that only if we truly seek God with all our heart, will we find Him. This is neither a mystical or a mental pursuit – neither occultic nor intellectual. To seek with the heart is to commit our will and affections to wanting Him; to open to His Word of Truth which teaches us of Him.

It is interesting to note a seeming contradiction to that text when comparing it to Job 11:7 – *"Can a man by searching find God?"* But the latter verse is a rhetorical question; one that makes a valid point, but not one that contradicts the former Jeremiah 29:13 reference. Both scriptures are highlighting the same fact: no one ever gets to know God merely by intellectual aspiration, but only by a heart quest. One can study the facts about God and analyze them – acquire information about Him, and grow in mental knowledge about Him – but that is neither the knowledge of foremost need to us, nor what God chiefly wants us to know. His desire is that we should know *Him* – have a *heart knowledge* of Him, not only a *head knowledge*; that we should *know Him*, not just *know about Him*. He wants this in order that He might bring to us and in us, all that He intends for us.

The Bible is clear in telling us that a mere intellectual pursuit of God is a futile exercise, not only because it misses His point for us, but because His greatness transcends the vain supposition of the most brilliant mind that God could be "learned." This is not to demean human intelligence, but simply to honestly acknowledge its limits – and to acknowledge God's directives as to how He may be known by us. Our Creator-Father seeks to make Himself known, and He wants to do it in a way that will allow Him to *apply* that knowledge to our lives – distilling it in a Person-to-person way that brings about the *change* and *transformation* we all need in our lives. This is what "knowing God" is about.

Ephesians 1:17–18 is a prayer for knowing God – the Apostle Paul's prayer for believers to *know God*:

> *"...that the God of our Lord Jesus Christ, the Father of glory, may give to you the spirit of wisdom and revelation in the knowledge of Him, the eyes of your understanding being enlightened; that you may know what is the hope of His calling, what are the riches of His inheritance in the saints..."*

These verses show his prayer as focusing two specific things:

1. *"...that God ... may give you the spirit of wisdom and revelation..."* The prayer invites God's action that would bring those for whom the prayer is offered, a present working of the Holy Spirit that would impart both *wisdom* and *revelation* to them. "Wisdom" refers to our receiving of *specific, practical, workable truth* from God. "Revelation" refers to being given the insight and understanding of *how that truth can be applied* to your life. Nothing here is mystical. The passion in the apostle's prayer is because of his desire that people *know* God; realizing that as they do, their lives will become increasingly affected and shaped by that knowledge.

    This NT concept of "wisdom and revelation" is perfectly in line with the thought expressed in Proverbs 1:7: *"The fear of the Lord is the beginning of knowledge."* It means that "fearing" God – *reverencing Him, understanding Who He is and what He is like, and responding to Him appropriately* – leads to a *change* and *transformation* in our person. When you or I understand God's heart and nature, it affects the way our lives are lived because we are coming to truly *know* Him.

2. *"...the eyes of your understanding* [literally, the "eyes of your heart"] *being enlightened* [opened] *that you may* **know** *what is the hope of His calling..."* Paul does not want the people *only* to have information. He desires that the knowledge they are gaining about God will become *incarnate* – that is, *"known"* in the intimate sense of "knowledge" – in the practical, penetrating application of God's intended purposes for us ("the hope of His calling").

So, the purpose of our studying the character of God is that we might know Him better and therefore respond to Him appropriately. God's desire is that, in our knowing Him, we might respond to His purposes for us. That's why we study "doctrine." It is not for the purpose of accumulating *information*, but for the practical benefit of our *transformation*. Doctrinal truth ought always target practical purpose, not philosophical investigation. It isn't given to us to dabble in or discuss as mere ideology, but that we might know the way to *Life*, and commit to Life's way to *live*.

The unfolding revelation of God

After the Fall of Man broke humankind's initially close relationship with God, the subsequent separation and loss of intimate communication presented a problem. Blinded and bound, human tendencies were away from God – wandering in sin, wallowing in bondage. But God initiated a progressive unfolding of revelation; first, to reestablish fellowship (communication/relationship) and then to restore understanding (insight into God's person and purpose for us).

To restore an understanding of Himself – of His nature and attributes, God, like a patient teacher, begins to re-educate humankind. One of the foremost ways He began was by disclosing Himself through various *names* – terms and titles which spoke of divine attributes and aspects of His nature and purpose. These were not varied "names" because God was changing His name in any way, but *descriptive terms* that were to help humankind gain an ever broadening picture of His greatness, goodness and glory. As each name was disclosed – always in life-settings and amid practical encounters as He showed Himself to ready hearts – another facet of *"the manifold wisdom of God"* was seen – an ever enlarging picture of what God is really like (Ephesians 3:10 – literally, the multi-faceted, or "multi-colored" glory of God).

Man's separation from God plunged him into spiritual darkness, but II Corinthians 4:6 speaks of God's grace in pouring light toward us all: *"For it is the God who commanded light to shine out of the darkness who has shone in our hearts to give the light of the knowledge of the glory of God in the face of Jesus Christ."* These words speak of a dual reality: the glory of God, and the face of Jesus Christ. In short, mankind in darkness, out of touch with the glory of God's Person, was in need of finding the light of that glory again. It is in this context that God *began*, step by step revealing Himself from season to season, as revealed in the OT, disclosing qualities of His character, attributes of His Person, by meeting people in circumstances where they sought or needed Him. When He responded, often it would occasion the revealing of yet another "name" – that is, a term or title summarizing that aspect of His being that "shone into the darkness" as divine grace invaded that human situation.

Following, we review a list of names by which God was progressively schooling mankind in the nature of His own fullness of being. But remember, our text above notes that a NT expression of the same realities about the Father are shown "in the face of Jesus." We will make a comparative study of some of these OT names and events when we see the NT names displaying "the glory of God – in Jesus" later, in Chapter 4. There, we will see Jesus Himself fulfilling that part of His mission involving His revelation of "the light of the knowledge of God" to humankind in darkness. And we will hear Him say, "Whoever has seen me has seen the Father." But now, let us look at 15 "names of God" from the OT.

We have grouped them in five main categories:

1. The Living God.

2. The Unchanging God.

3. The Almighty God.

4. The Saving God.

5. The Keeping God.

Relatively little elaboration of each is given here, as we reserve detailed development for later, when *Immanuel* comes – God with us. While in the OT the Creator-Father God says, "You may know me by this name," it is in the NT, when God becomes flesh among us, sending His Son to dwell among us, that we will see the incarnation of each Name.

Names of God in the OT

Here are the OT passages and names where God reveals features of Himself – attributes of His nature, traits of His character – as He *acts* in human interests, and *unfurls* new dimensions of Himself to become memorized in "a Name".

1. The Living God

- **Jehovah, I Am.** "[When] *they say to me, 'What is His name?' What shall I say to them? And God said to Moses, 'I AM WHO I AM'"* (Exodus 3:13–15). While both earlier and later passages of Scripture show God's primary and preferred name is *Yaweh* (Jehovah), this seldom spoken, hardly defined Name was held in deep reverence as "the Name," and reverently acknowledged as beyond definition – as, ultimately, God truly is. But here, in His words to Moses, we are given probably the closest and clearest explanation of what the idea Jehovah means – *"I Am that I Am"* – the One who is self-existent, beyond time and space, yet ever available and present to us.

- **El Olam, the Eternal** (Psalm 90:2) *"...from everlasting to everlasting, You are God."* Denotes His eternal nature. Psalm 90 speaks of the frailty and transience of Man. In strong contrast we see that the Lord is, *"...from everlasting to everlasting ... God."* In this Psalm attributed to Moses, noting the finiteness of human life – especially its fragility manifest in the death of those who perished during the wilderness journey – God is revealed as a timeless, enduring, "forever" kind of Person who has always been and shall always be.

- **Avi, Father** (Isaiah 64:8). *Avi* is the Hebrew word for "Father". The Aramaic equivalent to the word *Abba* that most people are familiar with. This name reveals the Father-heart of God; also referencing the same season of Israel's wilderness travel (see vs. 7–13), Isaiah notes the paternal patience that embraced them, even beyond the self-inflicted judgment that punished them.

2. The Unchanging God

- **Jehovah Ha Tsur, the Rock** (Deuteronomy 32:15) *"Then he forsook God ... the Rock of his salvation."* Deuteronomy 32 is a prophetic psalm of Moses, warning Israel of the disposition of the flesh to vacillate, to change, to lack sturdy commitment. It is in this setting that God is called our "Rock" five times, revealing His immutability – changelessness, steadfastness, absolute and utter reliability (vs. 4, 15, 18, 30, 31).

- **Jehovah Shammah** (Ezekiel 48:35) *"... and the name of the city from that day shall be: THE LORD IS THERE."* Reveals His omnipresence. (The historical context of this OT revelation is detailed in Chapter 4.)

3. The Almighty God

- **El Shaddai, the Almighty** (Genesis 17:1) *"I am Almighty God ... "* Reveals His omnipotence. (Historical context reserved for Chapter 4.)

- **El Elyon, God Most High** (Genesis 14:18–20) *"... Blessed be Abram of God Most High, Possessor of heaven and earth."* Reveals His exalted place of dominion, including His omniscience – seeing and knowing all things from His place *on high*, as the Most High. The setting is at Abraham's return from the night encounter resulting in recovering the hostages taken by the five kings. Melchizedek directs worship as Abraham tithes on the plunder he has gathered, and blesses him. As a priest of "the Most High," Melchizedek is seen by scholars as a spiritual continuum representing the faithful worship of the true and living God from the time of the patriarch before the flood. In short, "El Elyon" is noting the same God that was worshipped by the godly reach back to Adam; the "original" Creator-God, above all.

- **Jehovah Sabaoth, Lord of Hosts** (Psalm 24:10) *"Who is this King of Glory? The Lord of Hosts... "* In this prophetic Psalm of the King yet to come, David uses the name of God that reveals His position as Ruler of the angelic host.

- **Adonai Jehovah** (Genesis 15:1–2) *"Abram said, 'Lord God...'"* Abraham's understanding of the fact that his life is under covenant commitment to God, references Him in terms that acknowledge his submissive, servant role in relationship to the

One Whom he has come to know as his Owner and Master – the God of all his life, potential and destiny.

4. *The Saving God*

- **Jehovah Tsidkenu** (Jeremiah 23:6) *"In His days Judah will be saved ... that is His name ... THE LORD OUR RIGHTEOUSNESS."* In this, one of the OT most descriptive prophecies of the Messiah, the future day is spoken of when God's King will "execute judgment and justice" in the earth. As the one who is the ultimate equitable, just, mighty yet merciful, holy yet patient, powerful yet humble judge, He is our Righteousness.

- **Jehovah Rapha** (Exodus 15:26) *"...I am the Lord who heals you."* Upon Israel's escape through the Red Sea, their need of water and the problem of Marah's bitter pool is answered to by God's "healing" the bitterness supernaturally, and giving them rest at Elim (vs. 22–27). It is in this setting that God calls them to understand His nature as a healing God; to contrast what they knew of sickness and affliction in Egypt with the promise of His readiness to meet them as "The Lord Who heals".

- **Jehovah Nissi** (Exodus 17:15) *"And Moses built an altar and called its name The-Lord-is-My-Banner."* Another post-Egypt event, involving the encounter with the Amalekites – a battle that could have put an end to a future that was just beginning to open now that their enslavement was behind them. The picture of Moses, hands uplifted on the mountain as the battle is engaged in the valley, depicts his being in touch with One Whose banner was being "waved" in the invisible realm, and scattering the powers of the enemy. The Name, The Lord Our Banner, rises from this event as a reminder that He goes before His people when they engage hostility,

5. *The Keeping God*

- **Jehovah Jireh** (Genesis 22:14) *"And Abram called the name of the place The-Lord-will-provide."* He is our Provider. This is unquestionably one of the high points of OT revelation. In one encounter, close to forty years into his walk with God, Abraham is brought to a place of trust and surrender, as well as a place of insight and understanding. He not only shows his faith in God's faithfulness by his willingness to offer Isaac, but he "sees" into the future and lays hold of the truth of God's eventual plan to send a substitute – an only son – to provide for humankind's salvation (John 8:56). The Ultimate Provider of salvation is the Faithful Provider for all human need.

- **Jehovah Raah** (Psalm 23:1) *"The Lord is my shepherd..."* He is our Shepherd – leading, protecting, feeding, upholding. David's understanding of the shepherding task makes this tender psalm all the more significant, for the writer the Holy Spirit uses to provide this message was one fully in touch with the ways of a good shepherd. God has revealed Himself as entirely skilled at the demanding task of leading, protecting, feeding and bringing His flock to the fullest, highest and best for them.

- **Jehovah Shalom** (Judges 6:24) *"Gideon built an altar ... and called it The-Lord-Shalom."* He is our Peace. As Gideon is being ushered to a place of understanding about God that will prepare him as a judge-deliverer for Israel, he is awestruck and fearful when the Lord reveals Himself to him. Believing he will die for having "seen God," he is amazed to find life-purpose beginning for him, not ending. His discovering of the Lord as "God our Peace" creates the foundation of his becoming what he is intended to become, rising to the moment in the confidence of God's gracious embrace. In an era during which darkness prevailed on so many minds (the Book of Judges), this understanding stands in contrast to the view of God many held – not unlike the Canaanitish deities of anger, vindictiveness and raw, self-serving power.

In all these encounters, God showed Himself as the God above gods, the One like no other – the One Who calls us to know Him – and to build a life on Who He really is.

"Who is like the Lord our God, Who dwells on high,
Who humbles Himself to behold the things
that are in the heavens and in the earth?
He raises the poor out of the dust,
and lifts the needy out of the ash heap,
that He may seat him with princes – with the princes of His people.
He grants the barren woman a home, like a joyful mother of children."

(Psalm 113:5–9)

⁓ 3 ⁓

THE ETERNAL GODHEAD (PART 2): THE MYSTERY OF THE TRINITY

THEME TEXT

*"But when the kindness and the love of God our Savior toward man
appeared, not by works of righteousness which we have done,
but according to His mercy He saved us, through the washing of
regeneration and renewing of the Holy Spirit, whom He poured out on us
abundantly through Jesus Christ our Savior."*

(Titus 3:4–6)

We now begin to discuss the *Trinity of the Godhead* – the doctrine of
the Trinity.

The *Trinity* is one of three great biblical truths, each so consum-
mately grand that its revelation is, ultimately, incomprehensible –
that is, the human mind's capacity is exceeded because of the nature
of the Subject. The **Trinity**, the **Incarnation** and *Eternity* are not the
same as the truths God has revealed of Himself as *He has reached unto
us*. They are truths that *reach into the very nature and being of God
Himself*, and thus these three concepts transcend our grasp.

Just as the human mind cannot encompass "timelessness" (eternity), though we use words or the ideas of the physicist to attempt it;
and just as the human mind cannot compute how the infinite God
could confine Himself to finite human form (the incarnation of
Christ), though we worship in wonder to celebrate the birth of our
Savior, so it is with the idea of the Trinity. There is no way we can
truly apprehend the idea of three Persons Who are One. Nevertheless, the Bible reveals this truth.

Though the word "Trinity" does not actually appear in the Bible,
the concept is clearly present throughout Scripture. The idea in the
"Trinity" (derived from "tri-unity" – meaning "three in one")
presses us to the truth that there is so grand and expansive a richness

in the very essence of God's own being that it exceeds and transcends the limitations of our human definition of "personality". His grandeur shines through our inability to perfectly define or describe His being, and we are humbled by our inability to fully assess, analyze or inventory God.

To merely say, "God is bigger than life," may seem trite or mundane, but it is that fact that is basically revealed in the Bible's evidence: He is an entire *oneness*, complete in Himself (*"Hear, O Israel, the Lord our God is One"* – Deuteronomy 1:4); and He is so vast in the fullness of His very being, He exists as a true *threeness*, overflowing the boundaries of human perception (*"I and my Father are One ... and He will send the Comforter* [Holy Spirit]*"* – John 10:30; 14:16).

Our theme text (Titus 3:4–6) makes a wonderfully tender statement about the salvation that God has lavished upon us in His mercy. The "threeness" in the Godhead – the Trinity – is referenced:

> *"But when the kindness and the love of God our Savior toward man appeared, not by works of righteousness which we have done, but according to His mercy He saved us, through the washing of regeneration and renewing of the Holy Spirit, whom He poured out on us abundantly through Jesus Christ our Savior..."*

We see *the Father* ("God our Savior"), proactive in a majestic love that sends the Son to provide for our salvation (v. 4). Jesus Christ, *the Son*, is seen as the One through whom God pours His abundant mercy, grace and forgiveness to us – Jesus is the channel for God's love (v. 6). And we read of *the Holy Spirit*, shown as the One active to effect the works of salvation in us, as God extends His saving power work toward us. So since He has revealed the *Threeness in His Oneness*, let us study what He has revealed.

Why do we study "The Tri-unity" or *Trinity of God*?

There are three key reasons to study the doctrine of the Trinity:

1. Because the Bible teaches it.

2. Because it helps us understand more of God's Person (i.e., His "personality").

3. Because it helps us to understand God's workings – both in His acts of creation, and in His plan and works of redemption.

1. Because the Bible teaches the "Tri-unity" – the Trinity

The Trinity in the NT

▶ *"Jesus ... came up immediately from the water; and behold, the heavens were opened to Him, and He saw the Spirit of God descending ... a voice came from heaven saying 'This is My Beloved Son.'"*
(Matthew 3:16–17)

The Bible says "the heavens were opened" to Jesus. This does not mean that the skies were parted, but that the "invisible" around Him became "visible". He saw the Spirit of God descending like a dove and alighting upon Him. This was a miraculous visitation confirming the fact that He was the Messiah. The Holy Spirit was anointing Him, fulfilling the literal meaning of Messiah – "The Anointed One". Then, the Father speaks from heaven confirming Jesus' identity as His beloved Son. We clearly see the Trinity – each Person of the Godhead in this incredible scene. The Son is being baptized, the Spirit is being manifest, and the Father is speaking.

▶ *"...baptizing them in the name of the Father and of the Son and of the Holy Spirit."* (Matthew 28:19)

Jesus taught the concept of the Trinity in the baptismal formula that He Himself prescribed for us. From the human perspective, remember that Jesus was raised in the synagogues as a boy and would have been well acquainted with Deuteronomy 6:4, which so strongly affirms – "The Lord is One God!" Yet there is no conflict in His mind regarding the existence of the Trinity. Jesus knew beyond a shadow of a doubt that He had been sent as the representative of the Father, anointed by the power of the Spirit.

Several more scriptures might be considered in our study, each of which upholds Trinitarian doctrine. Read through each one carefully: meditate on the truth they reveal, but also notice that each one references the Trinity of God.

▶ *"And I will pray to the Father and He will give you another Helper."*
(John 14:16–17)

▶ *"The grace of the Lord Jesus Christ, and the love of God, and the communion of the Holy Spirit be with you all."*
(II Corinthians 13:14)

▶ *"There is one body and one Spirit ... one Lord, one faith, one baptism; one God and Father of all."* (Ephesians 4:4–6)

▶ *"Elect according to the foreknowledge of God the Father, in sanctification of the Spirit, for obedience and sprinkling of the blood of Jesus Christ."* (I Peter 1:2)

▶ *"By this we know that we abide in Him ... because He has given us of His Spirit. And we have seen and testify that the Father has sent the Son and Savior of the world."* (I John 4:13–14)

▶ *"The Holy Spirit will come upon you, and the power of the Highest will overshadow you; therefore, also that Holy One who is to be born will be called the Son of God."* (Luke 1:35)

▶ *"For He whom God has sent speaks the words of God, for God does not give the Spirit by measure."* (John 3:34)

▶ *"But the Helper, the Holy Spirit, whom the Father will send in My name ... "* (John 14:26)

▶ *"But when the Helper comes, whom I shall send to you from the Father ... "* (John 15:26)

▶ *"However, when He, the Spirit of truth, has come, He will guide you into all truth ... All things that the Father has are Mine. Therefore I said that He will take of Mine and declare it to you."* (John 16:13–15)

▶ *"Therefore being exalted to the right hand of God, and having received from the Father the promise of the Holy Spirit, He poured out this which you now see and hear."* (Acts 2:33)

▶ *" ... how God anointed Jesus of Nazareth with the Holy Spirit."* (Acts 10:38)

▶ *"Concerning His Son Jesus Christ our Lord ... declared to be the Son of God with power, according to the Spirit of holiness, by the resurrection from the dead."* (Romans 1:3, 4)

▶ *"But when the kindness and the love of God our Savior toward man appeared ... He saved us, through the washing of regeneration and renewing of the Holy Spirit, whom He poured out on us abundantly through Jesus Christ our Savior."* (Titus 3:4–6)

▶ *"How much more shall the blood of Christ, who through the eternal Spirit offered Himself without spot to God, purge your conscience from dead works to serve the living God?"* (Hebrews 9:14)

The Trinity in the OT

From the first moment we are introduced to God through Scripture we see that we are dealing with a phenomenon that transcends our intellectual grasp – *a multiplicity of personality in the singularity of God*. The opening verse of the Bible reads, *"In the beginning God created the heavens and the earth"* (Genesis 1:1), and the Hebrew noun used here – *Elohim* – is plural in form! So from the start, God's Word shows us that we are dealing with a plural entity (not "entities").

Only verses later, the Scripture reveals that in that plural-singular unity, interaction takes place between what we often refer to as "the members of the Godhead": *"Then God said, 'Let Us make man in Our image, according to Our likeness...'"* (Genesis 1:26). The Hebrew use, here and elsewhere involving God, uses a plural pronoun but the singular form of the verb; and notably, this is God referring to Himself! The noun *Elohim* (usually translated "God") almost always occurs throughout the OT the same as in Genesis 1:1 – in conjunction with a singular verb: *"In the beginning God* [plural] *created* [singular] *the heavens and the earth."*

Several other texts are offered here, where the use of the *plural pronoun* is used in reference to God:

▶ *"Then the Lord God said 'Behold, the man has become like one of Us, to know good and evil.'"* (Genesis 3:22)

▶ *"Come let Us go down there and confuse their language, that they may not understand one another's speech."* (Genesis 11:7)

▶ *"Also I heard the voice of the Lord saying: 'Whom shall I send, and who will go for Us?' Then I said, 'Here am I! Send me.'"* (Isaiah 6:8)

The Shema, Judaism's primary statement of faith begins with Deuteronomy 6:4 which contains the following statement, *"Hear, O Israel: The LORD our God, the LORD is One!"* A simplistic translation of the original Hebrew could read: "Yahweh, God of us, Yahweh is One." But, the word "God" in this verse is a masculine plural form with a first person plural suffix. Because of that, one could properly translate the text, "The Lord our Gods, the Lord is One!"

So we see that even in this great, monotheistic statement of Judaistic faith, an acknowledgement of the existence of this "plural" reference to God. It does not cause any special conflict to the Jewish people themselves, because they accept it as an idiosyncrasy of their language. They view it simply as encompassing the *vastness* of God and the *plurality* of the aspects of His nature.

Other OT references however, do more than merely hint at the mystery of the Trinity through the uniqueness of Hebrew grammar. Here are specific statements that make reference to the *plurality in the essence of God's being*:

▶ *"Behold! My Servant whom I uphold ... I have put My Spirit upon Him."*   (Isaiah 42:1 quoted in Matthew 12:18)

This Isaiah reference clearly distinguishes three parties involved in the action. The One who is speaking (the Father) is addressing the One who is called *Servant* in this verse (which is a reference to the Messiah – Christ), and is saying "I have put my *Spirit* upon Him."

▶ A few chapters later in Isaiah we see the Messiah speaking prophetically, testifying to the fact that, *"...the Lord GOD and His Spirit have sent Me"* (Isaiah 48:16).

Again, this Messianic statement observes God's Son (*"Me,"* the *Messiah, God's King*), God the Father (*"the Lord GOD"*) and the Holy Spirit (*"My Spirit"*), all in one verse. The distinction drawn between *the Lord God* and *His Spirit*, followed by *their* joint action *sending* the *Son*-Messiah clearly reveal the Trinity.

Values in looking at Trinitarian truth

Through these scriptures the Bible *obviously reveals the reality of and workings of the Trinity in the Old Testament*. It is His revelation of Himself to us, without which we would know nothing of either Him or this grand reality about His being, that stirs and humbles us. We do not examine it to suppose we can master its wonder, nor do we take notice of it to store ammunition for arguing with any who deny the obvious. But there are values to seeing more than merely the fact of the "three-in-one, and the one-in-three."

1. *It helps us understand God's Person*

It never ceases to amaze me how people consistently attempt to reduce God to a scientifically calculable entity – as though He could be taken into a laboratory and examined. Even though we can dissect or expound many texts about Him – in this case in regard to the Trinity – the only real conclusion we can make is that the Bible reveals certain *information* about God. This does not help us, with our finite minds and human intelligence, to truly *grasp* the enormity and expansiveness of *God*. How can we explain Him! How can we define God, when by His very nature He is beyond definition?

We simply cannot comprehend God, or the essence of His being – that He is Three in One, One in Three. At best, we are wise to embrace what He has revealed of the *fact* concerning His immeasurable breadth-depth-length-height and timelessness, and learn the *faith* that receives the benefits of opening to the small glimpse we are able to gain of His grandeur. The revelation of the Tri-unity of God through Scripture tells us two things about God.

- **His exceeding greatness is beyond man's intelligence or imagination**. We should *expect* God to be beyond our ability to totally define or express. The fact that we cannot fully apprehend God's nature does not mean that the revelation of the Trinity is incorrect or unreasonable. Rather it demonstrates that *finite* minds cannot – nor should be expected to – grasp that which is *infinite*.

- **His exceeding completeness in being requires multiple expressions to adequately release the richness of His Person**. For God to reveal Himself within the human limits of the time-space continuum requires language that introduces this mystery. It is the only way He can adequately help us see at one and the same time (1) the oneness and richness of His Person, but also to help us capture a glimpse of (2) The Father – The Son – The Spirit in their different functions within the Godhead.

Scripture reveals different operations, administrations and activities of Father, Son and Holy Spirit. But even though this is the case, we cannot say that the Father is the only One who performs a certain task, or the Son only does certain things. In these various functions of the Godhead, God again surpasses the boundaries of our best understanding, refusing to be contained by the limits of human comprehension.

- The Father may be seen as the *Source*, the Life-giver, the Creator.

- The Son may be seen as the *Substance*, the Transmitter, the Communicator, the Messenger, the Word.

- The Spirit may be seen as the *Stream*, the Life-breath, the Revealer, the Power, the Love of the Father.

Yet in all, let us remember, and always humbly regard the fact that whatever the distinct role, action or function we perceive any "member" of the Godhead to exercise, **The Three-in-One – always – are Co-equal, Co-eternal, and Coexistent** in being, power and holiness.

2. Because it helps us to understand God's workings

The Trinity helps us to understand God's workings in two respects – His workings in Creation and in Redemption. These are the two primary workings of God in regard to all of humankind. He created us, then due to Man's fall, He set into motion a plan of redemption.

- **The action of each member of the Godhead in Creation**

    i. *The Father's will*: The Father *determines* what will be done. The Bible says that all things were created by His will. The Father *wills* that things be (see Genesis 1:1).

    ii. *The Son's word*: The Son *declares* – speaking it into existence. The Father wills and the Son *speaks*. The Bible shows us that the Father is the Creator, but it also reveals Jesus as the *Word* who was with God "in the beginning" at the creation of the world (John 1:3).

    iii. *The Spirit's work*: The Holy Spirit *develops* – bringing life and power leading to the accomplishment of the Father's will by the Son's word. The Holy Spirit is the One who works to accomplish the Father's will as spoken by the Son (see Genesis 1:3).

- **The action of each member of the Godhead in Redemption.** [2] Using the paradigm revealed in Creation, see the parallel as redemption works toward bringing about the New Creation. When Jesus, as the Living Word, stepped into the midst of our fallen humanity.

    i. What the Father had *determined* in His purposes for Man – His originally intended goodness, righteousness, blessing, fruitfulness – He made possible to be recovered, as He "so loved the world He gave His only Son." As He achieved that, the *Son was sent*. Then,

    ii. Jesus *declared*. The Son of God spoke and actuated the will of the Father, through His life, ministry, death and resurrection. That *"declaration"* would shortly begin to take effect in the lives of those who would open to the working of the Holy Spirit. *Then, the Spirit was sent.* Now,

iii. The Holy Spirit *develops*; taking action to extend the Father's will (as determined), spoken by the Son's word-made-flesh (as declared), and now manifests the workings of redemption's full scope of grace.

(a) He brings the promise of new life *to us*, with the possibility of resurrecting us from our death in trespasses and sin, convicting us of sin, righteousness and judgment.

(b) He births the life of God *in us* by the power of regeneration, actuating the power of Calvary's triumph over sin, death and hell.

(c) He seeks to develop the character of Christ (fruit of the Spirit) and the *charismata* of Christ (gifts of the Spirit) so the likeness of Christ will operate *through us. That's how we are sent.*

What the Father determines, the Son declares and the Holy Spirit develops in you and me. And so the action of the Trinity in Creation, is also reflected in Redemption.

"For He Whom God has sent speaks the words of God,
for God does not give the Spirit by measure.
The Father loves the Son, and has given all things in His hand.
Then Jesus said to them again, 'Peace to you!
As the Father has sent Me, I also send you.'
And when He had said this He breathed on them
and said to them, 'Receive the Holy Spirit.'"

(John 3:34, 35; 20:21, 22)

❧ 4 ❧

THE ETERNAL GODHEAD (PART 3): THE SON – GOD REVEALED IN HUMAN FORM

THEME TEXT

*"In the beginning was the Word, and the Word was with God,
and the Word was God. He was in the beginning with God.
All things were made by Him,
and without Him nothing was made that was made.
And the Word became flesh and dwelt among us,
and we beheld His glory, the glory as of
the only begotten of the Father, full of grace and truth."*

(John 1:1–3, 14)

In John's Gospel, Jesus makes one of the most important statements in the entire NT. Thomas has asked Him, *"Lord, we do not know where You are going ... how can we know the way?"* (John 14:5). Jesus replies, *"I am the way, the truth, and the life. No one comes to the Father except through Me"* (John 14:6). Our familiarity with His words which isolate saving grace to the pathway of faith in Him, sometimes overlooks a second, profoundly significant part of the statement.

Jesus was expressing His "oneness" with the Father. He was not only showing the *way* to the Father, He *was* the essence of the Father's heart, shown through the Son in a human package. He continues: *"If you had known Me, you would have known My Father also; and from now on you know Him and have seen Him"* (John 14:7). When Philip responds by requesting, *"Show us the Father,"* Jesus' reply is in past tense, as though to say, "You've seen Him already!" – *"He who has seen Me has seen the Father; so how can you say 'Show us the Father'?"* (John 14:9).

Jesus wanted His disciples to grasp the fact that, for the whole time they had been together, His unbroken, perfect link with Father God was because of His own unique relationship with Him as Son. He had never once spoken from His own authority – only as a direct expression of the Father's will. He consistently affirms His works are not His, but the Father's (John 14:10; 9:3, 4; 10:37). As God the Son incarnate on earth, He is doing the will and work of God the Father in heaven.

Jesus is even more pointed in John 10:30, where He says explicitly, *"I and My Father are one,"* a gateway into this chapter where we will explore how the different attributes of God revealed in the "Names" of God (see Chapter 2), reflected and demonstrated in the Person and ministry of Jesus. To review these:

1. We observe Christ's character and attributes in their precise nature and quality as being the same as the Father – verifying Him as the Son;

2. Rejoice in and receive the promise those traits offer to our own personal need and circumstance – drawing on the grace the Savior wants to flow to us; and

3. Welcome our Lord, that those qualities with the attributes that may be transmitted into our own nature by the Holy Spirit's work may be grown in us.

Our theme text notes the fact the Bible equates the glory of Jesus, the Son, with that of God the Father. Jesus is God – and in becoming flesh manifests the qualities of God the OT revealed, including becoming the human expression of many of them in very direct ways. In Chapter 2 we noted we would provide the NT complement to the study of the Names of God, and again we have listed 15 names of God, grouped in 5 categories – this time, fulfilled in the Person of Jesus.

NT names of God, incarnate in God's Son

1. The Living God

*   **The 'I Am'** (Exodus 3:13–15; John 8:58). In John 8:58 Jesus unhesitatingly claims the "Name of God" for Himself. Jesus was being verbally assaulted by the Pharisees who hated Him because He confronted them with the reality that they represented only

in theory – God. They claimed to speak for Him, but refused to let Him fill their lives. They knew the Word of God inside out, but they did not allow the Word to enter from the outside-in. Their view of God had become so distorted that they projected a God of mercilessness and lovelessness – so concerned with religious rules and regulations there was no room for His own creature to simply "be human." Example: they persistently attacked Jesus, claiming He violated the Sabbath. Their criticism was born of their self-evolved, hyper-religious sabbatical require-ments which now made the day intended for human rest, worship and renewal, into a day of fear, legal nit-picking and discomfort. Their administration of a burdensome list of humanly contrived laws had removed the Father's intentions for the Sabbath – a day planned and set aside *for human benefit* (Mark 2:27). They had lost touch with the God who cared for Man, and by doing so had lost touch themselves with caring for either. But Jesus, facing down their anger, claims His place as "Lord of the Sabbath" (Mark 2:28), and thereby clearly announced Himself as God's Son. It is in that season of inter-change, John's Gospel reports this dramatic moment:

> *"'...It is My Father who honors Me, of whom you say that He is your God. Yet you have not known Him ... Your father Abraham rejoiced to see My day, and he saw it and was glad.' Then the Jewish leaders said to Him, 'You are not yet fifty years old, and have You seen Abraham?' Jesus said to them, 'Most assuredly, I say to you, before Abraham was, I AM.'"*
> (John 8:55–58; see also John 8:48–59)

Jesus was not only asserting His divinity, He was specifically laying claim to that *Name – Yahweh*; Jehovah; **"I Am that I Am"**, and applying it to Himself. The religious authorities understood very well what He was saying and were instantly infuriated, planning to execute Jesus for blasphemy.

Let us allow this passage and truth to sink deeply into our ears and hearts. Through the years there have been, and presently there are, those critics who will say, "Jesus never claimed to *be* God – He only claimed to be *an expression* of God!" But here, locked in the written Word is what the Incarnate Word said of Himself. Jesus stated very clearly in this text and other words and ways, that He is, literally and personally, "the self-existent One." As God the Son, He is the One Who came from beyond this world *into it*, so that Man could know God and eventually be brought beyond this world *unto Him*.

- **The Eternal One** (John 6:40; Psalm 90:2). God reveals Himself to us as *El Olam* (Psalm 90:2) – the Eternal One. In John 6:40 Jesus lays claims to this aspect of God's nature, and declares Himself as the Eternal Son who is able to give "everlasting life". He says,

   > *"And this is the will of Him who sent Me, that everyone who sees the Son and believes in Him may have everlasting life; and I will raise him up at the last day."*   (John 6:40)

   Jesus does not simply say, "God is everlasting". He says to us, *"I have come to give you that everlastingness."* It is this practical way in which Jesus was able to apply such profound truths to our lives that gives us the "Grounds for Living" that we are studying in this book!

- **The Everlasting Father** (Isaiah 9:6; John 14:9). It is an amazing thing that Jesus not only *shows* us the Father, but is called the *"Everlasting Father"* Himself. He fulfills the prophecy of a "son" who became a "father" (Isaiah 9:6). We have a Heavenly Father who created us and gave us life. We lost that life through sin, but the Son comes to "re-birth" that life in us by the work of the Holy Spirit. We have our Creator Father, and the Son who as the "seed sown into the ground" that multiplies (John 12:22, 23) became the *Everlasting Father* – joining us once more to our Creator Father God.

2. The Unchanging God

- **The Rock** (Deuteronomy 32:15; I Corinthians 3:11). In Deuteronomy chapter 32, God reveals Himself as "the Rock of our salvation". As Moses is giving a discourse on the details of God's covenant with Israel, he speaks of God's steadfastness and changelessness, using a great rock as the picture of God's stability and firmness of character. Jesus is manifest in that same way, and two verses in particular should be examined.

   i. In Matthew 16:18, Jesus responds to Peter's declaration, *"You are the Christ, the Son of the living God."* Jesus says, "Yes, you're right. The Father showed you that about Me." He then adds, *"...On this rock I will build My church..."* This passage is difficult to translate, as to whether Jesus *Himself* or the *confession made about Him* was in view. In either case, the message is that the Church Jesus prophesied would be founded upon Himself – the Rock (Greek, *petra*, a great or massive rock; contrast with Peter's name *Petros*, a piece of rock. This was clearly Peter's own understanding – that upon Christ, the Church is built up out of many smaller stones "living stones" – *lithoi zoontes* – that have received of Jesus' "rock-like" nature – I Peter 2:4–6.)

ii. In I Corinthians 3:11, the Apostle Paul shows Christ is the foundation for all life and living: *"No other foundation can anyone lay than that which is laid, which is Christ Jesus."* The term refers to the *bedrock* on which a house is built – thus the foundation upon which you can build a life (Greek, *themelion*, used in Homer as "basic stone," the foundation for a house). Similarly, in Matthew 7:24–27, Jesus refers to His teaching (includes His Self-designation as "Lord" and Son of God – see vs. 21, 22) as "the rock" upon which the wise build their lives.

- **The "Present One"** (Ezekiel 48:35; Matthew 28:20). Among the OT compound names of "Jehovah," *Jehovah Shammah – God is Present* – is introduced by Ezekiel as he prophesies hope to a demoralized remnant exiled in Babylon. This remnant's mood is reflected in Psalm 137, "How can we praise God in a distant land? The Lord is in Jerusalem and we have been carried far away" (paraphrase). But God sends Ezekiel to speak into their despair, not only revealing His presence in the prophet's message, but promising a future visitation of His presence to the temple they have seen destroyed: *"... and the name of the city from that day shall be: THE LORD IS THERE [Jehovah-Shammah]."*

    God manifested Himself in this name to tell us that He is faithful and that He will always *be there*. Jesus, the Son of God, shows us this same trait, revealed in some of the most tender words in the Bible – *"Lo I am with you always, even to the end of the age"* (Matthew 28:20). It is our Lord's claim as the Omnipresent God – the God who is *there!* It is a word for us all, whenever, as with those in captivity, we feel alone, distant and wondering if God is present with us any more! Jesus says, "I'm here!"

3. *The Almighty God*

- **The All-Powerful One** (Genesis 17:1; Matthew 28:18). In Genesis chapter 17, God reveals Himself to Abraham as *El Shaddai* – the Almighty God. In this context God makes a covenant with

Abraham, promising that he will be *"...exceedingly fruitful..."* that God will, *"...make nations of you, and kings shall come from you."* This would necessitate the birth of a child which Abraham does not believe his wife Sarah will be able to conceive or bear. He and Sarah attempt to help God fulfill His own promise, resulting in Ishmael's birth via Hagar, at Sarah's bidding. Even as Abraham tries to convince God to accept Ishmael as fulfillment of God's purposes (Genesis 17:18), God speaks to reveal Himself as *El Shaddai*, the Almighty God, for whom nothing is impossible. It is as the All-Powerful One that God makes the promise of the impossible to Abraham.

This parallels Christ's claim to be the Almighty God: *"All authority has been give to Me in heaven and in earth"* (Matthew 28:18). His mightiness is declared to be universal in scope. As God-among-us, Jesus is saying, "You are looking at El Shaddai – The One Who is omnipresent is also omnipotent."

- **The Most High** (Genesis 14:18–20; Colossians 1:16–17). Let us join this name with the next on our list. God, having created all things, is *above* all, *over* all and *knows all things* (*El Elyon*, God Most High); and, having created all things, is the Sovereign *God who rules over all beings*. This includes His rule over the entire angelic realm, making Him *Jehovah Sabaoth*, the Lord of hosts.

  When we assert God's claim as "The Most High" – Sovereign over all things – it is not uncommon to face human accusations: "If God really is all-powerful and all-loving, why does evil survive and succeed. He must either not be all-powerful, so He cannot stop it, or He is not all-loving, and He doesn't care." Because Jesus is the embodiment of the Father's sovereign power toward earth and humankind, and because He came announcing "The Kingdom (or rule) of God is here", believers need to be equipped with understanding to "be ready always to have an answer" (I Peter 3:15). The following is only a brief summary of a larger study concerning God, Man and the Kingdom of God, but it addresses doubts regarding God's sovereignty and love.

  When God's Sovereignty is sincerely (though ignorantly) questioned, remember:

  i. God, the All-Powerful One, as Sovereign Creator of all things, created our small planet as well.

  ii. In designing Man to learn His ways, He *sovereignly* entrusted the rule of this planet and its affairs to humankind.

iii. His decree in transmitting the government of Earth to Man means God's rule, *by His sovereign choice*, only functions on earth as Man functions in obedience to God.

iv. The breach in humankind's obedience has produced a broken rule, compounded in its devastation by the Serpent's usurping the role Man had in administrating earth's affairs.

v. The perpetuation of evil's *right and power* to rule earth was broken by Jesus – the Second Adam – re-establishing the possibility of the Sovereign God's rule being enforced wherever offspring of the Son of Man/Son of God learn to live, serve, minister and pray, "Thy Kingdom come."

vi. Thus, each redeemed human has been entrusted with "the keys of the Kingdom" (Matthew 16:18), and are charged to drive back the darkness of evil as they minister – giving place for the renewal of His reign in human hearts, life and experience.

vii. In the meantime, a world hell-bent for its own will and way will inevitably continue to receive the horrible fruit of its continuing folly, as each one disallows the benevolent rule of the Sovereign God to rule their hearts.

viii. Consequently, when bad things happen, as the product of a broken planet, a fallen human or a sinister devil, God continues to be blamed, doubted or cursed; not because He lacks sovereign power, but because that power is not welcomed.

ix. In this way, Man's or Satan's responsibility for evil's success, human sinning or natural disaster is thrown aside, and blinded humans argue against God instead of turning to Him.

x. In infinite patience, granting time for "all who will come to repentance" to do so, God refuses to defend Himself. Having shown mercy that preserves life; having given His Son to save and bring eternal life, He abides the wrath of Man with relentless grace, secure in the certainty of His own love, righteousness and power.

All of this is to assert that Jesus, as the One through Whom the Kingdom (or sovereign rule of the Most High) has been reintroduced to human experience, does so as the Most High Himself. He *now holds* "the keys of death and hell," (Revelation 1:18) and is soon-to-come as King of kings and Lord of lords (Revelation

19:16) when *"the kingdoms of this world have become the kingdom of our God and of His Christ"* (Revelation 11:15), and the universe shall sing in that hour, *"Alleluia! For the Lord God Omnipotent reigns!"* (Revelation 19:6) – and, astounding the reality of it all – as His Bride, we the redeemed shall be invited to rule together with Him (Revelation 5:9, 10). It is and will be **all because of Jesus** – the One who has come as God Most High!

- **"King of the Angels"** (Psalm 24:10; Hebrews 1:1–4). "King of the Angels" is the literal meaning of the name *Jehovah Sabaoth*, Lord of Hosts. Psalm 24:10 says, *"The LORD of hosts, He is the king of glory."* Hebrews 1:1–4 reveals that Jesus is also above the angelic realm, just as the Father is. This verse notes how, after completing His work on the Cross, Jesus sat down at the right hand of the Father, having become *"... so much better than the angels ..."* What does this phrase "better" mean, since we have already learnt that Jesus created the angels? It means that when Jesus became flesh, He walked a pathway as a perfect man that transcended even the excellence of unfallen angels. The pre-existent Son of God who created the angelic beings, and was so much higher than they, distinguished Himself beyond them even through His humanity.

- **He is Lord!** (Genesis 15:1–2; Philippians 2:8–10). God is also *Adonai Jehovah* – The Lord God. This name speaks of His position as Owner or Master. He revealed Himself in this way to Abraham in Genesis chapter 15 where Abraham was moved to address Him as "Lord GOD". Philippians 2:8–10 affirms Jesus' position as Lord also: *"... that at the name of Jesus every knee should bow ... that every tongue should confess that Jesus Christ is Lord ..."*

  Because Jesus lived the life of a servant, and was obedient even to death on a cross, He has been given a name above every other name. It denotes His "ownership" – He holds the title of "LORD".

4. The Saving God

- **Christ is our Righteousness** (Jeremiah 23:6; I Corinthians 1:30). Here we come to the most essential and most fulfilling expression of Christ's revealing the Father to us all: His nature and Person as Savior and Keeper. Jeremiah 23:6 contains a prophecy regarding the coming of Christ. God says that He will, *"... raise to David a Branch of righteousness."* "Branch" is a title of the

Messiah. God also says that, "... *this is His name by which He will be called: THE LORD OUR RIGHTEOUSNESS."*

Just as the prophecy predicted, through the triumph of the Cross, we can be declared "the righteousness of God" when we place our faith in Him Who is our righteousness. I Corinthians 1:30 declares: "... *you are in Christ Jesus, who became for us wisdom from God – and righteousness and sanctification and redemption..."* Jesus' personal purity, holiness and righteousness qualified Him not only for offering a perfect atoning sacrifice to the Father for our sins. His righteousness effected our justification before the Father, allowing Him to justly do even more than forgive us: God also rescinds the record of our sin, replacing it with the sinlessly righteous record of our Savior! (Romans 4:5–8). "Being justified" means I can be accepted by God "just-as-if-I'd" never sinned at all! Why? Because Jesus has been made "The Righteousness of God" for us before the Father (II Corinthians 5:21). Jesus is a wonderful Savior: able to save completely, and ready to save us notwithstanding our helplessness and unworthiness (Romans 5:6–11).

- **Christ is our Healer** (Exodus 15:26; Matthew 8:16–17). The healings Jesus performed were among the most notable aspects of His ministry. Many are listed and certain passages indicate countless other instances occurred. Understanding requires we see how Matthew 8:16–17 reveals that Jesus' healing ministry directly fulfilled Isaiah's prophecy – especially the forecast of Messiah's work as Healer: *"He Himself took our infirmities and bore our sicknesses"* (Isaiah 53:4).

  Further insight and faith rises for today when we compare Isaiah 53:4, Matthew 8:16–17, and I Peter 2:24. Study how Isaiah's *prophesied Healer*, Matthew's report of the *Fulfiller of the Healer prophecy*, and Peter's *application of the healing promise* to the living Church apply to us today. For then and now, the Bible blends *a three-fold cord* of scriptural promise, providing biblical grounds for divine healing being available today as faith may appropriate it. Jesus is Jehovah-Rapha – the Lord our Healer.

- **Christ is our Victory** (Exodus 17:15; Romans 8:37). At times in OT Israel, God led them by giving strategies and bringing victory in their battles. Jesus is the NT fulfillment of the Father's being a Leader in battle. In His Person we are declared "more than conquerors" in Him, because He has led the way in battle, through His Cross has triumphed (Colossians 2:14, 15). Having defeated the hosts of hell in the most immense of all spiritual battles, He now comes to lead us daily, making victory available to us in life's issues of spiritual warfare (Romans 8:37; II Corinthians 2:14).

5. *The Keeping God*

- **Jesus is the Creator-Source and the Conveyor-Source** (Genesis 22:14; John 6). In Genesis 22, when God provides a "replacement" for Isaac, Abraham is overcome with relief and filled with awe He names the place of the burnt offering *"Jehovah Jireh,"* saying, "In the mount of the Lord it will be provided." His identification as Father God our Source is rooted in His action as our Creator *and* Redeemer. "The Lord our Provider" is most commonly referenced regarding physical or material need. He *is* such a Provider, but both OT and NT passages show how the flow of promised physical-material provision is rooted in the promise of His spiritual-saving provision. In Genesis it is seen in the provision of a substitute for Isaac – a picture of Christ, dying in our place.

  In the NT, Jesus again evidences all the Father has been shown to be in the OT names – and the cases where they appear. In John chapter 6, where Jesus feeds the multitude, His action confirms His concern for humankind's simplest or greatest physical-material needs (vs. 1–14). But the message He gives at the same time, regarding His body and blood, reveal provision for the desperate human need of forgiveness and salvation (vs. 22–68).

  Understanding this we are wise to prioritize our spiritual need when coming to Him, but there is *never a need for hesitation or fear* requesting and expecting His provision in physical or material, economic or vocational ways. Never forget the foundation of Christ our Provider's care is what He has done for us in the Cross. Also, never intellectualize or spiritualize the promise of Christ's as Provider, confining it to the realm of "salvation only." If that were all, we would never complain, but Philippians 4:19 spreads the table wide with promise and invites us to expect heaven's supply at any and every point of need. Just as Jesus is the channel by which God's saving power is poured out into the midst of our humanity. He is the avenue by which all sufficiency flows to answer all arenas of our human need.

- **The Great Shepherd** (Psalm 23:1; John 10:1–20). Psalm 23 is the great pastoral psalm of the Bible, portraying the Lord as the Great Shepherd, watching over His sheep; concerned for their well-being; gently guiding, directing and protecting. Jesus is the incarnation of Psalm 23! John 10:11 reveals Jesus as the shepherd who went a step further – He actually gave up His own life for the sake of His sheep (see John 10:1–20; I Peter 5:4; Hebrews 13:20).

- **He is "our Peace"** (Judges 6:24; Ephesians 2:14–18). In Judges 6:24, Gideon has a face-to-face encounter with "the Angel of the Lord". Frightened by the consequences of such a meeting, Gideon is afraid for his life. But the Lord speaks to him saying, *"Peace be with you; do not fear, you shall not die."* In response to God's graciousness toward him, Gideon builds an altar and calls it "The-Lord-is-Peace". As the Prince of Peace forecast in Isaiah 9:6, Jesus literally brings us *peace* with God and peace between people who welcome all His working (see Ephesians 2:14–18). "He is our peace" – the One who has broken down every wall, and Who not only brings us into the presence of the Father, but Who is able to cause His reconciling grace to work through us as well, making us instruments of His peace (II Corinthians 5:17–21).

"Let praise rise to our blessed Savior!
He has been given to us from the Father's hand, and . . .
. . . He is the image of the invisible God,
the firstborn over all creation.
For by Him all things were created that are in heaven
and that are on earth . . .
All things were created through Him and for Him . . .
For in Him dwells all the fullness of the Godhead bodily,
and you are complete in Him . . ."

(Colossians 1:15–16; 2:9–10)

THE ETERNAL GODHEAD (PART 4): THE TRINITY AT WORK IN HUMAN PURPOSE

THEME TEXT

"Now there are diversities of gifts, but the same Spirit. There are differences of ministries but the same Lord. And there are diversities of activities, but it is the same God who works all in all."

(I Corinthians 12:4–6)

Just as a study of the Trinity helps both to humble and enlarge our understanding of God's Person and greatness, it may also help us to more deeply appreciate His individual purpose for us in our creation and His personal intentions for us in His redemption. Everything of His revealed purpose relates to these two areas – His work in *creation* and His work in *redemption*. In this chapter we will focus on our theme text as it opens the way to our examining the specific roles that the "members" of the Godhead play in the divine designed for each of us:

1.   The Father, introducing us to human life, having a designed purpose for each of us;

2.   The Son, rescuing us from human loss, recovering us for the Father's original purpose; and

3.   The Spirit, drawing us to, and growing us in, Christ – making us functional members of His Body.

Foremost, this all unveils a beginning insight into the richness of God's design in all things – in creation and redemption; activating a plan within our salvation unto eternal life that points toward responsible and meaning-filled vocation, service and ministry now, and high destiny eternally.

Our objective is to help each person to grasp something more of an understanding of God's heart regarding His plan and purpose for them. Dear One, God did not only send Jesus to save us from our sin, He sent Him to redeem and recover something of His treasured purpose in you. The horror of sin is not merely the awfulness and shame of its guilt, it is the damnable reality that each sinner's sin is the marring of a divine design.

In the coming of Christ, the whole Godhead was operating a plan that had more than "rescue" in mind – it has the "realization of an intended design" in mind. Within each individual's creation, a Master-plan had been conceived in heaven – one which sin destroyed, but grace is en route to recovering. Now, look with me at a brief overview of the operative workings of the Father, Son and Holy Spirit, and see how His sending Jesus represents His intention to see you and me brought back from loss, and brought into His hope for the fulfillment of all you and I were made to be (Ephesians 1:15–2:10).

With the *fullness* of God's purposes in redemption in mind, we will now go on to examine the role that each member of the Godhead plays in the redemptive process.

The Trinity at Work – Creation and Redemption

God the Father

Look at four aspects of the Father's "giving" toward humanity; each flowing from His heart which is as grand as His mind is wondrous and His hand exceeding mighty.

- **He gives human life** (Hebrews 12:9). God is called "the Father of spirits", acknowledging the fact our existence flows from His creative activity. He is the one who literally gives breath to our bodies and caused us to "live" (Acts 17:24–26). With the creation of the human race, He placed in humankind the capacity to relay human life from generation to generation, as He "breathed into man the breath of *lives*" (Hebrew, plural). This does not reduce the reality that each individual person is known to Him and of value to Him (Luke 12:24).

- **He gives individual created purpose** (Romans 12:3; John 1:3, 9; Proverbs 20:27). The "measure of faith" given to every person is that investment God has placed in each human being, incorporating not only their capacity to turn that faith toward Him and live, but involving each person's unique and distinct "motivation." By *motivation* I refer to that "creational gifting" God has place in each of us, inclining us toward and capacitating us for our vocation. "Lighted" by God (John 1:9, Proverbs 20:27), humans can live and fulfill their created purpose. Darkened by sin (Proverbs 24:20; II Corinthians 4:4) God's intended purpose for an individual cannot be fully realized apart from saving grace, but it either lays dormant or functions with a self-centered focus while the person lives separate from or in disobedience to Him.

- **He gave His Son to redeem humankind** (Colossians 1:12–14). Salvation in Christ is the way an individual returns (1) to God for forgiveness of sin and transgression, and (2) to the Father to see the recovery and fulfillment of his/her created purpose. Once he/she is "translated" from darkness to light, life opens to what Jesus described as "life to the full", or "life in all its fullness" – making possible the release of the potential the Father put inside us. *Gave His Son to redeem man* (John 3:16) – God sent Jesus to die on the Cross as the ultimate sacrifice to win back fallen Man and set him on the road to recovery.

- **He gives eternal life to those who receive His Son** (John 1:12; Romans 6:23). Salvation through faith in God's Son, first reconciles us to our Father-Creator: "*...as many as received Him, to them He gave the right to become children of God, to those who believe in His name...*" (John 1:12). It then opens the door to life purpose being found and pursued in His will. These graces are ours upon having entered eternal life. "Eternal life" is not only a term referring to life beyond this world, but the biblical term describing that "newness" of life we receive when we are restored to the Father through the Son. Eternal life is not only an endless duration of life, but an expanded dimension of life – both a "quantity" and a "quality". When we are told that "God so loved the world that He *gave* His only Son" so we would not "perish," please understand: "perishing" would not only have been the loss of our eternal souls in eternal judgment, but the loss of our intended, Father-created purpose for us in this life, as well as throughout eternity.

▶ *In summary re: the Father –*

Every person on earth is a "special creation" of the Father's *human* family, created and endowed by Him with unique purpose and motivation by reason of His "workmanship" especially focused on each one (Ephesians 2:10). Every person is beloved by Him, even before we understand our sin, our need or our lostness outside Christ. The Creator hears the cry of every one of His creatures, and He shows mercy to all mankind – even those not yet alive to Him through Christ (Romans 5:8; Lamentations 3:22, 23). However, the purpose of His temporal mercy is to bring each human being unto repentance and into a relationship with Him that will last eternally (Romans 2:4). This is available by receiving new birth in Christ, which brings us into His *redeemed* family. Only when we are saved through receiving the gift of eternal life in His Son, do the possibilities of "life, and life more abundantly" open to us (John 10:10). This "abundant life" essentially focuses the restoration of the individual to the potential fulfillment and fruitfulness originally intended by the Father-Creator for each person. In Christ, this "purpose" is "saved," just as surely as the individual's soul is saved!

This is the Father at work in creation and redemption. He gave us life and the incredible "treasure" of what He made us to be. He gave us His Son in order to retrieve that treasure, and the instant we open up to His Son He gives us the kind and quality of life that not only transforms us now, but gives us the hope of being with Him forever, in eternity.

God the Son

Now look at the aspects of the Son of God's "giving" toward humanity.

* **The Son Gave His life of His own accord** (John 10:17–18; 19:10; Luke 23:46). As the Bible says, "God gave His Son", but the Scriptures then show that the Son gave His life: *"Therefore My Father loves Me, because I lay down my life that I may take it again. No one takes it from Me, but I lay it down of Myself. I have power to lay it down, and I have power to take it again. This command I have received from My Father"* (John 10:17–18).

    Jesus tells us, (1) that the Father gave Him to the world, but, (2) that He was the one who chose to give His life. Later in John's gospel, in chapter 19 – on the day of the crucifixion – Pilate is urging Jesus to speak up for Himself. Pilate claims power over Jesus' life (John 19:10), but Jesus denies such power is Pilate's

(John 19:11). Pilate may be, as Rome's representative, able to sentence Jesus to death, but he does not control God nor can he conclude Christ's life unless Jesus willingly yields up His own life. It will be a short time later, Jesus will do this. Completing His work of redemption on the Cross, He will call out to His Father as He gives up His life: *"Father into Your hands I commit My spirit"* (Luke 23:46).

I Peter 3:19 and Ephesians 4:9 indicate that Jesus, upon surrendering His life at Calvary, "descended into hell" (i.e., *sheol*, the underworld – "Abraham's bosom", the abode of the righteous dead, until after the Resurrection: see Jesus teaching in Luke 16 in this regard. *He did not make this descent in order to suffer further in our behalf.* Rather, He went to "preach to the spirits in prison" (I Peter 3:19) – proclaiming the *worthiness of faith* that had long anticipated the coming Redeemer – the Seed of the woman (Genesis 3:15), and proclaiming the *justice of the judgment* of all who had rejected the truth of God and the way of faith.

Following the gift of His life, the Son of God rose from the dead, then ascended to the Father's right hand to make additional gifts.

- **The Son "pours out" the "gift of the Holy Spirit" to those who will receive** (Acts 2:32–33, 38, 39; 11:16–17). Before His crucifixion, Jesus told His disciples that He would send "the Comforter" – the Holy Spirit. Then, after His resurrection, He commanded them to stay in Jerusalem until they received the "power from on high" He would send – baptizing them with the Holy Spirit (Luke 24:49; Acts 1:5). On the Day of Pentecost, Peter told the inquiring crowd what had happened, expounding the prophecies, and explaining the supernatural visitation taking place, as people from many nationalities heard, in their native tongue, the disciples miraculously praising God in languages they had never learned.

  In pouring out the Holy Spirit upon His Church, Jesus was unleashing the power for His people do continue "all He began to do and teach" (Acts 1:1). This possibility opens as we, His people, learn, grow and obey Him, that we may move in the life and power of the Spirit, walking in loving submission and full obedience to God. No longer confined to the personal physical limits of His body, as during His ministry, now Christ is incarnating Himself in His whole Church by the power of the Spirit.

- **The Son gives servant-leaders to nurture and edify His people as He builds His Church** (Ephesians 4:7–16). Jesus having poured out the Spirit, knows that His people need to be led, shepherded, fed and cared for, and so He gives *ministry* to the Church. He gives apostles, prophets, evangelists, pastors and teachers (Ephesians 4). These gifts to the Church are *people* who will occupy various "servant roles" in the Church – their essential mission being to assist Christ's people to wholeness, to cultivate and nurture them in the Word, and to equip them for ministry in the power of the Holy Spirit.

It is crucial to remember, these "office gifts," as they are sometimes called, are to be respected and honored for the calling, gift and authority with which Christ has endowed them. However, and possibly even more crucially, these people-gifts are appointed by the Lord of the Church to *serve, to lay down their lives for the sheep, to **not*** "lord it over the flock" (I Peter 5:2, 3); and while they are to be lovingly and faithfully funded by the Body (I Timothy 5:17, 18), they are not to capitalize on their position to exploit a personal or financial advantage (I Peter 5:2). Their essential role is to be used under the touch of the Holy Spirit, and manifesting the character of Christ, to nurture and develop His life in His people, unto the advance of *their* ministry and effectiveness in touching the world in Jesus' Name.

▶ *In summary, re: the Son –*

Jesus gave up His life for us, to redeem us and restore us to the Father. Having achieved this "saving work," He set in motion His "building work" – the building of His Church (Matthew 16:13–19). To achieve this, He poured out "the gift of the Holy Spirit" on the Church at the beginning, and calls each of His own in every place and in every era to open to the same experience of being baptized with the Holy Spirit (Acts 2:38, 39). His life flowing into and through His Church is advanced by His gift of people who are gifted and assigned by Him to help build and shape the Church – the people of God. These ministries help in two ways: through assisting growth, they help believers "recover" the purpose of the Father creatively put in them from birth; and they equip believers in the Word and by the Holy Spirit, to learn to function in faith, faithfulness and power as members of Christ's Body.

God the Holy Spirit

Let us continue observing the Trinity in creation and redemption, looking at the Holy Spirit.

- **The Holy Spirit gives Himself to His ministry of "convincing" and "glorifying".** In the Gospel of John, Jesus begins to introduce His disciples to the ministry of the Holy Spirit – the Comforter (14:16–17). In 14:25–26 He adds to the subject, indicating the teaching ministry the Spirit will bring, and in 15:26 that the Spirit will "testify" of Christ. These contribute to, and ultimately focus on the "convincing/glorifying" activity of God the Holy Spirit as He magnifies the Person of Jesus Christ, God's Son, to the world – "He will *convict* the world of sin, righteousness and judgment" (16:8–11) and "He will *glorify* Me" – i.e., Jesus, the Risen Lord (16:13–14). Always remember He is moving on hearts, achieving this, even when we often do not recognize Him at work. The Holy Spirit goes before us, preparing hearts to receive the testimony of Jesus, and to draw people to Him as we bear witness to His life, grace, love and power.

- **The Holy Spirit gives "wisdom and knowledge" in Christ, unto the Father's "hope".** Ephesians 1:17–18 are part of the Apostle Paul's prayer for believers to gain heart-insight (*"the eyes of your heart being enlightened"*) that they might see the *"hope"* of the Father's *"calling"* in their lives. This clearly evidences that once we come back to the Father through the Son, the Holy Spirit desires to bring us into a place of understanding as to *exactly what the Father had in mind for us when we were conceived in His mind.* His unique, creative investment in each of us is what is being referenced as "the riches of the glory of *His* inheritance" *in us!* (Contrasted with *our* inheritance in Him – Ephesians 1:13, 14). It is the Holy Spirit's reconstructive, redirective program, designed to bring us *back into* and *up unto* the Father's will and purpose for us; to actuate what Jesus paid for, to be realized since He has redeemed us unto the Father.

- **The Holy Spirit gives "grace gifts" (charismata) to enable the believer's ministry.** As well as the "creational-motivational" gifting and ability the Father has seeded in each of His own human creatures; and as well as the "redemptive-restorative" power of salvation through the Son's gift of Himself; the Holy Spirit is a Giver of distinct gifts, too. I Corinthians 12:7–11 lists nine distinct "manifestations" of the Holy Spirit. They should not be confused with those gifts of the Godhead that are given by the Father and the Son. These are "resourcings" the Holy Spirit seeks to add to the Body – distributing "as He wills" (I Corinthians 12:11), and as believer's earnestly welcome and desire His resourcing (I Corinthians 12:31; 14:1).

The purpose of these specific gifts – distinctly said to be given by the Holy Spirit – is to extend the graces and power-life of Christ Himself *through* the ministry of the believer, supplying supernatural gifts that will enhance our work as representatives of Jesus – agents of the Kingdom of God – moving in His life, love and power wherever we go. Jesus gives us the gift of the Holy Spirit, but when the Spirit comes to dwell in us He is loaded with packages! He desires to release much more in us and through us than we could ever imagine. These gifts are given "for delivery" not for accumulation. They are given to us to be given to others – as the flow of the power of God reaches through the Body of the Church to people – both saved and lost – who need what only He can do. Many have noted these three basic categories:

i. **Gifts of insight** – knowledge, wisdom, discernment.

ii. **Gifts of power** – faith, miracles, healing.

iii. **Gifts of utterance** – prophecy, tongues, interpretation.

After describing the various gifts of the Holy Spirit in verses 7–11 of I Corinthians, vs. 12–26 go on to compare the Church to the human body. The point is to show that such a wide diversity of spiritual gifts should lead to unity, as each gift contributes something necessary for life, growth and development. Each person plays their part and no one can succeed alone. There is no room for pride or arrogance.

▶ *Summarizing – the whole: Father, Son and Spirit –*

All in all, the splendor of this full and expansive work of the Godhead brings us to a new place of amazement. How wonderful – that Father God should have, before-all-time, had a plan for me! How wonderful – that the Son of God should have, before-all-time, determined to die to rescue sinners and see the Father's plan fulfilled! And how wonderful – that the Spirit of God so fully and faithfully pursues us to bring us to Christ, then equips us with resources beyond ourselves that by the Spirit's enablement we become empowered *ministers* of Christ's life, love and power.

"And we have such trust through Christ toward God. Not that we are sufficient of ourselves to think of anything as being from ourselves, but our sufficiency is from God, who also made us sufficient as ministers of the new covenant, not of the letter but of the Spirit; for the letter kills, but the Spirit gives life."

(II Corinthians 3:4–6)

PART 3

The Fall of Man:
Knowing Revealed Anthropology

⚬ 6 ⚬

THE FALL OF MAN (PART 1)

THEME TEXT

*"Therefore, just as through one man sin entered the world,
and death through sin, and thus death spread to all men,
because all sinned."*

(Romans 5:12)

The doctrine of Man as revealed in God's Word is important for us to understand, for it reveals man as a *special creation* of God. Man is not merely a being who has reached some advanced point of ascent on an evolutionary scale. Man is not an "animal" who has become ever more sophisticated due to the passage of aeons of time. Man is a distinct being, created with a distinct purpose by the hand of God at a specific time in the distant past. God made Man to enjoy specific benefits and blessings, and to have a specific status. That status is one of relationship with God.

Genesis 1:26–3:24 describes the entire sequence of events from God's decision to create humankind – to give them (the first pair) dominion over all God's creation and set them in a garden paradise, to the tragedy of their disobedience and fall from their original state and their eventual banishment from the garden. That pair were created to be founders of a new race of beings we refer to as "Man" – not as a gender reference, but as a specific order of being profoundly and uniquely created in the image of God Himself – Creator of all things.

God had provided the means for Man to be fulfilled in every dimension of life imaginable. On Man's part, he was required to be morally accountable and obedient to His Creator; to acknowledge his submission to the One who made him, and thereby realize his highest possibilities. God did not place Man in submission to Himself in order to exploit Him, but to release all the amazing possibilities of the potential God had invested in him at his creation.

In the face of this "test" – to live obediently and accountably before an obviously benevolent Creator Who had made him with rich possibilities – Man chose to believe a lie and responded with disobedience. And so Man fell from his original state in the most disastrous and damaging occurrence in the history of our planet. To understand the devastation of this "Fall," let us examine biblical revelation concerning Man.

Three things can be asserted about Man at Creation: *state, status,* and *station.*

1. **State:** Man's state revealed something of the image and likeness of God. He reflected the person of God – what God is like.

2. **Status:** Man has a relationship with God. He is "related" to Almighty God – the One who created him.

3. **Station:** Man was appointed ruler over all creation as pertaining to this planet.

God gave Man the capacity of having fellowship with Him at a level unknown among the rest of earth's creatures. There is no comparison with any creature, from amoebae to animal to angel: Man was unique (and still is, though fallen and broken by that fall). Man's rejection of the terms God had given, his loss of the place he had been provided with, and his violation of the trust God had mandated, separated him from his Life-source and his grounds for governance over the domain he had been assigned. *His* **state** *was* **marred,** *his* **status** *was* **forfeited,** *and his* **station** *was* **surrendered.** Let us look more closely at the implications of the Fall.

Created in the image of God

When the Bible talks about Man being made "like" God, it uses two words: *image* and *likeness.* Genesis 1:26 says, *"Then God said, 'Let Us make man in Our* **image,** *according to Our* **likeness** . . . ' "* The word that is translated "image" is the same word that would be used for "shade". Perhaps a clearer derivation of that word for us would be "silhouette". If a strong light was shone directly at you and projected onto a flat surface, then the outline could be traced and a silhouette or "likeness" produced. This likeness would be a representation of you, but it wouldn't be exactly as you are. There would still only be one of you. A number of other people might even "fit" the silhouette, but there would still only be the one person – you – who cast the original likeness. The picture that the biblical word creates shows that man bears a strong resemblance to God. Man is not precisely the same, but there is a marked similarity.

How are God and Man alike? There are at least three ways:

1. **Man is a creature capable of reason.** This ability separates Man from *all* of the other creatures that God made. There are ways in which we can scientifically measure the relative intelligence of animals, and we tend to find that certain animals are capable of responding to certain stimuli in a way that causes us to say, "Why, they are almost human!" But these are simply terms we use, because in reality they are nowhere near *human*. Animals can exhibit conditioned responses, even great awareness and sensitivity, but they don't possess the capacity for reflection or reason. They may possess the ability to respond and perceive, but they cannot reason analytically as Man can.

    Man can reason, and in that sense He reflects the likeness of God. Of course the "silhouette" differs vastly from the Person Himself. Man is a mere shadow of God because of the finiteness of his capacity for reason. Man's intellectual capabilities are in no way approaching the omniscience of God, Who *knows all things* – far more than merely being able to "process" and "analyze" incoming information. Therefore Man can *reason*, but has limited *knowledge*.

2. **Man has a free will.** Man reflects God's likeness in the sense that he possess a free will and has the capacity of self-determination. Again there is a vast difference between Man's capacity to make his own private choices and his ability to fulfill exactly what he wants to do. *God is sovereign, all-powerful and omnipotent.* Just as God is omniscient and not merely a creature of reason, He is also omnipotent and not merely a creature of self-will. God possesses *all the resources* He needs in order to fulfill whatever He wills to do. God can make choices and He can do exactly what He chooses to do. We can make choices, *but Man is limited in his capacity to fulfill what he chooses to do.*

3. **Man is self-conscious.** Man is self-aware and able to respond to, and abide by, "moral" conduct. God endowed him with the capacity to tell right from wrong. If we compare that ability with the conditioned responses of other creatures, we see that Man's self-consciousness distinguishes him apart from the animal creation.

It is not proper to call Man an "animal" at all, though contemporary science has conditioned our culture to think of man in these terms. Evolutionists maintain that Man is a mammal, and an animal which has achieved an advanced hierarchical position in the animal kingdom. But the Bible never refers to Man as an animal. An increasingly humanistic culture has embraced the prevailing notion of Man being merely a sophisticated animal, because thereby a certain degree of irresponsibility on man's part becomes allowable, and morality becomes merely a matter of relative opinion. Since we would not necessarily expect animals to make good moral judgments or abide by certain regulations, today's Man justifies himself by claiming to be something other than that which the Bible reveals.

It cannot be because it is *unreasonable* to believe in the notion of a God who created Man in His image, that people choose to disregard the biblical account of creation. If you trace the evolutionary hypothesis back to any of the stages in its development, at every point there is at least as much faith required to believe in that process as there is to believe in a God who created all things at a beginning, and created humankind distinctly and uniquely at a later time. It is simply a question of deciding what you choose to put your faith in – a mechanistic system of evolution, or a purposeful creation.

Man tends to opt for the evolutionary theory because it relieves him of any *accountability* to a Creator, to a moral standard, to revealed truth or to deal responsibly with regard to his own sinfulness. Man's excuse for his behavior can then become, "I can't help it. It's just the way I am"; his answer to issues of accountability: "To whom?" or, "Who says anything makes any difference anyway – it's all relative!" But the Bible maintains that Man is the way he is because he fell from the position he was created for, corrupted the nature he was created to possess, and lost the higher destiny once within his potential.

Two ways Man is "modeled" on God

If we further extrapolate the biblical words that give us the terms "image" and "likeness", we arrive at the analogy that Man is *modeled* on, or *shaped* like God. In the sense that you might buy a toy car that is an exact scale replica of a real car, Man is a also a "model" of God. A toy car might represent the real thing in every aspect and detail, but it is far from being the *actual* thing. I want to make note here, that while such analogies help us to understand Man's make-up and resemblance to his Creator, we can only take them so far. We must not begin to invert the analogy and think of God in terms of being confined to a finite, physical body such as ours. We must indeed, never lose sight of the vast and incomparable nature of the Living God. There are, however, two ways in which we can say that Man is like God in model, shape or resemblance:

1. Man has a moral capacity.

2. Man has an eternal capacity.

1. Man's moral capacity

I have briefly mentioned that God gave Man the ability to tell right from wrong. The enormous difference between God and Man in this regard, is that the Bible tells us that God is absolutely holy. He can do *no wrong*. This is a very difficult concept for us to grasp – the absolute holiness of God. Some may argue, "Why then did God not make Man *exactly* like Himself in this regard? It must be God's fault that Man sinned." But this argument merely exhibits Man's blame-shifting tendency. The issue is that God offered Man clear parameters that would allow him to walk in both continual obedience to God, and high fulfillment of his potential. But Man chose to violate those parameters.

2. Man's eternal capacity

Man possesses an eternal spirit, but as a created being, is not like God in the sense that he has *always been*. God has always existed and will always exist. In contrast, humans have not been pre-existent, though each one will exist eternally. The childish image of humans existing as a kind of angelic being in heaven before birth, and the "coming" to earth to take a bodily form, then automatically returning to heaven after death, is sorely confused and, sadly, nonetheless genuinely believed by some. Not only do humans not "pre-exist," neither are we a kind of "recyclable" being, as in the teaching of reincarnation. The beginning of existence for mankind is conception in the womb. We have but one life to live, and the choices we make will determine our eternal destiny.

The Bible says that it is appointed to Man *once* to die and then comes a time of accounting before God (Hebrews 9:27). This determines our destiny for eternity – an eternity in the presence of God, or an eternity of separation from Him. So Man's eternal capacity is like God's in terms of endlessness, but not in terms of God's pre-existence.

What position did Man fall from?

In summary, the Bible tells us that Man's *state* was that of likeness to God, his *status* was that of relationship to God, and his *station* was that of ruling over creation. There are four statements following that show how Man's likeness to God was manifest. How did God's likeness reflect in Man, and what did Man fall from? What attributes did Man sacrifice when he chose the route of disobedience rather than obedience?

1. Man was endowed with knowledge and understanding

▶ *In the spiritual realm*

> *"...they heard the sound of the* LORD *God walking in the garden in the cool of the day, and Adam and his wife hid themselves from the presence of the* LORD *God among the trees of the garden. Then the* LORD *God called to Adam and said to him, 'Where are you?' So he said, 'I heard Your voice in the garden, and I was afraid because I was naked; and I hid myself.'"*   (Genesis 3:8–10)

This brief and tragic vignette reveals to us that Man had a knowledge and understanding of God in the spiritual realm. The evidence in Scripture reveals that there was a fellowship and communion between God and Man – a sense of partnership, and a *walking* with God that existed prior to the fall. This was not something that simply "happened" after the fall as God begins to inquire of Man.

The Lord had initiated a relationship that had an ongoing flow of life to it. Adam said, "I heard Your voice." He recognized God's voice immediately because of their ongoing fellowship. We have no idea how long God and Man *walked together* in the garden before the Fall. But we do know that it was long enough for Man, endowed with knowledge and understanding in the spiritual realm, to have a well-established relationship with his Creator. This explains why there is still something that resonates in the heart of humankind; something that still cries out after God. Christian writers and philosophers have said for years: there is a God-shaped vacuum in every one of us, and only God can fill it. Augustine's words express it well: "You have made us for yourself, and our souls find no rest until we find it in Thee."

▶ *In the natural realm*

Man was also endowed with knowledge and understanding in the natural realm. Scripture indicates that Man had an intellectual capacity which far surpassed the state he found himself in after the Fall. Genesis 2:20 says, *"So Adam gave names to all cattle, to the birds of the air, and to every beast of the field. But for Adam there was not found a helper comparable to him."*

In part, this verse states that God is showing Adam that he has need of a helper that is comparable to him. That in itself would provide a fascinating study. However, the remarkable thing about this text, which is often overlooked, is that Adam was solely responsible for the naming ("taxonomy") of all the creatures. Taxonomy is the branch of biological science concerned with the classification of organisms into groups based on similarities of structure and origin, etc. The Bible tells us that all the animals were brought before Adam and that he named them all. This is an incredible intellectual accomplishment! The Bible does not elaborate on specifically how Adam did this, but the biblical text does infer that the names he chose were appropriate to the types and kinds of creatures.

▶ *In the domestic realm*

In Genesis 2:23–25 we see that Man is endowed with a knowledge and understanding of the domestic realm – the husband/wife and parent/child relationship (see also Genesis 1:27).

The Bible tells us something of what the relationship between the first ever "couple" was like. At least two things are outstanding.

Firstly, the *equality* and equal partnership of man and woman is evident. Genesis 1:27 says that *"God created man in His own image . . . male and female He created them."* God created Man or *humankind*, which consisted of male and female. We have tended to use the word "man" in terms of the male gender, but God created "Man" viewing *them* as male and female co-equals.

From the very beginning the man and the woman's equal status was established. God says in Genesis 2:18, *"I will make a helper comparable to him."* That the Bible reveals this comes as quite a surprise for those who have attributed a somewhat inferior status to women, or for those who blame the Bible for the demeaning treatment men have often shown women throughout history. This was clearly never God's intention. To the contrary, God created men and women for equal partnership, and redemption opens up the way for couples to recover the fullness of His original purpose – *perfect partnership*. (Space and subject focus do not allow development of this concept here, but the above paragraph does not propose "perfect partnership" (egalitarian relationship in marriage) as either a right or as automatically achievable by simply becoming married. *"Redemptive partnership"* is the terminology this author uses to describe the pathway to answering the NT summons that a couple grow in mutual responsibility and maturity in Christ – which growth can become fruitful to the recovery of the full "grace of life" (I Peter 3:8) originally known to the first pair.)

Secondly, the Bible describes man and woman as enjoying *perfect communion*. Genesis 2:25 says that Adam and his wife *"...were both naked and were not ashamed."* What does that mean? The concept central to these words is not Adam and his wife's *nudity* (though they likely were), but the focus is on the *openness* and *transparency* of relationship they enjoyed. They had nothing to hide from one another because no violation of their relationship had occurred.

2. Man was positioned to enjoy and maximize every potential

Genesis 1:28 shows God bestowing His blessing upon Man and giving rulership of the earth over to him. God is appointing Man as a king over the earth, and also giving him authority over the other living creatures (see also Genesis 2:8 which shows God placing Man in the garden paradise as the pinnacle of all His creation).

There was nothing to obstruct or restrict Man in any way. In his Eden paradise there was no sickness, no death, and nothing to hinder what he could become. Man was given *dominion* – he was allotted a specific realm of authority; he was made king with a broad domain of resource for development. God told Man to *"be fruitful and multiply"*, to *"fill the earth and subdue it."* God was not merely instructing Man to "have children" to populate the earth; the implication is far greater. God wanted Man to "bring out" of the earth all the possibilities that were latent within it.

We cannot begin to imagine what unfallen Man might have achieved as he began to learn and master his environment. We are talking about phenomenal potential that was lost. We have no conception of what might have developed in terms of an unspoiled, untainted technology under the brilliance of Man in his unfallen state. We can however, glimpse a fragment of that potential through the amazing accomplishments of many brilliant "fallen" minds throughout the centuries.

3. *Man was accountable to moral law*

In Genesis 2:9 it says that, "*. . . out of the ground the* LORD *God made every tree grow that is pleasant to the sight and good for food. The tree of life was also in the midst of the garden, and the tree of the knowledge of good and evil.*" Then, in Genesis 2:16 God says to Adam, "*. . . of every tree of the garden you may freely eat; but of the tree of the knowledge of good and evil you shall not eat, for in the day that you eat of it you shall surely die.*"

God issued specific parameters to Man. The purpose of this was to demonstrate Man's "creaturehood". The parameters were placed there as a reminder that, although Man had been given a huge domain with vast areas of privilege and potential, he was still a finite being. And as a finite being, left to his own devices, Man, despite his potential for brilliance and accomplishment, still had the capacity to lose his way. The parameters provided Man a method of accountability to God.

God did not place a tree of forbidden fruit in the garden so as to *tempt* Man – not in any way. The tree and the accompanying prohibition was only a reminder of Man's limits; that he was a "creature" and not the Creator. It was an abiding statement regarding Man's dependency; that he relied on a source beyond himself – upon God *Himself*. The tree was placed and grown in the garden with the intent of pointing Man's eyes *upwards* – to his Creator; to enable him to acknowledge his dependency on God, and his abiding trust in His benevolent will and purpose.

No prohibition of God is ever forced upon us to taunt or to tease. People tend to take the view that if something is "out of bounds" or forbidden, then it is "human nature" to want to access it. But that is *fallen* human nature. It did not characterize the nature of Man prior to the Fall. God's boundaries were entirely benevolent, established in order to *protect* Man from falling and all it would mean.

Aside from God's issuance of clearly defined parameters to Man, we also have to deal with the fact that satanic temptation entered the garden (Genesis 3:1–4). No doubt some will legitimately ask, "Why did God allow such an influence in His paradise?"

Firstly, we need to realize that there was every reason for sinless Man to simply reject the temptation that was being put in his way by the devil. Since the fall, every single member of the human race has been tainted with the curse of the fallen nature, but at that point in time there was no sin in Man – only innocence. Man, however, failed to deny and overthrow the device of the devil.

Secondly, why was the temptation allowed? Because without a moral test there can be no verification of moral excellence. Man, created with moral excellence, failed the test – not because he was incapable, but because he chose to. Without such a moral confrontation there could be no verification of Man's submission to God, nor growth in that submission with its accompanying cultivation of character and moral muscle.

4. Man was subject to just reward or retribution

Man knew that he could enjoy either the reward of obedience or the retribution of disobedience. His reward was to enjoy the infinite possibilities of developing the creation around him, having dominion over all of it (Genesis 1:28). Man's reward was, at the very least, the subduing of an entire planet, and beyond that, who knows? We can only speculate on what Man may have achieved in the future had he not fallen.

In contrast to the reward for obedience, there was also the risk of retribution, and this was made clear to Man from the outset: "... *for in the day that you eat of it you shall surely die*" (Genesis 2:17). God tells Adam, "If you disobey you will die." Adam disobeyed and he died instantly in terms of his relationship with God, because he died *spiritually*.

Man also died domestically because there came a defilement of the family relationship. Adam began to call his wife "Eve", but she was not called that before the fall (Genesis 3:20). God essentially created *Man* – male Adam and female Adam. Now Adam calls his wife something else and that "renaming" has great significance – he sees her in an entirely different light. There is also the issue of blame. Adam blamed his wife for eating the forbidden fruit. This, too, caused a withering of their relationship.

Thirdly, Man died *biologically*. From that time onwards, even though it was 930 years later, Adam's body began to decay and deteriorate. Why did he live as long as he did? There could be speculative reasons for this, but perhaps a valid one is the absolutely pure and unpolluted environment that Adam lived in. The atmosphere of the earth and Adam's diet would have been radically different. Interestingly, God originally created Man as a vegetarian. The Bible does not instruct us to become vegetarians, it simply states that Man was originally created that way. After the flood there was a cataclysmic change in the environment of our planet, and the Bible says that after that time God allowed both the meat of animals and fruit of the trees for Man's food.

Man, endowed with knowledge and understanding, and enjoying an unparalleled richness of position fell, and the implications of that fall are phenomenal as we will explore further in the following chapter, as we examine Man's responsibility for our present human condition.

THE FALL OF MAN (PART 2)

THEME TEXT

*"For the creation was subjected to futility,
not willingly but because of Him who subjected it in hope."*
(Romans 8:20)

Before the fall, Man was positioned to enjoy and maximize every potential that a benevolent, loving Creator had provided for him. Man was intended to retain a relationship with the Almighty that would cause all his creative possibilities to flow forth in fullness and richness. Man was also responsible for moral accountability. He had to adhere to the parameters that God set for him in order to acknowledge his dependence upon God, and also to verify the moral excellence which he possessed.

If Man obeyed God's moral law then he would reap the benefit of rich reward. He could partake of the tree of life and know the flow of divine life abounding in him. But if he chose disobedience, eating from the tree of the knowledge of good and evil, there would come instead of reward, the retribution of death; of severance; of removal from the source of his life and wholeness, and removal from the destiny of high purpose and fulfillment that God had given him.

Now we come to the awful truth that Man fell. Satan lured and tempted Adam and his wife. The serpent's first point of attack was to question what God had said, *"Has God indeed said, 'You shall not eat of every tree in the garden'?"* (Genesis 3:1).

Satan first of all gives the woman reason to doubt what God had said, and then goes on to contradict God outright. He suggests that if Adam and his wife obey God it will be to God's advantage and their disadvantage: *"You will surely not die. For God knows that in the day you eat of it your eyes will be opened and you will be like God, knowing good and evil"* (Genesis 3:4).

This utter lie could be equally translated, "Die? You will not die!" In other words, the serpent was saying that God had falsely threatened them with death, and he urged them to break away from their dependency upon God.

The tactics of the enemy have never changed since. He is always trying to persuade us to deviate from God's beneficial guidelines, telling us that it will be to our advantage to do something else. He seeks to break the continuous flow of our communion with God that makes our lives fruitful and fulfilling.

Creation subject to futility

As Man fell there came a cataclysmic change, and disaster struck the earth. The Bible says in Romans 8 that even creation was "subject to futility" and describes the struggle of the present world situation. I have chosen this text for our study, firstly because it gives insight into the heart of God toward mankind, and secondly, because it speaks of the human circumstance and a great hope for the future.

> *"For I consider that the sufferings of this present time are not worthy to be compared with the glory which shall be revealed in us. For the earnest expectation of the creation eagerly waits for the revealing of the sons of God. For the creation was subject to futility, not willingly, but because of Him who subjected it in hope; because the creation itself will also be delivered from the bondage of corruption into the glorious liberty of the children of God."* (Romans 8:18–21)

These verses show us that this was a situation that God did not desire to bring about. He "subjected" creation to futility in the hope of bringing about a future deliverance. This "hope" includes the provision of His plan of redemption for mankind, but beyond that the establishment of a "restored" world that surpasses our comprehension.

In the context of this great passage, the aim of the Apostle Paul is to show us *life in the Spirit of God*. An exposition of Romans 8 demonstrates one grand point upon another: Life in the Spirit is:

1. Ordained by God to bring us into a life of victory over the sin which has infested our flesh.

2. Intended to bring us into a life of victory over circumstances, where we dynamically address matters in intercessory prayer by the power of the Spirit.

3. Intended to bring us into a place of victory in our relationships, and

4. Ultimately intended to bring us into a place of victory over death itself, when at the coming of the Lord Jesus Christ, we will rise through resurrection to be with Him.

In addition to these great themes, the Bible also reveals a gargantuan concept; declaring that eventually – in ways that we can hardly describe and at which the Bible only hints – there will be an impact of the victory-life of the Spirit that will ultimately affect *the entire cosmos* (vs. 19–21, Greek, 3x usage of *ktisis*, references *the whole of creation* – see G. Kittel, Vol. 3, p. 1028). The whole of creation is anticipating, with anxiety and expectation, the day that God's redeemed sons and daughters will come into their own – this at some time in the future, beyond the present order of things. This event will occur at some point in the future, so of primary importance is our *present* moment – living obediently for Christ in the "current" order of things. Although millions around the world have put their trust in Jesus Christ as Savior and Lord, still a vast proportion of mankind is as yet unaware of their part and responsibility in these matters.

In addition to this, the philosophy of our culture tends to seek *escaping* responsibility, rather than *admitting* it. In the light of this, let us examine three aspects of the present human condition that are the result of the fall:

1. Man is responsible for the human condition.

2. Man is incapable of self-recovery or redemption.

3. Man is dependent upon divine grace for restoration.

Responsibility for human condition

Man carries the responsibility for the present human condition in three areas. Firstly, as it bears upon Man's own experiences, relationships and circumstances humanly speaking. Secondly, as it bears upon the environment of the natural world. And thirdly, in regard to the infestation of the demonic into the spiritual dimension of life – the infection that has taken place as evil has penetrated our world.

There has been a dramatic affect upon Man's own nature, upon the natural environment around him, and upon the spiritual realm.

These three effects are the result of three specific areas of violation that occurred at the fall of man. These are the areas of **Choice**, **Calamity** and **Control**.

The issue of choice

Man is not a "victim of circumstance", despite the fact that everything about the climate of our culture argues for this. Mankind has a great disposition towards shifting blame.

- Man will either blame natural circumstances: " . . . For there *is* no God," the argument might offer, "and all this is the result of random chaos." Or,

- Man will seek to direct blame back towards God: " . . . For God obviously is cruel if He allows this kind of suffering . . . " etc. But the Bible discloses that things are the way they are because God is fully willing to tolerate the blindness of those who mock His love and His power, while at the same time waiting, patiently subjecting the created order of things to futility, because of a greater hope He has – a hope that is being worked out in the process of redemption, that the results of Man's Fall might eventually be overthrown.

The issue of Man's choice is really at the center of the human condition. Rather than victims of circumstance, we are the offspring of disobedience. *"In the day that you eat of it you will surely die."* The "death syndrome" that has infected the human race is the result of sin – the wages of sin is death. What took place in Adam has also been transmitted to us genetically – the inclination towards sinning. This is the reason behind the present human situation: Man made a *choice*.

However, we cannot simply take the view that Adam sinned, and that thereby we are helpless victims of his choice. Each one of us makes our own separate choices. Who of us can plead innocence? Increasingly infesting our culture and taunting a million minds is another great ploy of the enemy: "Look at it this way – mankind may have entered into a sin situation because of Adam, but I can't be responsible for that, so I'm simply a victim of circumstance." God doesn't ask any of us to be responsible for Adam's sin: we are guilty on our own – each of us, all of us – are responsible for our own sin.

We may have inherited Adam's *disposition* towards sin, but we exercised our own *decision*. By our own freewill, each person chooses to sin ourselves. In addition, we find many ways of justifying our sin, of excusing and pardoning ourselves – especially concerning sins of oversight or neglect. But nonetheless, our nature is damaged. When Man fell it was like a delicately tuned instrument was dashed to the floor. When it was picked up again, it just didn't work right any more.

So ultimately, the human condition is not the result of an unloving God, or of hereditary or environmental influences upon us. It is the result of choices that we make ourselves.

I Timothy 2:14 tells us that by reason of *conscious disobedience* sin entered the human arena. Ephesians 2:2–10 details and develops the sinning nature of mankind and the grace of God in response. This scripture underscores the fact that fallen mankind are "sons of disobedience". Man's choice has brought us to this condition.

The issue of calamity

The human condition for which Man is responsible, involves not only human nature and circumstances, but also the natural world around him. Wherever we look we see evidence of natural disaster. Our news reports are full of them: earthquakes, flooding, tornadoes and other environmental disasters happen, resulting in damage, devastation and loss of life.

We read in our insurance policies that the world calls these events colloquially "acts of God". Yet this is another example of the fall of Man bringing to bear on the human environment, something for which mankind is unwilling to accept responsibility. Man is respons-ible for the choices which have brought about the condition of our *own* nature, *and* Man is also responsible for the conditions of the *natural world*.

One could argue that the world is the way it is due to geological peculiarities, or specific meteorological problems. But the Bible tells us that when God created this habitation for Man it was *perfect*; it was *good*. We cannot describe the geological state of the planet at that time. All we know is that is was perfect. It was not created for the confusion, chaos and destruction that it has experienced since through the many disasters that strike us. We are talking about an historic reality – things are not as they once were.

We do know from the Scriptures that the world before the Great Flood, during the period of Noah, was different. The Apostle Peter confirms this fact in his second epistle, saying that following the flood, "... *the world that then existed perished, being flooded with water*" (II Peter 3:6). The Bible tells us that there was a "breaking up" of the fountains of the deep, as recorded in Genesis 6–8. There was a breaking up of the terrain, and also the subterranean cavities of the earth. We also know that when the world when it was created, all the land was in one place, and that later the earth was divided. The division was not only linguistic, national and ethnic, but a literal division of separate continents. All these elements point to the fact that the world had a very different structure at the time of human-kind's creation than it does today.

We have no way of measuring how devastating the results of the Fall on our planet have been. The impact of the devastation of sin upon mankind is seen in the fact that, at one time it had reached such an intensity that God had to pronounce judgement upon it by means of the deluge of the Great Flood.

All of these factors lead to an earth, a shadow of its former glory, ripe for calamity and disaster, subject to futility. The creation, once perfect, is now infested with disorder, disease and disaster. The fall of Man teaches us that Man is accountable for his own condition, and for there being distilled upon this plant, conditions that were not in the original environmental arrangement.

The issue of control

The issue of *control* is a most devastating aspect of Man's fall, primarily because it resulted in the entrance of evil into the world. The issue of control has to do with *who* is really in charge on this planet.

Psalm 115:16 says, "*... the earth He* [the LORD] *has given to the children of men.*" The earth was given by God to Man as his domain (Genesis 1:26–28). This verse in Psalms is consistent with our earlier study of Genesis that revealed God placing the rulership of the earth in Man's hands. God's decree was that Man should have dominion over the earth, and God is always faithful to His decrees. What He says He will do, He abides by.

Satan came and lured Man into disobedience, and Man, in submitting himself to that disobedience was doing more than suffering the devastating results of his own severance from God. Man's rule of this planet was forfeited and given into the control of the one to whom he had given his allegiance – the Enemy – by submitting to his destructive lies. At that point the earth came under the control of the devil. Man gave Satan legal right to rule by voluntarily submitting to him.

In Matthew 4 we see a reenactment of the first garden's terrible scene, as Jesus stands before Satan in the wilderness. Jesus is not in the garden paradise of Eden as Adam was – already surrounded by an abundance of fruit; being tempted to plunder the *single* tree that is out of bounds – He is in the wilderness with nothing around Him at all, reaching the end of a 40-day fast. Just as this scene was played out with the first Adam, now the "second Adam" – a second order of man (I Corinthians 15:45–47) – has stepped into the human scene.

> *"The devil ... showed Him all the kingdoms of the world and their glory. And he said to Him, 'All these things I will give You if You will fall down and worship me.'"*　　　　　　　　　(Matthew 4:8–9)

The issue at stake here was not stones turning into bread, or Jesus jumping from the pinnacle of the temple to prove Himself. The issue was the control of the planet. Satan offered Jesus all the kingdoms of the world in their glory if He would bow down to him.

There are two points to note here:

1. **Jesus did not contest Satan's right to make that offer**. This does not mean that Jesus would not have rebuked the "serpent" as he posed this temptation, although the Scriptures do not reveal the details to us. "Who do you think you are offering the glory and the powers of the kingdoms of this planet?" Jesus could have said. Nevertheless, Jesus recognized Satan's evil offer as legally valid, because He knew that through the fall of Man, the power of control of the planet had been submitted to the Evil One. And that power he exercises wherever he can to this day, with vengeance, destructiveness and viciousness.

2. **Jesus did not accept the terms of the offer**. Jesus refused to bow to Satan and take the kingdoms of the world. However, we know for certain that Christ has come to take the kingdoms of the earth back to Himself. *The Son of God became a man, because only a man could reclaim the kingdom.* Since the rule and control of this world was given to Man – and since Man subverted that authority through disobedience and gave control to the enemy – now the Son of God has come as a man, God in flesh, in order that we might experience what was intended for Man, and *this man* comes to break the power of sin, death and hell and reinstate humanity to the possibility of being qualified to rule again. Through Christ that possibility is ours once more. Revelation 11:15 says that ultimately, *"The kingdoms of this world have become the kingdoms of our Lord and of His Christ, and He shall reign forever and ever!"*

Incapability for self-recovery or redemption

Revelation 11 looks forward to a time when Christ's rule is total and complete. This is a certainty, but in the present time we are locked in an ongoing struggle against the Adversary as he seeks to dominate the people of the world who are living in darkness. It is this "darkness" or "lostness" that we must briefly examine now.

Man, through his Fall, is totally and completely incapable of self-recovery or redemption. There is nothing he (we) can do to reinstate himself to his original relationship with God and the realization of his (our) destiny under God. Neither can he reclaim the dominion given to him by God as a king. Man is helpless to regain his position. There are four terms that the Bible uses to illustrate that this is true:

1. *Dead* – **Man's spiritual condition.** *"And you He made alive who were dead in trespasses and sins ... even when we were dead in trespasses..."* (Ephesians 2:1, 5). A dead man can do nothing for himself. Man is biologically alive, but spiritually dead. Man can do his best in the circumstances in which he finds himself, maneuvering and manipulating his way through life, but spiritually he is severed and disconnected from the *source* of his life, and the full richness of his creative potential.

2. *Lost* – **Man's moral condition.** *"All we like sheep have gone astray; we have returned, every one, to his own way"* (Isaiah 53:6; see also Luke 15:1–32). In Luke 15 Jesus describes Man's condition as being like that of a "lost sheep" that has wandered away. The moral condition of Man is that he cannot find his way. Man is always wandering through life, meddling with things that hold no lasting worth or value – even things that will become destructive to him. No matter how efficiently Man may seem to "manage" life, he is incapable of recovering the moral excellence he formerly possessed.

3. *Sinful* – **Man's natural condition.** *"...you ... walked according to ... the spirit who now works in the sons of disobedience"* (Ephesians 2:2). Man's nature tends towards sin and willingly, by personal choice, walking in the ways of this fallen world. The context of this verse suggests that Man also tends to irresponsibly go along with what the rest of mankind is doing – to "follow the crowd", being manipulated by the dark powers. The Bible calls Satan the "prince of the power of the air" in this regard because he controls Man's environment and culture, like a puppet master.

4. *Hopeless* – **Man's eternal condition**. *"... having no hope and
    without God in the world"* (Ephesians 2:12). The most devastating
    aspect of Man's state now is that, outside of Christ, his eternal
    condition is hopeless. The lack of *hope* is such a characteristic of
    modern society that those who know Christ should at this
    moment shout aloud, "Praise God for hope in Christ!" Jesus
    came to bring us hope for tomorrow under the providence of
    God's rule. Man without Christ though, is *hopeless* because he
    has no ability to redeem himself and is therefore condemned to a
    lost eternity.

Dependence upon Divine grace

The hopelessness of Man's condition outside of Christ brings us to
the last point of this chapter. Man can do nothing for himself and so
he is utterly dependent upon divine grace. Even from the moment of
disaster in Eden, as Adam and his wife are fearfully hiding from God,
knowing that they have sinned, we see the evidence of the grace of
God towards man. From the very onset of the human dilemma we see
revealed the heart of a loving, merciful and redeeming God.

The Fall of Man is undoubtedly the greatest disaster that ever
impacted this planet, but we stand now facing a reality that is as
precious to us as it must have been to Adam and his wife. The Creator
could have justly extinguished their lives in that moment, but
instead He quietly questions them, "What is this you have done?"
God could have justifiably unleashed a flaming bolt of wrath upon
them, but instead, mourning, and remembering how they walked
together in fellowship in the cool of the evening, simply speaks to
His friends.

God will, of course, deal with Adam and his wife justly, and they
must suffer the very real retribution they were warned of in the
beginning, but first He addresses the Deceiver.

* Turning to the serpent, He announces the ultimate defeat of
  the Serpent: *"...I will put enmity between you* [the Serpent] *and
  the woman, and between your seed and her Seed; He shall bruise
  your head and you shall bruise His heel"* (Genesis 3:15). In this
  short phrase is encapsulated the titanic struggle that will take
  place between good and evil on the earth, with God ultimately
  claiming victory through Jesus Christ, the last Adam.

* Even in announcing judgment on the Serpent, the nature of
  God's love and grace resounds with hope for the fallen pair.

There will be a Deliverer! This is often referred to as the first messianic prophecy in the Old Testament and is known as the *protoevangelium*.

- Then the Lord turns to the couple, and we read that a creature was slain to provide tunics of animal skin. Rather than raining down devastation on Man, God instead sets about meeting their immediate need. We can summarize the characteristics of divine grace as displayed by God the Father as follows:

  i. **Patience** with the sinner. God didn't destroy Man – *"The Lord God sent him out of the garden of Eden"* (Genesis 3:23).

  ii. **Provision** for our need – *"The Lord God made tunics of skin, and clothed them"* (Genesis 3:21).

  iii. **Promise** of a Savior – *"He shall bruise your head, and you shall bruise His heel"* (Genesis 3:15).

So the story of the Fall of Man ends with a promise, but that promise is contingent upon mankind – one by one – acknowledging that we can only receive it by *grace*. We not only have a Creator who has purpose for us, but also a Redeemer who has come to restore that purpose to us – the Lord Jesus Christ. As we move on to our next topic of study, we shall see how that sovereign, divine grace reaches towards us so magnificently and majestically.

PART 4

The Plan of Redemption:
God's Restoration Program

✍ *8* ✍

THE PLAN OF SALVATION (PART 1)

THEME TEXT

"And you shall call His Name JESUS,
for He will save His people from their sins.
... Nor is there salvation in any other,
for there is no other name under heaven
given among men by which we must be saved."

(Matthew 1:21; Acts 4:12)

We believe that while we were still sinners, Christ died for us – the just for the unjust. Freely and by divine appointment of the Father, Jesus took our place on the cross, bore our sins Himself, and received the condemnation for those sins, dying in our place. Jesus fully paid the penalty for our sins and signed, with His own life blood, a pardon for everyone who believes in Him. He bought for us the right – upon our exercising a simple faith in His atonement – to be cleansed from sin and forgiven. This is the essence of God's *plan of salvation*.

Our study of God's plan brings us to Acts chapter 2, with the Apostle Peter's sermon on the Day of Pentecost – the first ever sermon in the history of the newly-born Church. Peter says, in essence, that redemption came about as the result of a divine, long-term plan. *Salvation* was something that God, in His foresight, conceived prior to the creation of Man; prior even to the establishment of the present order of the created world.

Peter refers to prophetic scriptures which show that this plan was the result of centuries of preparation and work by God. He quotes from the words of the prophet Joel, written 800 years before the birth of Christ, yet clearly making reference to the promise of the Father and indicating a long-term plan. He also quotes from the Psalms of King David, dated 1,000 years before Christ. Finally, Peter says to the gathered crowd:

"Repent, and let every one of you be baptized in the name of Jesus Christ for the remission of sins; and you shall receive the gift of the Holy Spirit. For the promise is to you and to your children, and to all who are afar off, as many as the Lord our God will call."

(Acts 2:38–39)

Within Peter's message we have direct reference to God's plan of salvation and its culmination in Jesus' death and resurrection. The evidence of Scripture reveals that God had long since prepared this plan by which Man could know remission of sins and a reinstatement of his relationship with God, should created Man ever fall from grace – a plan conceived before the foundation of the world.

Throughout this chapter and the next we will examine four aspects of God's plan of salvation:

1.   The choice of the plan

2.   The subject of the plan (Man)

3.   The process of the plan

4.   The price of the plan

The choice of the plan

1. The plan was born in the mind of God

The Apostle Peter, in his epistle to Christians living in various parts of Asia Minor, says that we are not redeemed from the "aimless conduct received by tradition from your fathers" by "corruptible" things such as silver or gold but, *"... with the precious blood of Christ, as of a lamb without blemish and without spot. He indeed was foreordained before the foundation of the world, but was manifest in these last times for you who through Him believe in God, who raised Him from the dead and gave Him glory, so that your faith and hope are in God"* (I Peter 1:19–21).

Here we see two things that underscore the plan of God. First, that the Redeemer, Jesus Christ, was *foreordained* before the foundation of the world (v. 20). Second, the reference to the "lamb without blemish" in the preceding verse, takes us back in time – even beyond the 1,450 years since the Exodus, when a spotless lamb was the sign of the coming Redeemer – to the garden of Eden. While we are not told specifically what animal was slain by God in order to provide a covering for Adam and Eve after their fall, it is reasonable to assume that it was a lamb. God's first response to Adam and Eve's sin was to announce the coming of a Redeemer in His address to the serpent (Genesis 3:15); then an animal was slain to provide a covering for the couple (Genesis 3:21).

This presents a vivid picture of the coming Savior and the way in which He would provide atonement for sin. It was God's first "lesson" to Man regarding salvation and the way in which Man would regain his relationship with his Creator. Such "sacrificial" acts came to be regarded as essential to walking in fellowship with God and worshipping Him.

In the next chapter of Genesis we see that Cain's offering to God is rejected, and yet Abel's is accepted. Why? Because Cain insisted on making an offering that came from the work of his own hands. Abel's offering was received by God because he was acknowledging that it took a *sacrifice* in order to be able to approach God and worship Him.

Peter reminds us that from earliest times there was a plan, ordained and set in motion by God, so that Man need not be ignorant of the process of salvation.

There are other references in Scripture which confirm this, most notably from the lips of Jesus Himself. In Matthew 25, Jesus refers to God's long-term plan of salvation in parables spoken in conjunction with a series of prophecies on the Mount of Olives. Within days, Jesus would fulfill the prophecy of the "lamb who was slain". Jesus' message was being delivered on the Monday or Tuesday following His triumphal entry into Jerusalem; on Friday, He would be put to death.

In Matthew 25:34 Jesus speaks of when He will come again: *"Come you blessed of My Father, inherit the kingdom **prepared for you from the foundation of the world.**"*

The Lord Jesus, who is about to be slain as the Lamb of God, is talking about the promise of blessing upon the redeemed, bequeathed in advance by the will of God, and ordained by Him before the creation of the world – the promise of salvation fore-ordained by divine decree.

So it is that at the festival of Pentecost, Peter comes to preach to the Jewish people, many of whom had shouted for Jesus crucifixion: *"Jesus of Nazareth ... you have taken by lawless hands, have crucified and put to death; whom God raised up ... "* (Acts 2:22–23). "Despite your lawlessness," Peter says, "this was God's plan. He meant for this to happen from the very beginning. It is the fulfillment of His great plan to bring about Man's redemption."

God's long-term plan had a victorious ending! The death and resurrection of Jesus Christ had resulted in the outpouring of the

Holy Spirit that the Jews were now witnessing – an undeniable verification of His authenticity.

2. The plan was given from the heart of God

The plan of redemption was born in the mind of God before the foundation of the world, and the plan was also born from the *heart* of God. When we deal with the subject of God's foreknowledge and His long-term planning, it is important that we understand that God is not just a massive intellect. The Bible does not say that God is "mind", it says that He is "love". All the attributes of God revealed in the Bible are adjectives that describe traits of His nature, so that when the Scriptures say that *God is love* – it means that He is the *personification of love*. God's plan of salvation was not a technically conceived "fail-safe" mechanism, but a rescue plan conceived out of a heart of love for His creation.

Romans 8:20 reveals that *"...creation was subject to futility, not willingly, but because of Him who subjected it in hope."* How was creation made subject to futility?

- **By the fall of Man**. God informed Man that the earth would not yield its fruitfulness so readily anymore; Man's sweat and toil would now be required (Genesis 3:17–19). Before the fall, Man was established by God as lord over creation under God's headship, and while he occupied that office, it appears that creation was far more cooperative with his endeavors. We cannot tell from Scripture to what degree this was so, but it is clear that following the fall, Man had to work hard to harvest the food he needed.

- **By God**, with the hope that the plan of redemption would bring about the eventual recovery of what had been lost. God did not choose to "frustrate" His creation willingly. Although He did not desire to follow this course of action, with great regret He carried out the retribution that Man's sin warranted. It needed to be done, but it was done with *hope*. In other words, He did it because He had a plan – a plan that would ultimately deliver Man from his sin, and also deliver creation from its "reduced" state of potential and productivity. It was a plan born from the heart of God.

II Peter 3:9 says: *"The Lord is not slack concerning His promise, as some count slackness, but is longsuffering toward us, not willing that any should perish but that all should come to repentance."*

This verse shows God's all-surpassing patience with Man. The preceding verse states that a thousand years is like a day to the Lord, and one day as a thousand years. Time is not an issue with God when it comes to completing His will. He is willing to take as long as He needs to accomplish what He desires to do. Peter infers that, with the passage of time, people tend to think that God has forgotten what He promised to do. However, God always accomplishes what He purposes to do, and the primary reason, as Peter states, is because of His heart toward us. God is not willing that anyone should perish, but that everyone should come to repentance.

3. Foreknowledge versus predestination

We need to further address the issue of God's *foreknowledge*. The fact that God *knew* even before Man was created that he would fall and that salvation would be necessary, gives rise to a philosophical problem for many. If God knew that redemption would be necessary, and He knew that not all would accept salvation, then why did He create Man, knowing that some would be lost for eternity?

God's foreknowledge

First, we must not confuse the *foreknowledge* of God with the concept of the *predestination* or *election* of God. When the Bible speaks of God's predestination, it describes the *provisions that He makes*. When the Bible speaks of God's foreknowledge, it describes *the facts of which He is aware*. In truth, the foreknowledge of God is beyond our grasp, as is anything pertaining to the phenomenal qualities and attributes of God. He transcends us in every way.

Yet, we can establish that God can know all things because He is eternal, and resides "outside" of time as we understand and experience it. All of Man's experiences are linear – they take place in time and space. There are things yet to happen, choices yet to be made, people yet to be born, but God has knowledge of all these things from His unique position of encompassing time. He sees the end from the beginning. That means that everything that will take place in time, as far as God is concerned, has already taken place.

However, the fact that God knows the outcome of all events does not mean that He is somehow manipulating Man's free will. Man is still able to make free will choices. Although God knows what Man will choose, this does not *make* it happen.

By contrast, *predestination* refers to God's *provision* for those who believe in Christ. By way of an example, we could say that predestination is like being scheduled to fly to a specific place on an airplane. If you get on the plane, then at the appointed time you arrive at the place where the plane is headed. If you don't get on the plane, you'll never arrive at your destination. Similarly, when God sees that a person has put their faith in His Son Jesus Christ, what God *predestined* or *prepared* for them becomes reality.

Some Christians would hold the view that God predestined some to salvation and some to damnation, arguing that this must be so since God knows the outcome of all events. He knew that some would refuse the plan of redemption, but He allowed them to come into being anyway. They contest that God is a God of sovereign election. This is the essence of extreme Calvinism, which may be contrasted with a moderated view of Calvinism which honors the truth of God's sovereignty without exaggerating it beyond God's own appointment of His assigned dimension of "sovereign choice" within the responsible power of the human will.

The problem with the exaggeration of extreme Calvinism is that it provokes questions which faithful biblical exposition would not invite. A kind of fatalism appears, prompting one to ask, "If God had all this planned in advance, how can what I do make any difference? If we are either elected for salvation or condemned to damnation by God, what say can we have in the outcome?"

But God is not partial in that manner. The Bible says that He is not willing that *any* should perish, but that *everyone* might come to repentance. God willingly opens His arms to us, having died for us on the Cross, and invites each one of us to come to Him and to enter into salvation. *Salvation* is what has been *predestined* for us in Christ. While the Father does indeed have foreknowledge of who will accept this free gift and who will not, He does not and will not make this choice for us. He has chosen that all salvation shall be *in Christ, and Christ alone* (Acts 4:12). That is His elective choice, and none can challenge it. But His offer is to *whoever believes in Him* (John 3:16), and that truth will never violated by Him, nor should any philosophy of God however "biblical" its claim, be allowed to dim the glory of the Sovereign's will that human choice be free to receive or free to reject.

In addition there are at least five reasons why God created Man in view of the costs involved. God created Man because:

- **Love must express itself.** Love cannot exist centered in itself. By its very nature, love must expand. Love has the capacity to create and bring others into being, and will do so for the sake of expressing itself. This includes multiplying, sharing and risk-taking.

- **The objective mandated the risk**. What was God's objective in creating Man? It is often said that God created Man for fellowship. But surely that is an unworthy reason for God to have created Man? God, who is all-sufficient within Himself, did not create Man because He was lonely – He had countless angels for fellowship. God created Man to verify His love and justice, and to bring "many sons to glory" (Hebrews 2:10).

- **The glory and blessings that would be offered to the redeemed recommended it**. The price of the process was worth paying for the product. It is God's desire that we should share even grander levels of His fullness. The greater good and blessing that would be bestowed upon mankind warranted God's creation of Man as a race. The Bible says that through redemption, we have been made joint-heirs with Christ (Romans 8:17). A "joint-heir" is someone who has been made a full participant in everything that is *His*.

- **No one needed to be lost**. God offers salvation freely to all, and when all people stand before Him, each one will be silent in recognition that He is just and loving, and that they have no excuse (Romans 1:19–20).

- **The greater cost was His**. He became flesh and suffered and died so that Man might be redeemed. The price of salvation was His. The infinite One entered the realm of finiteness and has committed Himself to that for eternity – Jesus the Son became a man and is forever a man in heaven. The sinless Son of God experienced what it meant to become flesh, to live in the midst of a sinful environment, and to suffer horribly on the Cross at the hands of those whom He created. He paid the ultimate price – His own life to redeem ours.

God not only created Man knowing that he would sin, but He created man knowing that He Himself would be the "lamb that was slain from the foundation of the world". God knew that He was preparing an inheritance for those who believed, that they would become joint-heirs with Christ forever and ever. Thus, the plan of salvation was born in the mind of God and came forth from the heart of God.

∽ 9 ∽

THE PLAN OF SALVATION (PART 2)

THEME TEXT

"Blessed be the God and Father of our Lord Jesus Christ,
who has blessed us with every spiritual blessing in the heavenly places in
Christ, just as He chose us in Him before the foundation of the world . . .
having predestined us to adoption as sons by Jesus Christ to Himself . . .
by which He made us accepted in the Beloved.
In Him we have redemption through His blood,
the forgiveness of sins,
according to the riches of His grace."

(Ephesians 1:3–7)

The word *forgiveness* is unquestionably one of the loveliest words in the Bible. It represents both the power and the tenderness of God. It is as strong as steel and as soft as velvet; there is a glory about the truth of forgiveness that touches the deepest places of our hearts. The precious blood of Christ not only paid the price for our forgiveness, but broke the power of sin in our lives, and broke the power of the enemy to bring condemnation upon our heads.

Our theme text here in Ephesians makes mention of the *long-term* aspect of God's plan and direct reference to the *price* of our redemption. The *plan* is revealed in verse 4: *"He chose us before the foundation of the world"*, and the *price* in verse 7: *". . . redemption through His blood, the forgiveness of sins."*

Redemption means that God has said to us: "I want to put in your hands the promises of My Word, the testimony of My Son Jesus, who has paid the price. Your hands that are unmarked, unscarred, can receive the gift of salvation, because His hands were pierced to pay the price."

The *subject* of God's plan of salvation is *Man* – you and me. The purpose of the plan is to *redeem* Man and has three elements that God seeks to accomplish:

1. Remission for man's sins.

2. Recovery of God's likeness in man.

3. Restoration of man's state.

The subject of the plan (Man)

1. Remission for sins

The Greek word for forgiveness is translated in several passages of Scripture as "remission". Remission means forgiveness. When we get a bill, and it says "Please remit", we know that means we are to return payment. Jesus Christ *paid the price* for our sin, and so "payment" for our sin has already been "returned". We can therefore enjoy fellowship with God when we accept His free gift of redemption. The word *remission* is used in the following verses:

▶ *"This is My blood of the new covenant, which is shed for many for the remission of sins."* (Matthew 26:28)

▶ *"Repent, and let every one of you be baptized in the name of Jesus Christ for the remission of sins ..."* (Acts 2:38)

In the context of these two verses, the word *remission* means that God has literally "sent away" our sins – He sent away the record of wrongdoing that indicted us. He took our sins from us and *sent* them to the Cross where all sin was accounted for. Through Jesus, there is provided a remission for sin. Therefore, Man who was separated from God by sin, is now able to come back to Him.

2. Recovery of God's likeness

Man in his fallen state was shattered and broken, and his ability to reflect God's likeness severely marred. In addition to being separated from God, the traits of God that were "stamped" upon us by the Creator – the divine genetic that God installed in Man – were shattered like a broken picture and lost. Although a person may be good, beautiful, or display any number of worthy characteristics, outside of Christ their ability to reflect the image of the Creator is distorted and disabled.

God, however, seeks not only to *remit* Man's sins, but to help Man to *recover* His likeness. God seeks to restore the inner part of our character so that the loveliness of Christ becomes evident in our lives. Redemption not only offers Man forgiveness of sins, but provides a program of recovery for Man's character that will bring him back into wholeness.

The second epistle to the Corinthians reveals: *"Now the Lord is Spirit; and where the Spirit of the Lord is there is liberty. But we all, with unveiled face, beholding as in a mirror the glory of the Lord, are being transformed into the same image from glory to glory, just as by the Spirit of the Lord"* (II Corinthians 3:17–18).

This passage points to the ministry of the Holy Spirit Who, as a part of the plan of salvation, comes to restore the image and likeness of the Lord in us. We are *changed* into His likeness by God's Spirit working in us. God desires that we not only come to the cross and have our sins forgiven, but that we also come and look in the "mirror" of His Son revealed in His Word, so that we begin to be transformed. The word "mirror" conveys the idea of "reflection" as well as "looking into". The more we look at the "mirror" of the Word that reflects God's glory, the more we will be changed into His image and likeness, and as we are progressively transformed, we will "reflect" God's glory more brightly.

The Apostle James confirms the idea that the Word of God acts as a mirror and begins to change us (James 1:22–25). He also goes further by saying that when Man comes to the Word, reads it and goes away unchanged, he is like someone who looks at himself in a mirror and immediately forgets what he looks like.

The Apostle Paul also stresses the fact that we need to come to God with "unveiled face". This means to open ourselves to God's shaping influence in a "transparent" way. If we do this, then we can come to God's Word, see the beauty of His character revealed, and we will *want* to become like Him. We will *want* to be changed. How does it happen? We are transformed into the image and likeness of God by the power of the Holy Spirit working in us. The word "transformed" that we use so often in this context is the root of the word *metamorphosis* – the process by which something changes progressively from one thing into another.

This is not something we can in any way accomplish ourselves, it happens only *"... by the Spirit of the Lord"* (v. 18) – by the Holy Spirit taking the Word of God and applying it in our lives, causing the Word to be activated in us. This is why so much emphasis is placed upon Christians having regular times of reading and studying the Bible. Even by reading just a small portion of the Bible each day, a shaping process is continually taking place.

3. Restoration of "state"

God's plan of salvation also includes the provision of *restoration* for Man from his fallen state. We have already noted that when God created Man He bestowed upon him the privilege of *dominion*. The first chapter of Genesis reveals Man before the fall as the ruler of all things in the natural realm of the planet.

God has not only "covered" the sin of Man, He has made provision to recover the broken character of Man. He brings us back from the place of separation and begins to fill us with the character and life of Christ. In addition to all of this, God also wants to *reinstate* Man to the position he was created to occupy – a position of dominion and authority endowed with God's love.

There are two scriptures that show the way in which God wants to restore the *state* of Man with regard to his dominion and authority. First, *"Do not fear, little flock, for it is your Father's good pleasure to give you the kingdom."* (Luke 12:32). Then, in Matthew 11:12 we read: *"From the days of John the Baptist until now the kingdom of heaven suffers violence, and the violent take it by force."*

The common denominator in these two verses is the word *"kingdom"*. "To give you the kingdom" refers to a restoration of authority. It is the restoration of Man to the state of living under and by God's ruling power. The context of Luke 12:32 is that of Jesus delivering the sermon on the Mount. He precedes this statement with the words "Do not fear..." because He has just been telling the crowd not to worry about the basic needs of life. Jesus is saying that we should not fear because it is the Father's pleasure to restore us to rulership in life (Romans 5:17). Anxiety about the necessities of life – food, clothing, relationships, and so forth – need no longer dominate or crush us. We no longer need to be driven by the incessant motivation to "survive", but should become dependent upon God for provision.

Jesus says *"Do not fear, **little flock**..."* indicating that the listeners *belong* to God. The barrier of separation has been removed, and now God desires to do more – to reinstate the rulership of mankind.

Jesus has been speaking about the restoration of Man's authority in reference to the fundamental needs of life, and in Matthew 11, He speaks about Man's authority with reference to confrontation with the powers of hell. When the Bible says that the "violent" take the kingdom by force, the word is referring to a holy, divine strength that is "breaking in". It is the sheer force of life in Christ which is breaking into the present order of the created world and overthrowing it. We could summarize these two aspects by saying that, in restoring our dominion, God is concerned with the issues of *welfare* and *warfare*.

God ultimately wants to see Man restored as a *dependent* with *authority* – the critical balance that was in place before the Fall. Gaining a balanced understanding of Man's position in this regard is vital. It is easy to allow the fact that God has given us spiritual authority to go to our heads. We must be mindful of the fact that this resource of power flows through people who have learned that they are entirely dependent upon Him for it.

Followers of Christ are not "lions" who are running headlong into battle. They are like God's "lambs" who have been endowed with the power of the "Lion". Jesus showed by His example that we are to walk in the humility and simplicity of dependence upon God, without fear of the adversary. Maintaining such an attitude will save us from presumptuous arrogance.

Having said that, we are called to make an assertion of kingdom authority in the reality of spiritual battle. As followers of Christ, we are called to "move out" and claim dominion. If we don't, then there will be areas that God's kingdom will not penetrate. God wants there to be men and women who know that although they are His "sheep", they are also "soldiers" who need to march out and possess the land – soldiers who will advance His kingdom. While we are not covering these topics here, advancement of the kingdom includes binding and loosing, laying claim to the promises of God, and intercessory prayer. Every believer has been given the ability to move under God's authority with appropriate humility, knowing that every need will be met by God, and with dominion over all the powers of hell.

So then, God calls us to a place of *remission* for our sins; to *recover* His image and likeness by the work of the Holy Spirit, and to be *restored* to a place of authority and dominion, first in our own lives, and then as His agents in reclaiming and advancing His kingdom.

The process of the plan

Sin penetrated mankind and set in motion the "death syndrome" when Adam and Eve chose to disobey God and violate the boundaries He had set for them. After speaking first to Adam and Eve, God then confronted the serpent who deceived Eve: *"I will put enmity between you and the woman, and between your seed and her Seed..."* (Genesis 3:15).

God was speaking of the struggle between good and evil that would ensue, and was also pointing to the fact that a Redeemer would come. God says that this Redeemer will be an "offspring" descended from Adam and Eve – not by natural birth, but by the miracle birth of the Messiah. In this way, God uses Eve as His agent. He informs the serpent that although he managed to deceive Eve, God will use *her* Seed to crush the serpent's head and break his power.

1. The preparation of human understanding

This was the first of a series of prophecies and lessons that God gave to Man by *type* – in other words, by using metaphorical illustrations. Sometimes the Scriptures call these illustrations *shadows* – they hint in a small way at something that God will do in a much greater way; they are shadows of what is to come. God showed Man a shadow of redemption. He was preparing Man for the coming Redeemer, and the preparation began immediately before Man was exiled from the garden of Eden.

The Bible says that the Law of Moses was a shadow of the good things that God was going to bring forth through His Son, Jesus Christ the Redeemer: *"For the law, having a shadow of the good things to come, and not the very image of the things, can never with these same sacrifices which they offer continually year by year, make those who approach perfect"* (Hebrews 10:1).

There are two things to note in this verse. First, the context and primary point of the text is that the Law in itself is incomplete and unsatisfactory. It was adequate as a preliminary announcement and a means of teaching Man about the ultimate sacrifice that the coming Messiah would make. God still honored those who practiced and observed the Law, but it was always a temporary arrangement. The proof of its temporary quality is seen in the fact that the same rituals needed to be constantly repeated year in and year out.

When we speak about the Law in this context, we are not referring to the Ten Commandments, which are abiding, but to the ordinances of the Mosaic Law and the various aspects of the sacrificial system. These ordinances could never *perfect* Man. Even the Ten Commandments cannot perfect Man – they can only direct him.

Second, in contrast to this, the writer of Hebrews goes on to say that while the Law required repeated sacrifices every year, Christ once and for all sacrificed His life and settled Man's debt completely and forever.

Therefore, the object of the Law was to point towards Christ, and as such, it was laden with elements that foreshadowed the way in which He would redeem Man. The Law was full of *types* of redemption. A good example is the Ark of the Covenant – the embodiment of the presence and glory of God which resided among the people of God. The Ark "enclosed" the unbroken Law of God which was preserved inside it, just as in Christ, the Law was unbroken within Himself. The Ark was made of wood completely covered with gold, representing Christ's humanity and His divinity.

The Bible also provides *types* of Christ through lessons taught to individuals. When Abraham was on the verge of sacrificing his son Isaac, God provided a "substitute" – a ram caught in a nearby thicket.

Throughout the OT Scriptures, we see God giving Man lesson after lesson through types and shadows. He was preparing mankind by presenting the plan of salvation in ways which Man could understand. All of this is summarized in one verse: *"Therefore the law was our tutor to bring us to Christ, that we might be justified by faith"* (Galatians 3:24).

Why didn't God provide salvation immediately in Eden when Man had sinned? Could God have allowed Christ to step into the garden at that point and let Him destroy the serpent on the spot? If God had done that, then Man would never have understood all that was involved in his accountability to God. Man would never have grasped either the heart of God or the ways of God. The truth of God would have been seen from a greatly limited perspective. God knew that what had to take place was a "schooling" process that would continue until the actual presentation of the Redeemer.

2. The presentation of a Redeemer

Jesus Christ was presented to Man as his Redeemer when the Word became flesh and lived among us. The Bible says that when Jesus came into the world, fully understanding the mission God had given Him, He said:

> *"Sacrifice and offering You did not desire, but a body you have prepared for Me. In burnt offerings and sacrifices for sin You had no pleasure. Then I said, 'Behold, I have come – in the volume of the book it is written of Me – to do Your will, O God.'"* (Hebrews 10:5–7)

This statement is a quotation of the messianic Psalm 40:6–8. The verse in Hebrews says that these words were uttered by Christ *"...when He came into the world"* (v. 5). The amazing thing about this particular scripture is that it relates to us a *conversation* that took place between the Father and the Son. The second Person of the Godhead is just about to step out of the presence of the Father into the realm of humanity to become a microscopic entity in the womb of a virgin in Nazareth.

Jesus acknowledged the fact that the OT system of sacrificial offering was not God's highest desire, and He says to the Father: "You've prepared a body for me, and here I am. All the Scriptures that have been written over the centuries have spoken about My coming. Now I come to fulfill them." And in a moment, the presence of the Son was no longer at the right hand of the Father.

God had been constantly preparing Man until finally the time was right to announce the arrival of the Redeemer on earth. As the Apostle Paul notes, "... *when the fullness of the time had come, God sent forth His Son, born of a woman, born under the law, to redeem those who were under the law,* [3] *that we might receive the adoption as sons*" (Galatians 4:4–5).

After God's schooling process had been completed, after all the types and shadows had been established and centuries had passed by, God sent His Son – the Redeemer – at the right time to fulfill His plan.

The price of the plan

Approximately 33 years later, Jesus knelt in a garden and His humanity cried out, "If it is possible for there to be another way to fulfill the plan, then let this cup pass from me ... " But there was no other way, and so He said again in the garden the same words He said before He stepped out of glory: "*Nevertheless, not my will but your will, O God be done.*" And then He obediently went to Calvary to suffer on the Cross, where the *price* of the plan was paid.

The sinless Son of God died an agonizing death on the cross, and in so doing, completed all the requirements with which God had commissioned Him. On the Cross, He paid the debt of mankind to God.

1. Christ suffered

Jesus the perfect, unblemished sacrifice, suffered the penalty for our sin. He lived life as a human and was tempted in the same ways that we are tempted, but He did not fall. He lived a sinless life, fully in harmony with the Law of God.

> "[He] *was in all points tempted as we are, yet without sin.*"
>
> (Hebrews 4:15–16)

Although Christ was utterly blameless, He took our place on the Cross. Unlike the sacrifices of the Law, which required continual repetition, the all-sufficiency of Christ's sacrifice meant that it took place "once and for all".

> *"Christ also suffered once for sins, the just for the unjust, that He might bring us to God."* (I Peter 3:18)

2. Christ died

Jesus the Savior gave His life and died in our place to win our salvation.

The purpose of Christ's coming and His death on the Cross was to redeem fallen Man and to bring about the destruction of the devil and deliverance from the fear of death. This does not mean that the devil has been annihilated, but that his power is broken in the lives of those who belong to Christ.

> *"Inasmuch then as the children have partaken of flesh and blood, He Himself likewise shared the same, that through death He might destroy him who had the power of death, that is, the devil ... Therefore in all things He had to be made like His brethren, that He might be a merciful and faithful High Priest ... to make propitiation for the sins of the people."* (Hebrews 2:14, 17)

In the OT, the High Priest had to be "one" with the people he was representing before God. Therefore, the incarnation of Christ was an essential and indispensable part of the plan of salvation.

> *"And from Jesus Christ, the faithful witness, the firstborn from the dead ... To Him who loved us and washed us from our sins in His own blood ..."* (Revelation 1:5)

God provided the *payment* for the price of sin by sacrificing His own Son who paid with His own blood. Christ paid the price of our sin and broke the power of sin in the lives of those who identify themselves with His work on the Cross. God's ultimate intention is to one day remove us completely from the presence of sin and take us into His presence forever.

> *"Thanks be unto God for His unspeakable gift!"*
>
> (II Corinthians 9:15)

∼ PART 5 ∼

Salvation Through Grace: His Glory in Our Humanity

✑ 10 ✑

THREE STEPS TO LIFE: GRACE, REPENTANCE AND ACCEPTANCE (PART 1)

THEME TEXT

"For Christ also suffered once for sins, the Just for the unjust, that He might bring us to God..."

(I Peter 3:18)

There are three great truths at the heart of the Gospel: That salvation is by *grace*, and that it is appropriated by *repentance* and faith in Jesus Christ as we *accept* Him as our Savior. This results in the phenomenon known as the "new birth" in each believer. Jesus said *"You must be born again"* (John 3:7), and the Scriptures confirm that *"...if anyone is in Christ he is a new creation; old things have passed away; behold all things have become new"* (II Corinthians 5:17).

The Apostle Paul dealt with these three steps to life extensively throughout his epistles; we begin by examining the words he wrote from his prison cell in Rome to the believers at Ephesus (Ephesians 2:1–10). Paul mentions initially that it is *"by grace you have been saved"* (v. 5) – a comment he makes in parentheses as he talks about us being made alive in Christ. He then goes on to express more fully the essence of this amazing truth:

> *"For by grace you have been saved through faith, and that not of yourselves; it is the gift of God, not of works, lest anyone should boast."* (Ephesians 2:8–9)

Man is incapable of attaining salvation by any means other than receiving grace by faith, Paul explains, because God made alive *"you ... who were dead in trespasses and sins"* (Ephesians 2:1). This "deadness" is the separation from God that has occurred since the fall of Man, and he describes the many ways in which Man sins. Paul says that before acknowledging Christ, we *"walked according to the course of this world"* (v. 2). Everyone who is living outside of Christ is in a state of agreement with the world and its system, and as such, is "sinning", often in ignorance. We live in a culture that is more interested in pleasing *self* than pleasing God.

The Bible says that there is also sin that results from bondage. Man walks *"according to the prince of the power of the air, the spirit who now works in the sons of disobedience"* (v. 2). In addition to Man's natural propensity to sin, there is the factor of demonic provocation and manipulation. But we cannot simply "blame" our sin on either our cultural environment or demonic influence. *"... we all once conducted ourselves in the lusts of our flesh, fulfilling the desires of the flesh and of the mind, and were by nature children of wrath ... "* (v. 3). Every one of us by choice has indulged in fulfilling our own sinful desires. The text aptly sums up the condition of sinful Man after the fall, and then makes a pivotal statement of the NT:

> *"But God, who is rich in mercy, because of His great love with which He loved us, even when we were dead in trespasses, made us alive together with Christ (by grace you have been saved), and raised us up together, and made us sit together in the heavenly places in Christ Jesus."*   (Ephesians 2:5–6)

In the face of Man's persistent disobedience and errant ways, God sovereignly intervenes with an outpouring of His mercy. God's Word describes how His grace brings us from death to life, and how He has elevated us to a position of being "seated with Christ". This is not something that awaits the day of our rapture – the time when we will go to be in God's presence eternally – but something that has happened now. Those who have accepted Christ as Savior are now *in Christ* and can function from that position. The "heavenly places" that the text refers to is the "invisible realm".

In Christ, we now dwell in two different realms – the tangible realm of our physical being on earth, as well as the "heavenlies". This does not refer to a mysterious, invisible place; it means that our spirits have been made alive in Christ. Before accepting Christ as Savior we were spiritually "dead", but now God has "revived" our spirits and, through Christ, we can have the intimate relationship with God that was previously impossible.

God's grace has the power to bring us from death to life; from failure, guilt, shame and sin to forgiveness, and into a relationship with Him where we can function within His grace and know dominion and rulership in Christ. The rule of Christ comes as He exercises His Lordship through us, as we walk in relationship with Him.

Grace versus works

Grace is the foundation of the life of authority we have been given in Jesus Christ, and grace is also the foundation from which we accomplish "works" for God.

> *"For we are His workmanship, created in Christ Jesus for good works, which God prepared beforehand that we should walk in them."*
> (Ephesians 2:10)

This means that having received grace from God – the forgiveness of sins and the free gift of salvation – we can enter into the fuller purposes of God for our lives and destiny in Christ, setting about certain tasks or "works" that God has prepared specifically for us to do. It is critical for believers to understand the principle of this truth, because many have misunderstood it. *Grace* and *works* have become "divorced" in the minds of some believers.

The grace of God affects our salvation. Grace is God's work; He alone accomplishes it. His grace "works" salvation in us and this, in turn, produces a pattern of life that results in works that are glorifying to God. *Grace brings about works.* Many believers mix up this equation. Either they think, "If I do great things for God, He will lavish His grace upon me." Or they mistakenly think that since they cannot earn their salvation, they might as well passively accept the situation, and works are irrelevant. Both of these extremes miss what God intends.

A life of grace is not a life without works, but grace becomes *productive* through works. The main thrust of the Apostle Paul's message is that God's gift of salvation by grace is free; we cannot earn it. When we allow His grace to flow through us, "what we do" to help extend His kingdom becomes effective. Grace does not mean that *no works* are involved, it just means that *our works* are not involved.

Salvation by grace

We have seen that God sovereignly intervened on Man's behalf to offer salvation in His mercy and grace. We have also noted that we cannot earn this free gift by accomplishing things for God, but that His grace working in us will result in "good works" preordained by Him. For the remainder of this chapter and throughout the next, we will look at two distinct aspects of salvation by grace. Salvation is:

1. **Entirely God's doing** – He alone could accomplish what needed to be done by sending His Son to live a sinless life and pay the price for our sins on the Cross.

2. **Entirely conditional** – the conditions are not works, as we have already established, but have to do with *repentance* and *acceptance*.

Salvation is entirely God's doing

We will never really understand *grace* unless we view it in the light of the *Law*, *Sin*, and *Works*.

Law

You will often hear people coin the phrase "We are under grace, not under law." What this means is that we are not saved on the basis of our performance according to a written code. We are saved on the basis of the performance of Christ – that is where our salvation lies.

What is the Bible talking about when it speaks of the Law? There are two fundamental meanings used throughout Scripture.

▶ *The Creation Ordinance*

This refers to the original agreement made between the Creator and His creature. It was a law that declared Man's position of dependence upon God, and explained the obedience that was required in order for the relationship to be maintained. That law was violated by Adam and Eve after an unspecified length of time spent enjoying God's paradise, the garden of Eden. The law was founded on moral obedience whereby Man had to observe certain boundaries – i.e. he was forbidden to eat the fruit of one specific tree in the garden – and was informed of the consequences of breaching the law.

Man broke the Creation Ordinance and *"thus death spread to all men"* (Romans 5:12). What Adam became – a fallen man subject to sin and death – has been transmitted to the entire human race. We have inherited his disobedience and the penalty of death – each one earning it by the action of our own freewill choice.

Man also inherited from Adam an "awareness" of what it is to sin –
our conscience. Man has an intuitive sense of responsibility to One
higher than himself. Systems of humanistic philosophy do everything in their power to contradict this truth and stamp it out, but it
exists nonetheless. It is impossible for Man to quench the things that
God has instilled in him. The sense of need for a relationship with
and accountability to One greater than ourselves remains – even if
Man, in his lostness, cannot readily identify who or what that is.

Man's perception of accountability results from the "in-built"
knowledge that he has violated a basic ordinance of God. This law
has been written into human nature. What is "morally right" in
human terms is subject to varying interpretation in different
cultures, but the knowledge of transgressing "in-written" law is
universal.

▶ *The Mosaic Law*

The Law of Moses was given by God because He was establishing a
covenant with a group of people that He was going to use as
instruments of redemption for all the world. God called Abraham
and birthed the nation of Israel for the purpose of begetting a people
through whom He could extend salvation and mission to the rest of
the world. The Church, with Jesus Christ at its head, is the present
projection of that goal, and the expression of "Abraham's seed" – the
Israel of God; the people through which His promises are being
fulfilled. That is why Peter called us "a holy nation" (I Peter 2:9).

As God set into motion the initial process of bringing that nation
to Himself, He saw the need to school them in His ways. This
included domestic practicalities, social issues, ethics and moral
consciousness – all of which were encapsulated in the Mosaic Law.

God desired to bring Man to a place of recognition of two things by
instituting the Law. First, He wanted Man to understand his inability
to ever, by any works, measure up to the excellence that was required
of him. The Bible says that the Law was a teacher that would bring us
to Christ. It not only pointed us to the Savior that was coming, but
also to our abject need of Him.

Any laws that God made, Man would inevitably violate, and so the
Law is a reminder of our incapability – apart from His new life in us –
to live in obedience to Him. The first law of the Creation Ordinance
explains *why we are separated from God*; the Mosaic Law illustrates *the
way in which God would seek to restore Man*. The Law did not possess
the power to bring Man back into relationship with God – it was put

in place to give Man a spiritual "compass", just like the compass of the in-built conscience that God gives each person.

Praise God that now there is a new law – the law of the Spirit of life in Christ Jesus! (Romans 8:2). This new law means that the law of sin and death at work in Man can be broken through faith in Christ. The Bible describes Jesus as,

> "...*having wiped out the handwriting of requirements that was against us, which was contrary to us. And He has taken it out of the way, having nailed it to the cross."* (Colossians 2:14)

The Bible says that every time we sinned, it violated something of God's Word that was written down, and created a record of every offence and failure we were guilty of. But now – thanks be to God! – in Christ, our criminal record is wiped clean! And through Christ, His sinless record has been posted to our name!

Sin

Sin is the act of transgressing or violating the law. The Bible says that *"sin is lawlessness"* (I John 3:4). We tend to think of sin as bad deeds that have been committed. Sin is essentially *whatever disregards the divine order.* Sin occurs when we disregard God's law and decide to become "a law unto ourselves."

Take the example of water: if you submerge yourself under water without the aid of any breathing equipment for more than perhaps ten minutes, you will begin to die. The order of creation is *constructed* that way and it is the *law.* This is not an issue that can be subject to any kind of philosophical debate – it is the law and the created order has no choice but to abide by it. Similarly, sin is an act that seeks to contravene the *divine order.* Man was not *constructed* or *created* by God to sin.

As well as the issue of Man's *construction*, we also need to be aware of the *conditions* according to which Man was intended to function. Using water as our illustration again, we see that one of the *conditions* in the created order is that we need to *drink* water. We cannot submerge ourselves under water for long, but we do need to drink water, and if we don't consume a certain amount of it, then we will dehydrate and die. Both these infringements of the created order amount to the same thing – death.

Man tends to excuse his own sin on a number of grounds. We live in a culture that continually persuades Man to rationalize his actions. Man says to himself "I must shake free of all rules and regulations in order to live a truly liberated life. It won't matter what I do as long as I am not hurting anyone else..." Man justifies his sin on the grounds that "everybody else is doing just the same as me, therefore I can't be held responsible."

However Man tries to justify his actions, he never escapes from his sense of need for God, however that is manifest. I am persuaded that many people come to Christ not because of guilt regarding the sin in their lives, but because of their awareness of a deep void and a sense of aimlessness. When they hear the truth, it resonates with their spirit, and they just *know* that it is *right*.

Sin is anything that violates God's divine order. It is not simply a list of things that are "wrong" to do. As a result of disregarding the divine order, we are dead in sin (Ephesians 2:5). We have no power by which we can restore ourselves to life. No one by "trying to be good" or by "trying to change" can make any difference in their standing before God or restore their relationship with Him.

Society often refers to the sin of mankind as *sickness*. They say that a person is *sick* because they act a certain way or do certain things. Man is not sick – Man is *dead!* The Bible says Man is spiritually dead and there is no way a "dead" person can do anything about their condition. They cannot work their way out of being dead. Man may have biological life, intellectual life, emotional life, even a strong sense of moral awareness, but Man cannot produce spiritual life.

Referring back to our illustration of water, if someone is pulled from a swimming pool after being under water for a long time, it may be possible to resuscitate them, but they are not able to resuscitate themselves. The recovery must be brought about by another person. The great truth of salvation by faith apart from works is that God does just this for us.

Works

Despite the fact that Man is incapable of bringing about his own recovery, he has invented other *systems* of belief in which he puts his faith. This is Man's attempt to bring about that which only God can do. Human systems cannot save (Ecclesiastes 7:20). Aside from numerous world religions, there are at least three systems we can name that rely heavily on *works*.

▶ Reincarnation

This system says essentially that through living successive lives, you can work towards a state of harmony with the cosmic energy of the Creator; that if you are sincere about living a good life and being good to others, you will accumulate the wisdom you need to "master" life, and through progressive lives, become the being you were intended to be – godlike. (See John 3:3–8, 16–18.)

▶ Christian works systems

Most religions are works-based systems and even some Christian traditions have relied upon works rather than grace. This is the belief that God has saved us, but we must adhere to a set of regulations in order to retain our salvation (Ephesians 2:8–10). For these believers, their salvation, along with their sense of relationship with, and confidence in, God, is dependent upon their works. These Christians have usually been taught that they are dependent on Jesus for their salvation, but that if they do not perform certain works, they will lose their salvation.

Clearly no one is perfect enough to constantly observe such a list of requirements, and so this results in a vast amount of guilt and condemnation in people – even though they are born-again. Works-based theology breeds crippled Christians.

Of course, it is also possible to breed a very reckless kind of Christian who embraces the other extreme – suggesting that since grace saves without works, that grace is now a license to sin. This kind of believer may not understand that he or she has a responsibility to walk in obedience and grow in Jesus Christ; to live a pure, holy and just life before the Lord. While we are growing into that Christ-like person (and all of us are) we tend to sin and fail from time to time. We are not walking on a knife-edge of disaster, with God holding on to us tentatively or reluctantly. God loves and accepts us in Christ despite our times of weakness and failure. If we live in the warmth of God's grace and don't presume upon it, then we will walk with greater confidence and peace, trusting in Him to help us. As we do, God will be able to continue to produce the likeness of His Son in our lives.

▶ Humanism

Humanism is the works system which is in greatest proliferation in our world today. It is not a "religious" system in the sense that it requires certain rules to be observed, but is the product of fallen human logic. Humanism in its strictest sense is a totally secular approach to life which denies the existence of God, placing Man at the center of all things and glorifying "self". Humanism is a generic term that encompasses a broad spectrum of thought and has alternatively been called *rationalism, atheism* or *secularism*. The tradition of humanism can be traced back to the teachings of ancient Greece.

In addition, there is also a humanistic strand of thought that says, in essence, "I believe that I should try to be good to my fellow man and be generous and decent." This is the belief that "being a good person" or "being true to your own inner convictions" is enough to make God look kindly upon you (Romans 3:21–24; I John 1:8). Many people are absolutely sincere in this belief, but at the heart of this kind of mindset there is pride. There can be a fundamental smugness that leads people to say, "I don't need to acknowledge God in order to be 'good'. I'm pretty good anyway. I'm certainly a lot better than..." But this attitude is just as errant as a false religion. Each person is on equal terms before God, and each person will have to give account of his or her life before God.

Grace

Works will never get us to God. It is only by grace given by God in His mercy that we can come to Him and know the cleansing power of the blood of Jesus, and the regenerating work of the Holy Spirit in our lives. Grace is imparted to us through our faith in Jesus Christ.

The Apostle Paul confirms that it is *"not by works of righteousness which we have done, but according to His mercy He saved us..."* (Titus 3:5).

> *"For by grace you have been saved through faith, and that not of yourselves; it is the gift of God, not of works, lest anyone should boast."* (Ephesians 2:8–9)

▶ *The meaning of grace*

Grace then is the provision of God's works in place of ours. None of Man's systems of works are effective in any way, but God's works are complete and all-powerful. The root idea of this Greek word grace – *charis* – is *"gift"*. A *gift* is something that is given without any condition. The only "condition" is that the giver loves the person they are giving the gift to and so they decide to pay for it. God loves you, and He paid the entire bill for your salvation. That is grace. We can't do anything to earn it.

▶ *Forgiveness is a free gift*

A gift is free and does not cost us anything personally, however there is a *price* involved in giving it. In terms of the grace of God that leads to the forgiveness of our sins, God is not simply saying to us, "There's no charge because I love you." God paid an enormous price to win Man back to Himself – the life of His Son. The wages of sin are death, but grace means that God paid the price for us. God performed the work and paid the price that made forgiveness possible through grace (John 3:16–18).

Our appropriation of grace comes about through *repentance* and *acceptance*, resulting in new birth. Grace is offered equally to us all that we may come and drink of the water of life freely. Grace is God's unconditional provision for Man's salvation – unconditional in the sense that God gave it without restraint and without measuring our worth in any way. He has poured Himself out to us in the gift of salvation through Jesus Christ, and this gift is abundantly and freely available to us, not based on any works that we can perform ourselves. In the next chapter we will see that the only condition for receiving God's grace is *acceptance* which necessitates an understanding of repentance and a willingness to respond to God.

An appropriate conclusion and summary may be found in the beautifully coined acronym:

GRACE = God's Riches At Christ's Expense

"For you know the grace of our Lord Jesus Christ,
that though He was rich, yet for your sakes He became poor,
that you through His poverty might become rich."

(II Corinthians 8:9)

THREE STEPS TO LIFE: GRACE, REPENTANCE AND ACCEPTANCE (PART 2)

THEME TEXT

"If we confess our sins, He is faithful and just to forgive us our sins and to cleanse us from all unrighteousness."

(I John 1:9)

While the free gift of salvation is given from God unconditionally on His part, receiving salvation is *entirely conditional* on Man's part. In order to be *saved*, Man must first go through the process of *repentance* and *acceptance*. These two conditions lead to the experience of Man being "born again" – of having his spirit brought back to life and restored to a condition capable of communion with God the Father. As a background to our study it will be helpful to reflect on the following statement of faith:

> "We believe that upon sincere repentance, godly sorrow for sin, and a whole-hearted acceptance of the Lord Jesus Christ, they who call upon Him may be justified by faith through His precious blood; and that in place of condemnation, they may have the most blessed peace, assurance and favor with God. That with open arms of mercy and pardon, the Savior waits to receive each penitent who will, with unfeigned contrition and supplication for mercy, open the door of his heart and accept Him as Lord and King." (Declaration of Faith, ICFG)

There are several phrases in this declaration which deserve a brief definition and will help us as we go on to examine some biblical passages relating to repentance and acceptance.

The conditions for receiving salvation

1. **Repentance** – the act of turning from your own way to God's.

2. **Wholehearted** – unreservedly and without restraint or condition.

3. **Penitent** – a person who is repentant for their sins.

4. **Unfeigned** – genuine and utterly sincere.

5. **Contrition** – remorse and regret; a heart that is humbled before God.

6. **Supplication** – a plea or earnest request.

In the last line of this confession, we speak of accepting Christ as "Lord and King". This is an important distinction to make. Coming to Christ for salvation and receiving Him as Savior is distinct from the act of repentance and acknowledging Him as Lord. That is not to suggest that they may not – or should not – both happen at the same time – ideally they should. A person submits to the *Lordship* of Jesus when they carry out the act of repentance and accept God's grace. Submitting to Christ's Lordship means *surrendering your will to Him and allowing Him to rule your life*. It means putting your own will and desires in second place to God's will.

There are two basic responses that a person makes as he comes to repentance. The first is the act of *responding to the Holy Spirit*, because it is He who convicts us of our sin, and the second is the act of *receiving Jesus Christ* as Savior and Lord.

1. Responding to the Holy Spirit

Jesus told His disciples about the coming of the Holy Spirit and the distinct ministry which the Spirit would carry out on the earth. The Holy Spirit was Jesus' gift, sent to mankind after Jesus ascended into heaven. Jesus said that the Holy Spirit would come as the "Helper" – to carry out a specific ministry in the life of all believers, and also to convict Man of his sin, and therefore make him aware of his need for a Savior.

John 13–16 contains a series of discourses by Jesus, all of which took place in the upper room with His disciples the night before His crucifixion, in which Jesus is leading up to the announcement of the coming of the Holy Spirit.

Jesus refers to the Holy Spirit as the "Helper" and the "Comforter". This description is not limited to "comfort" in the general sense of the word, but also means to *exhort*, to *strengthen*, and to *encourage*. This is the Holy Spirit's ministry to believers. There are four specific aspects of the Holy Spirit's ministry in terms of Man's response to Him which we need to examine:

▶ He awakens an awareness of Man's sin

In John 16:8 Jesus says, *"And when He has come, He will convict the world of sin, and of righteousness, and of judgment,"* speaking of the "convincing" and "convicting" ministry of the Holy Spirit. He comes to cause Man to have a deep-seated awareness of his own personal sin and need. Everyone understands what we mean when we say a person has "convictions" – it has to do with deeply held feelings and beliefs. Similarly, the Holy Spirit comes to give Man "deep feelings" and convictions regarding his fallen state.

Jesus says that the Holy Spirit will *"convict the world"* – all those who are outside of Christ; all those who formerly possessed no convictions regarding their standing before God. You have probably seen unbelieving people grow uncomfortable as they come into a place where the presence of God is manifest. Sometimes unbelievers will also show a hunger or interest around someone who is filled with the Holy Spirit. This is because the Holy Spirit is doing His work of *conviction.*

Jesus goes on to say why the Holy Spirit has come to convict Man about his sin:

> *"...of sin, because they do not believe in Me; of righteousness, because I go to My Father and you see Me no more; of judgment, because the ruler of this world is judged."*   (John 16:9–11)

Jesus reveals the fountainhead of all sin: *"because they do not believe in Me."* People sin against God in rejecting the Witness that has been sent – Jesus Christ – and therefore rejecting God's gift of salvation through Him. The Light has come into the world but mankind still chooses darkness rather than light. This planet has been visited by God! His arrival was announced, and He came to live among us. He died for our sins in a demonstration of love that transcends anything of human measure, and rose from the dead as He prophesied.

Yet still Man dwells in darkness. Even though, on the basis of intellectual analysis, some of the finest minds in human history have drawn the conclusion that there is no logical way to escape the truth of who Jesus was and what He did, still many choose to rationalize and to reject God's free gift.

There are many who will seek to preempt an encounter with God by labeling Christians as "fanatics", or simply deciding to close their minds to anything which might challenge them. But an honest confrontation with Jesus Christ will always bring the conviction of our need of Him. The Holy Spirit brings Man to a place where he is aware of his own sinfulness, and aware of Christ's righteousness.

▶ *He draws Man to repent and acknowledge God*

Man not only needs to acknowledge the fact that he has sinned and violated God's law, he must also acknowledge that he has rejected God's Son Jesus Christ. As well as following his own selfish desires, Man has violated God's offer of salvation. Each person, under the conviction of the Holy Spirit, needs to come to a place of recognizing that it is only through Jesus Christ that this situation can be rectified. They must come to a realization of the fact that only Christ is all-sufficient; only He can meet their deepest needs – the greatest of which is the need to be cleansed from sin and forgiven, which is the beginning of God's restoration program.

The Bible informs us that,

> *"If we say that we have no sin, we deceive ourselves, and the truth is not in us. If we confess our sins, He is faithful and just to forgive us our sins and to cleanse us from all unrighteousness."*
>
> (I John 1:8–9)

In conjunction with the act of acknowledging Christ – who He is and what He has done for us – comes the act of *repentance*. The Bible says that *"...the goodness of God leads you to repentance."* (Romans 2:4). God prompts us to respond to His Holy Spirit's urgings to lead us into repentance. We respond to the Holy Spirit by obeying His call to "return" to God and forsake the "self-way" that characterized our life up to that point. This act of repentance leads to us being able to *accept* God's gift of salvation. The Holy Spirit convicts us, making us aware of our sin, and of Christ's ability to deal with our sin, then leads us into the act of repentance and acceptance.

The Greek word for repent is *metanoeo* which is a construct of the words *meta* meaning "after" and *noeo* meaning "to think". In other words, repentance is a decision on our part to "think again" – literally to have a change of mind that leads to a change of action – a turning around to pursue another path. Repentance is the taking on of a new mindset as the Holy Spirit makes us realize that we need a

Savior. It is a deliberate act of the will as we decide to "turn around" and follow God's way instead of our own. Although repentance may involve emotion, it is primarily an *act of volition*.

The implications of repentance are threefold:

1.   It means recanting our former ways and experiencing a "reversal".

2.   It means assuming an attitude of humility and teachability.

3.   It means an ongoing submission to God's shaping in our life.

I John 1:9 says that having confessed our sins and repented before God, we are cleansed – our sins are forgiven and the record of them wiped clean. The Holy Spirit's ministry also involves breathing a peace and assurance into our hearts that confirms to us we have indeed been forgiven.

▶ *He reinforces the reality of Satan's broken rule*

We note in John 16:9–11 that the Holy Spirit also comes to *proclaim judgment on the devil*. The Holy Spirit is not coming to convince us of our judgment, because Christ bore our judgment, but to show us that Satan has been judged. In other words, the devil's power has been broken. The Holy Spirit tells us that we no longer have to live bound by the devil and his ways.

On the Cross, the Lord Jesus bore the judgment for our sins, but there was another judgment taking place at the same time. Jesus not only broke the power of sin in the flesh, He also broke the power of the enemy so that we would not need to live incarcerated by the devil's snares. The Holy Spirit working in us "educates" us and helps us to realize that we are no longer subject to the world system that is controlled by the enemy. We are no longer subject to the traits of the "sons of disobedience" (Ephesians 2:2); we are no longer subject to the bondage that we previously lived under. Jesus said, in effect, that when the Comforter comes, He will say to you, "You don't have to bear that any more. You can be set free, because the ruler of this world has been defeated"!

Jesus has come to set us free from the power of the enemy and cause us to have peace with God. This happens to a person when true repentance takes place.

▶ *He will point to the pathway of restitution where needed*

This is a part of repentance that relates to doing everything possible to set right the wrongs that you have done in the past. It is likely that, for the majority of sins that we have committed in the past, we won't be able to do anything about them. But when we truly understand the fullness of all that Christ has done for us, and as the Holy Spirit progressively frees us from the character traits of the past, there will inevitably come a desire to do all that we can to rectify events of the past in which we injured, betrayed or hurt other people. Restitution isn't a requirement for salvation, but restitution is the response to the Holy Spirit of a truly repentant heart. Restitution is *works* that follow repentance.

The Holy Spirit may lead us to request forgiveness of someone whom we have hurt, or to try to resolve matters that were left in a bad state. For example, one day I received a letter that contained a single dollar bill. The letter was from a person who was studying for ministry at a Bible college. While they were training for ministry, the Lord brought back to their mind something that had happened more than 20 years previously in our own church. They described an occasion when they took something from the church, the worth of which was as little as 30 or 40 cents. To make restitution they decided to send a dollar bill, saying, "The Holy Spirit brought this back to my mind and I wanted to make it right."

Restitution is not something that we can always do. There are hosts of things that we just have to surrender as being "covered" by the blood of Jesus Christ. We need to understand *that is enough* – it is totally sufficient to cleanse our sins completely. But if the Holy Spirit prompts you to do something that is within your power to set right, then you may also make restitution.

A biblical example of restitution can be found in Luke 19:

> *"Then Zacchaeus stood and said to the Lord, 'Look, Lord, I give half of my goods to the poor; and if I have taken anything from anyone by false accusation, I restore fourfold.'"*   (Luke 19:8)

Jesus had singled Zacchaeus out from the crowd and told him that He would be visiting his house that day. Zacchaeus was the chief tax collector and had great wealth. The biblical account of this story says that Zacchaeus was seeking to see "who Jesus was". Jesus immediately responded to Zacchaeus' offer of restitution by saying, *"Today salvation has come to this house..."* (Luke 19:9).

Jesus was not saying that Zacchaeus deserved salvation because he had "paid" for it. Jesus was telling us that this act of restitution revealed evidence of the reality that already existed in Zacchaeus' heart. It wasn't necessary for salvation, but restitution manifests itself in the lives of people who truly respond to the Holy Spirit's prompting.

2. Receiving Jesus Christ

The Holy Spirit comes to lead Man in repentance which results in:

- Man recanting his own self-way as he becomes aware of his sin.

- Man returning to God, who alone can provide the righteousness through Christ that Man lacks.

- Man's becoming aware of the fact that Satan's bonds have been broken because Christ has judged and defeated him. Now Man is free from those bonds.

Man must *accept* the gift of God of salvation, and *accept* Christ's Lordship in his life. All the benefits of salvation we have been discussing are freely provided by God, but we must *receive* His gift. Repentance and acceptance go hand in hand. Our repentance does not *earn* us the right to receive salvation from God, but it is that which *appropriates* it – meaning to "receive" or "take for one's own use".

When we accept Christ, we receive God's saving grace, the entrance of His presence within us by His Holy Spirit, and the potential of all the resources of God's power. The Bible says, "... *as many as received Him, to them He gave the right to become children of God, to those who believe in His name*" (John 1:12).

When we receive Christ, we receive His righteousness, by which we are *justified* (Romans 5:1), and we receive His forgiveness so that we are *no longer condemned* (Romans 8:1).

> "Therefore having been justified by faith, we have peace with God through our Lord Jesus Christ." (Romans 5:1)

Justification is the act of God by which He declares the guilty sinner acquitted of all charges against him. The Judge of the universe says, "Not guilty." There is no grander biblical theme than the grace of God by which He *justifies* sinful Man – that Jesus, in dying for us, swallowed up all the sin, guilt and shame of mankind in Himself; that Jesus, the Son of God, became forsaken by God for our sake.

Jesus did not simply perform an act of atonement for our sin by dying on the Cross; He literally took all the sins of every person upon Himself. At the moment of His death on the Cross, the entirety of humanity's sins were invested in Him. And Jesus so completely dealt with all mankind's sin that God was able to declare, "All man's sin has been sufficiently judged and paid for. It no longer exists as a record to hold against Man that he should pay the penalty, if he puts his faith in My Son." Jesus rose again triumphant because neither the sin of the world, nor death itself could contain Him. He proved the power of what He had accomplished on the Cross, and now the Father declares all who believe in Him "Not guilty"!

How could Jesus die for sins that had not yet been committed, by people not even born? Because Calvary was an eternal moment during which the Eternal God was accomplishing something timeless, encompassing the totality of human history.

Since we have been "justified" through Christ, we now have peace with God, which means that we no longer need to live under the condemnation of His judgment. Even though we may stumble and fall from time to time, the Bible says:

> *"There is therefore now no condemnation to those who are in Christ Jesus, who do not walk according to the flesh, but according to the Spirit."* (Romans 8:1)

Jesus came to set us free from condemnation, to cast down the accuser of the brethren, that we might stand in the confidence of knowing that our sins are forgiven and we are at peace with the Father. Salvation is a gift by *grace*, but *repentance* and *acceptance* are the means by which we must receive it.

> *"But God, who is rich in mercy, because of His great love*
> *with which He loved us, even when we were dead in trespasses,*
> *made us alive together with Christ (by grace you have been saved) ... "*
> (Ephesians 2:4, 5)

❧ PART 6 ❧

Baptism and the Lord's Supper: Ordained Ordinances

BELIEVE AND BE BAPTIZED

THEME TEXT

"And He said to them, 'Go into all the world and preach the Gospel to every creature. He who believes and is baptized will be saved; but he who does not believe will be condemned.'"

(Mark 16:15–16)

There is no more fundamental assignment to the Church than to baptize those who believe and receive the Gospel. We are to:

1. Go into all the world,

2. Preach the Gospel,

3. Baptize in water, and

4. Make disciples of all nations.

Water baptism is a central part of our mission.

There are dynamic reasons for this rite – a Christ-commissioned activity which is taught in the NT as being parallel to the practice of circumcision (Colossians 2:11, 12). Not only should baptism be observed, it needs to be understood. Only as leaders in today's Church understand and apply the power-ministry intended to be released as believers approach, experience, and come through the waters of baptism, will the Savior's full intention for this practice become effectual.

Many Christians who have been baptized in water, do not realize what they have received by covenant from God for carrying out this simple act of obedience. They are not living in the *resources* that God has made available to them through water baptism. This does not invalidate the worthiness of their obedience to Christ in having been baptized, but this chapter is intended to point the way to the fuller pathway of participation *in* baptism, and appropriation *of* its resources.

Water baptism is not optional. According to the Word of God, baptism in water following a person's commitment of faith in Jesus Christ, should be seen as: a *sign of faith*, a *sign of obedience* and a *key to enablement*.

A sign of faith – a new reality

Water baptism is a sign of faith. It is a sign indicating a reality that "something has happened" to the person being baptized. The fact that *Jesus commanded* us to be baptized is a vital point to note. This is not a doctrine that was "invented" by the Church. Faith in Jesus as Savior includes accepting the clear directive He has given, alerting us fully to the importance of water baptism. There is no escaping the mandate, yet its clarity has caused some to raise a question.

In the words, *"He who believes and is baptized..."* Christ the Lord links these two events so closely, some have wondered, "If a person doesn't do *both* are they saved?" But Jesus resolves the question with His next words, saying, *"...but he who does not believe will be condemned"* (v. 16). Notice, Jesus does **not** say, "He that does not believe **and is not baptized**." The absence of the parallelism He might have made while commanding baptism, makes the Savior's intention clear. His disciples *are* to be baptized, but it is *not water baptism that saves* a person. It is, by Jesus' emphasis, an essential expression of faith in Him, and there are spiritual dynamics waiting to be released when our obedience to baptism is given, but water baptism is not the key to salvation: the Cross is, and the Savior Who died there and has risen again!

1. Questions raised over water baptism

▶ *Some people question its relative value.*

"Since water baptism is not essential for salvation, why should we need to do it?" The obvious, and categorically conclusive answer as to why we should be baptized is: Jesus commanded it! But there are also spiritual provisions for the believer that are intended to be released, doors to be opened, chains to be broken, when water baptism is obeyed. Let us come and fulfill the conditions, and enter the doorway to receive the promises!

▶ *Some fear condemnation if circumstances make it impossible for them to be baptized.*

For example, someone may experience a death-bed conversion, and have no chance to be baptized. Are they acceptable before God? Of course! In fact, it seems as though God Himself anticipated the question and arranged the marvelous conversion of the thief who was crucified alongside Jesus as an unforgettable example. Repentance and faith in Jesus as Lord and Savior are all that is needed to go to heaven. The thief prayed, *"Lord, remember me when you come into Your kingdom."* Jesus turned to him and said, *"Today you will be with Me in paradise"* (Luke 23:42–43). Other physical circumstances may obstruct water baptism in a few cases, but the Bible removes doubt regarding the certainty of one's salvation in such cases.

▶ *Questions often rise around the practice in some churches of **infant baptism**.*

While we do not make argument against this practice, it is important to understand what – at best – its value may be. First, *no* ritual of water baptism provides for a person's salvation. Some traditions may practice this in ways that lead people to believe their baptism as a child constituted the eternal establishing of their relationship with God. This is a serious misapplication of the truth, making salvation the product of religion, human works, and non-biblical suppositions. However sincere, we can be sincerely wrong. The truth is, the Bible makes clear that personal faith in Christ, by one's own heart decision, is essential to salvation (Romans 10:9–10).

▶ *Then, how should we deal with someone asking about this?*

I believe that in dealing with sincere souls who ask what meaning their earlier baptism holds, we should never demean its occurrence. I encourage the person to honor the spiritual concern and intent of their parents, "who cared enough to take the steps they understood as important to honoring God with your life." At the same time, I answer their question, "Should I be baptized now, as an adult?" with the Word of God. When Philip led the Ethiopian to Christ on the desert road, the man said, *"Here is water. What hinders me from being baptized?"* Philip responded by saying, *"If you believe with all your heart you may."* And he answered and said, *"I believe that Jesus Christ is the Son of God."* God's Word reveals, (1) a ready reception of Jesus Christ recommends, (2) a ready will to be baptized (Acts 8:36–38).

I encourage people to answer the summons of the Spirit in their heart, and to obey the command of Jesus in His Word. We hold that *when* a person has made their own, conscious, decision to receive Christ as their Savior, *it is time* to be baptized – baptism is to follow repentance. And in coming to the waters of baptism in obedience to Jesus, we should help each person to be prepared to receive *everything that is intended* for us when we are baptized!

2. What happens when we are baptized?

Romans 6:4 says that there is a dynamic *burial service* intended at baptism:

> *"Therefore we were buried with Him through baptism into death, that just as Christ was raised from the dead by the glory of the Father, even so we also should walk in newness of life."*

When you are baptized, you are being *buried* just as Jesus was buried, and you are being *raised again* just as Jesus rose again. There is a full *identification* with the power of what Jesus Christ has accomplished for you. When Jesus died He died for your sin, and when He was buried, the *body* of your sin – sin in the flesh – was buried along with Him. When He rose again, He rose having defeated sin and death.

Just as the person being baptized is saying, "Lord Jesus Who died for me, I acknowledge You as my Savior," so let each one say, "Jesus, Who was buried for me, I want to leave behind, in this watery grave of baptism's waters, my sinful practices, my selfishness, all clutching ambitions – all to be left behind. They remain in the tomb, and I want to rise to newness of Your life by the power of Your Spirit!" So baptism is intended to be a moment of our saying, "I'm dying to my old ways" (doubts, fears, passivity, pride, argumentativeness, rebellion, etc.) and one of declaring our entrance into the new life dimensions of "burial and resurrection" from the power of our past.

> *"In Him you were ... buried with Him in baptism, in which you were also raised with Him through faith in the working of God who raised Him from the dead."* (Colossians 2:11–12)

In this regard, it is always important to remember that it is the power of *faith's appropriating these things in Christ*, that releases such delivering grace through water baptism. It is the Holy Spirit's power at work that makes this possible: the water of baptism itself has no inherent power, but obedience through faith releases the dynamics of God's grace in this process of deliverance. (Incidentally, in the early Church, preparatory and follow-up ministry to baptism was practiced in the Spirit's power, often dealing with demonic bondages residue to the past life of new believers. This is a vital, biblical ministry which we administer regularly. Because certain exaggerations and aberrations have attended some "deliverance" ministry practices, we emphasize sound, biblical, spirit-discerning counsel in these regards. Still, we will not let the folly of fanaticism turn us from the wisdom of incorporating this needed ministry within ours. My booklet and video, *"The Finger Of God"* gives a brief summary on this subject which this volume in hand does not contain for lack of space.)

3. Why we baptize by full immersion

It is through the clear biblical figure of speech in Romans 6:4 – the burial of a dead body – that we feel the practice of baptizing by full immersion in water is the most biblically fulfilling. We will not war with others who baptize by sprinkling or effusion (pouring of water over the brow or head of a person), but notably, neither of these expressions fully reflect the extent of the biblical description of baptism. Full immersion is consistent with the definition of the Greek verb *bapto* – meaning "completely dipped" – a word also used to describe a sunken ship – totally submerged. Again, while we do not enter into strife with others in Christ's Body over this subject, we minister with the convictions we do for these reasons.

A sign of obedience – a new rule

As Matthew 28:18–19 reveals, baptism also confronts the new believer with a call to submission – to yield to a new rule in their lives – a new authority:

> *"Then Jesus came and spoke to them saying, 'All authority has been given unto Me in heaven and earth. Go therefore and make disciples of all nations, baptizing them in the name of the Father and of the Son and of the Holy Spirit.'"*

In sending His disciples to preach, baptize and disciple the nations, He gave them His authority and directed them to minister in His Name. Among other things, it means that each spiritual leader is charged with calling believers to be baptized, and to do it under the authority of Jesus' command.

The issue of baptism has nothing to do with church tradition or pastoral authority. Many people object to being *told* by their pastor or minister to be baptized, because they feel their freewill has been violated. They argue, "I would only be doing it because you told me to and not for the right reasons..." But the "right" reason is because *Jesus* commanded it, not your pastor! Pastors teach about and lead people to water baptism because Jesus' mandate was to "make disciples ... baptizing them in the name of the Father and of the Son and of the Holy Spirit", "*... teaching them to observe all things that I have commanded you*" (Matthew 28:20). Faithful leaders assist new believers past resistance, should it be manifest; disallowing fears, pride or incipient rebellion to rob them of a highly pivotal moment, and of a mightily releasing entry into their new life in Christ. Each needs to see beyond church history, tradition, or even pastoral authority. The issue of water baptism is ultimately the issue of *Christ's authority* in one's life. Will you accept the Lordship of Jesus in your life? Will you welcome His Lordship and His power awaiting you, so essential for the release of His fullness working through your life? Will you submit to Him Who saved you, to fill you to over-flowing, and to take up the reigns of your life and direct it for the whole of your future? Say "Yes!" Amen!

A key to enablement – a new release

Just as there comes a *new reality* in your life as you confess your commitment to Christ in baptism, and a *new rule* as you submit to His Lordship, there also comes a *new release* through the key of enablement. Acts 2:38–39 says:

> *"Then Peter said to them, 'Repent, and let every one of you be baptized in the name of Jesus Christ for the remission of sins; and you shall receive the gift of the Holy Spirit. For the promise is to you and to your children, and to all who are afar off, as many as the Lord our God will call.'"*

Here we see that the release of the power of the Holy Spirit in a person's life is directly linked to baptism in water. This has caused some to ask, "If I've already been baptized with the Holy Spirit, do I still need to be baptized in water?" The short answer to that question is, "Yes, you do!" Being baptized with the Holy Spirit does not make you exempt from the call to water baptism. This exact thing happened to Cornelius and his household. They were baptized with the Holy Spirit first, but were then immediately baptized in water. The Scriptures also make clear that this is not the usual sequence of events, but that such a case was not inappropriate.

With the enabling power of Holy Spirit fullness waiting at the waters of baptism, one other potential is present. Before we leave this chapter, take note of the words of I Corinthians 10:1–2, 6:

> *"Moreover, brethren, I do not want you to be unaware that all our fathers were under the cloud, all passed through the sea, all were baptized into Moses in the cloud and the sea ... Now all these things became our examples ..."*

Earlier in this chapter, we referenced the ministry of "deliverance" in conjunction with water baptism. An added note here is worthy.

In this text, the Apostle Paul notes how Israel was freed from their oppressors when they went through the Red Sea, and he uses the figure of the believer's baptism to show this is the way they were *separated* to Moses – that is, they were (1) not only delivered from death through the blood of the Lamb, (2) not only separated unto a new leader by their passage through the sea, but, (3) severed from their former oppressors, whose power was broken as they were drowned in the sea!

In short, they entered into a new realm; into a new release of life as they were completely delivered from the slave-masters of their past.

Sometimes, new believers in Christ come for baptism who are still plagued by slavery to habits and bondage from their former life outside Christ. While there is no question that they have received Jesus as Savior and been totally forgiven – justified in Him – still, some seem unable to shake off the shackles of the past. Ministry at the time of baptism is appropriate to be brought to bear on such challenges; if not at the immediate setting, pre- or post-baptismal arrangements are practical. As they allow Jesus Christ to "bury" their former self under the waters, it is time to fully appropriate Jesus' power to bring full freedom at all points – *through* Holy Spirit fullness, *by* separation from past bondage, and *with* deliverance unto full liberty, and entry into the victory life of our Lord Jesus Christ!

"Thanks be unto God Who gives us the victory through our Lord Jesus Christ ... Who always leads us to triumph in Christ!"

(I Corinthians 15:57; II Corinthians 2:14)

THE FULL SCOPE OF COMMUNION

THEME TEXT

*"And they overcame him by the Blood of the Lamb and
by the word of their testimony..."*

(Revelation 12:10–11)

The night before His crucifixion, Jesus celebrated the Passover with His disciples. The next day He would accomplish the work of redemption of which the Passover celebration was a mere shadow. For His disciples, the Lord's Table (Supper), or Communion, would from that moment on transcend the Passover in commemoration of a far greater deliverance. Our theme text, especially in its larger context, lends a clear statement on the extent of Jesus' accomplishments on the Cross:

> *"Now salvation, and strength, and the kingdom of our God, and the power of His Christ have come, for the accuser of our brethren, who accused them before our God day and night, has been cast down. And they overcame him by the blood of the Lamb..."*

There are five key elements of Communion that I want to highlight in this chapter. They are:

1. Communion is a celebration of victory.

2. Communion is a proclamation of redemption.

3. Communion is a declaration of dependence.

4. Communion is an examination of self.

5. Communion is a reception of provision.

1. Communion is a celebration of victory

There are four passages of Scripture in the NT that refer to the occasion when Jesus instituted the Lord's Table (Matthew 26:26; Mark 14:12; Luke 22:14; John 13). After they had celebrated Passover together Jesus introduced the concept of Communion to His disciples and spoke these words,

> *"This do in remembrance of Me."* (Luke 22:19)

Jesus said that Communion was an act during which we were to *remember* Him. This surely means to remember Him along with all that it implies – His death; His resurrection; His overwhelming victory; His majesty, and His glory. My observation over many years, however, has been a mentality in the Church at large that has somehow "reversed" these words of Jesus.

During most of my early life as a believer, the observance of the Lord's Table was of a mood and in a manner that led me to believe "Do this in remembrance of Me" meant that Communion was to be a morose commemoration – at the very least, an extremely quiet, pensive, sober and often guilt-laden event. Later, studying the Word of God and observing the presence of the Holy Spirit in our celebrations that, while not irreverent, were of a reverence defined more by faith than fear, by joy than by guilt, I came to learn differently.

Defining the intended point of remembrance

Since Jesus asks us to remember Him, we legitimately ask the question, "What exactly is it about Himself or what He has done for us, that He wants us to remember?" In the light of the Cross, where Jesus announced "It is finished," I have become convinced His call "to remember" is a call to *never forget the triumph, no matter what your trial!*

Our theme text in Revelation 12 states quite clearly that through "the blood of the Lamb," a great triumph has been accomplished over the works of darkness; that a massive release of the power of the Kingdom of God has been made available to mankind. Joined to this, notice in Colossians 2 a clear description of the Cross, as the occasion when Satan was so confronted and overcome, is made:

"He has taken it [our debt of sin to God] *out of the way, having nailed it to the cross. Having disarmed principalities and powers, He made a public spectacle of them, triumphing over them in it."*

(Colossians 2:14–15)

Returning to Revelation 12, we read that *"They"* – speaking about *you and me* – have overcome him (Satan) "by the blood of the Lamb and by the word of their testimony." In short, the Word of God is pointing to the fact that Satan, the accuser of the brethren, who relentlessly seeks to defeat, discourage, depress, denounce and disarm us with the sense of our own inadequacy and failure, has a point of accounting. He must retreat from every claim where the Blood of Calvary is made the Testimony of the Saints! When he would cause us to feel our unworthiness – to feel alone or distant from God's goodness and grace, or to feel resigned to our circumstances, supposing there is no hope of rising above them – we are to announce his utter defeat at the Cross. And we do it *not* so much by addressing him, as by *praising the Lamb!* As we appropriate the power of the blood of Christ in our lives, and declare our faith in Him, we participate (that is, "receive our share" – the basic idea of *koinonia, communion*) in Jesus' great victory at the Cross!

Through the power of His Cross Jesus vanquished the power of hell. So great was His accomplishment that I am persuaded, when we come to the Lord's Table, that the thought uppermost in our minds should be to celebrate Jesus' victory.

Coming to the table with thanksgiving

In each of the Gospels where Jesus is introducing the Lord's Table, He begins by *giving thanks*. Jesus gave thanks. He would very shortly kneel in a garden and sweat blood (Luke 22:44) with the pressure of His imminent suffering. But as He sits amid the celebrations in the upper room, recalling with His disciples the victorious deliverance of Israel from her oppressors by God, He breaks bread for them, takes the cup and *gives thanks* – still with the thought of victory over oppression in His mind. Though about to enter the conflict, Jesus knew the outcome would be the triumph of redemption's provision. Through His Cross, He would overcome oppression and bondage, and all the works of darkness – *so He gave thanks*.

The Greek word translated "thanks" is *eucaristao*, the word which gives rise to the term "the Eucharist" – another term used in some church traditions for "Communion." It is yet another reminder that Communion is intended as a time of thanksgiving, not a mournful or morbid event. Jesus is our Risen Lord, who is not asking us to sorrowfully remember the agony of His Cross, and somehow attempt to feel a little more "faithful" for agonizing over it with feelings of guilt. I am not arguing against feeling a humble gratitude for the enormous price He paid in His suffering, but I am saying this: when Jesus says, "When you take this cup, *remember*," that His call is to rehearse how He conquered the power of the Enemy – how He once-for-all paid the price of sin and death to deliver us from condemnation and unto hope. It is the counterpart to Israel's annual remembrance of the Passover – a celebration of *release from bondage!* – the NT call to celebrate the fact that through His Cross, we have been given an abiding place of victory over our slavery and our oppressor!

2. Communion is a proclamation of redemption

As well as being a time of thanksgiving and celebration for Jesus' victory, the Lord's Supper is also a proclamation of redemption:

> *"For as often as you eat this bread and drink this cup, you proclaim the Lord's death till He comes."*　　　　　(I Corinthians 11:26)

In the verses preceding this text, the Apostle Paul has reiterated the details of the Lord's Supper, relating to the Corinthian congregation the proper way to celebrate it. In directing them to "proclaim the Lord's death," He is saying that each celebration of Communion is a proclamation of the Gospel – a restatement of the fact, "Jesus Paid It All".

In other words, every Communion event is a sermon! When we take the cup we are testifying that we have been *redeemed* from that which would have harmed or destroyed us. When we break the bread we are testifying to the fact that that there is healing available here – through the broken body of Christ. We proclaim to all present that there is forgiveness and cleansing of sins through the blood of Jesus, inviting all who do not know Him to come and enter in. Their partaking of the elements of The Lord's Table will not save anybody, but they may come and join in as our proclamation of His finished work welcomes their receptivity of the Savior, and be saved through faith in Him!

The Lord's Supper is a statement about how deliverance has come into the world, and it is also a precious time of sharing fellowship with other believers. When you come to the Lord's Table and think about all that Jesus has made possible for you, that is a good time to tell others about it. The word "communion" is related to the word "common". In other words it is something we have together as a mutual benefit. That is why I Corinthians 10:16, 17 observes that as we partake of "one bread" we are acknowledging that we are "one body." We share in common experience the *uncommon wonder* of Christ's redemption, and we proclaim to one another the ongoing ways in which the greatness and all-sufficiency of Christ's work on the Cross and daily care for us continually manifest "The Wonder Of It All".

3. Communion is a declaration of dependence

In John's Gospel Jesus makes a bewildering statement that puzzled His disciples:

> *" 'Most assuredly, I say to you, unless you eat the flesh of the Son of Man and drink His Blood, you have no life in you. Whoever eats My flesh and drinks My blood has eternal life, and I will raise him up at the last day. For My flesh is food indeed, and my blood is drink indeed. He who eats My flesh and drinks My blood abides in Me, and I in him.' ... Many of His disciples, when they heard this, said, 'This is a hard saying; who can understand it?' "* (John 6:53–56, 60)

This event follows closely on from Jesus having miraculously fed five thousand people. This context is very significant, since Jesus goes on to talk about Himself being the "bread of life". In concluding, He makes the above "hard saying" (strange statement) about His body and His blood. On the surface of it, we can understand why His disciples found these words a "hard saying" – it sounded to them like a bizarre form of cannibalism.

Jesus clarified it completely:

> *"It is the Spirit who gives life; the flesh profits nothing. The words that I speak to you are spirit, and they are life."* (John 6:63)

Jesus was interpreting His words for His disciples so that they could understand what He was telling them. He was not speaking of a literal eating and drinking. He was describing a power-filled way of partaking of the Lord's Table – "my body and my blood." He explained these were "spiritual" words – words that were filled with "spirit and life" – words with dynamic spiritual intent and which were life-determinative in consequence.

Jesus was saying that when we come and partake, we are showing our absolute dependence upon Him for life and salvation. It is our third aspect of examining the meaning and power of Communion – the declaration of dependence. Thus, we believe that in participating at the Lord's Table we "remember" we are utterly reliant on Christ as the source of all our life. As our "food and drink" He keeps us alive. We have no life outside of Jesus.

While we do not believe that the bread actually becomes His body, nor that the cup literally becomes His blood (transubstantiation), we partake of them as far more than simple symbols or emblems. As that, they *do* represent Jesus' body and His blood, but as we partake of them in vibrant worship, praise, thanksgiving – in true and living biblical "remembrance" – there is visitation of spiritual dynamism the Holy Spirit will bring about. Coming to the table of Communion, we declare that we are dependent upon:

- The vertical flow of the Holy Spirit's power to nourish us with the flow of Jesus' life. *We need Jesus.*

- The horizontal flow, because Jesus' life flows through me to others in the Body of Christ. *We need each other.*

Communion therefore, is not only a reminder that I draw my life and nourishment from the Savior, but that the way He often channels His life to me is through the lives and ministry of other believers. In the kingdom of God there is no room for "lone rangers" – we are all dependent upon one another.

4. Communion is time for self-examination

Communion provides us with a time to examine ourselves; receiving the Apostle's strong counsel to the Corinthians regarding coming to The Lord's Table:

> *"But let a man examine himself, and so let him eat of that bread and drink of the cup ... For if we would judge ourselves, we would not be judged. But when we are judged, we are chastened by the Lord, that we may not be condemned with the world."*
>
> (I Corinthians 11:28, 31–32)

When we read the word "judged", our first thoughts are of condemnation or being in jeopardy of hell. But this passage is directed toward believers, not unbelievers. It is referring to "chastening" (literally, to be humbled or shamed), something that God occasionally calls us to when our persistence in sin, ignorance or disregard for His ways, has transpired. That is when the Table becomes an occasion for "a Parental showdown" – for God to *tell us off*, to *straighten us up!*

The aspect of self-examination is not a call to dredge up the past, repeat remorse for sin that has already been forgiven, or to so scrutinize our walk as to urgently seek to find "something wrong" so as to partake "worthily". If our "worthiness" qualified us for Communion, none of us could come! Thus, partaking in a "worthy" manner, as the Scriptures direct, means to come with a full heart of gratitude, humbly teachable where necessary, and magnify the *full worth* of Christ's redemption – singing again, "Thou Art Worthy!" "Worthy is the Lamb" is not only the song of the ages (Revelation 5) but today's song of the saints as well.

So Paul advises that before we come the Lord's Table we examine our hearts, so as to save ourselves from being chastened by the Lord. The Lord calls us to come to His Table as His disciples, and disciples accept *discipline*. And note: true NT discipline does not *forbid* people coming to the Lord's Table, but *invites* them to partake of the spiritual dynamic and deliverance that comes when sin is confessed, the soul is unchained, and the life of Jesus flows into His people.

So when you come to celebrate and share and receive life in Communion, let us all allow that life to come to bear on the places where we need strength, development, growth, maturity, and release.

5. Communion is a reception of provision

In the context of avoiding the chastening of the Lord by examining or "judging" our hearts, Paul also has this to say:

> *"For he that eats and drinks in an unworthy manner eats and drinks judgment to himself, not discerning the Lord's body. For this reason many are weak and sick among you, and many sleep."*
>
> (I Corinthians 11–29–30)

This "unworthy manner" mentioned refers to any attitude that demeans and devalues the importance or the provision of Communion. "Unworthy" means *"to fail to ascribe full worth to something".* The Apostle was not threatening death if an unworthy soul partook of Communion, but that sick souls and suffering, ill bodies could find provision for their health if they would "ascribe the full worth" to what Communion is provided to give us. In short, those who might "get sick and die" because of partaking "in an unworthy way," are not those being struck down by God, but who are not partaking in a way that invites His provision to raise them up – to life, health and strength. Let us come and receive the *full provision* that Christ desires to give us, as we learn to ascribe *full worth* to the divine resources of the Lord's Table.

Communion is not only a testimony of the forgiveness of your sins, it is a testimony of God's provision for every matter in your life. Jesus' blood paid for your sins, your healing, your provision, your peace of mind – for everything you need. When we receive this provision, we are attributing "full worth". This is why Paul says that some of the Christians have fallen sick or even died, because they have not given full recognition to the depth of Christ's work on their behalf, and have not sought humbly before God to receive it through the act of Communion.

When we come to the Lord's Table we partake in the name of Jesus who is our provider. There is holiness, health and wholeness made available to us by His provision. We should come in the spirit of celebration for His victory, proclaiming His redemption, declaring our dependence upon Him, examining our hearts, and receiving the provision He has for us. Jesus said, *"Father, if it is Your will, take this cup away from Me; nevertheless not My will, but Yours be done"* (Luke 22:42).

Now, we may partake of the cup of blessing because He drank the cup of suffering.

(This hymn lyric, written by the author, is sung to the folk melody, "All Through The Night". It is proven to bring rich rejoicing, sung briskly in the spirit of faith and victory the Cross affords us.)

Hail to the Cross

By Jack W. Hayford

Come with me to Calv'ry's mountain, Come to the Cross.
Come and wash in Calv'ry's fountain, Come to the Cross.
To the place where Christ died for us, where He paid the
    "blood-price" for us,
Come and lift this joyous chorus – Come to the Cross.

Praise the Lamb who bled and died there, there at the Cross;
Jesus who was crucified there, there at the Cross.
Through His Blood, that crimson token, all hell's power has
    been broken:
"It is finished" has been spoken – there at the Cross.

Here is reason for rejoicing, here at the Cross;
Grounds for highest praises voicing, here at the Cross.
Here the sin-curse Jesus severed; here He bought us life forever;
Here He'll keep and leave us never – Here at the Cross.

Here is heav'n's eternal treasure: God planned the Cross;
Wealth of love in endless measure, God planned the Cross.
Since His Son has bled and died there, all my hope for life is
    tied there,
For God says I'm justified there – God planned the Cross.

Jesus saves and Jesus heals us, all through the Cross.
By redemption's power He seals us, all through the Cross.
In the wake of human sinning, Jesus brought a new beginning,
By His death this promise winning – All through the Cross.

By the Cross we are forgiven – Hail to the Cross!
By the Cross we'll enter heaven – Hail to the Cross!
Through God's love and grace amazing, we shall join in
    endless praising;
So this anthem now we're raising – Hail to the Cross!

PART 7

The Baptism with the Holy Spirit: River of Release

༺ *14* ༻

THE BAPTISM WITH THE HOLY SPIRIT: THE TERM AND THE TIMING

THEME TEXT

"But you shall receive power when the Holy Spirit has come upon you; and you shall be witnesses to Me in Jerusalem, and in all Judea and Samaria, and to the end of the earth."

(Acts 1:8)

What makes a believer, after they have come to Christ, go on living like a believer, is the fact that the truth is incarnate in them. The truth goes on living and growing inside them and they begin to grow and change. This is the ministry of the Holy Spirit working in the life of the believer.

The Holy Spirit has been *poured out* and lavished upon us – the Church – that we might receive power and enablement from "on high" as Jesus said we would (Acts 1:8).

We begin our study of the power of the Holy Spirit in believer's lives in the first chapter of Acts because it reveals two reasons why Jesus gave the gift of the Holy Spirit to us.

Why does Jesus give us the power of the Holy Spirit?

1. For the sake of causing His life to be so manifest in us that we become *evidence* for the case that He is alive and still ministering in the world today. The Holy Spirit brings verification that Jesus is not dead, but alive. This happens through us verbalizing our

own experiences of the life of Christ to others by our testimony, and it happens as the person of Jesus is manifest in our lives through our character and our actions.

2. So that the ministry of Jesus will continue by the Holy Spirit working through us. Jesus seeks to work through each believer by the power of the Holy Spirit so that the Father's will is accomplished. Jesus continues His ministry on earth, but now we are His hands and feet.

There are two important points to note here:

*   It is impossible for the person of Jesus to be manifest in our character except by allowing the Holy Spirit to come in and dwell in us.

*   We cannot have the power of Jesus flowing through our lives unless the Holy Spirit comes and "overflows" our lives.

The Holy Spirit comes to *indwell* the believer so that the *person of Jesus* can be seen in us, and He comes to *overflow* our lives so that the *power of Jesus* can happen through us. All that Jesus came to do and to say continues through us as we cooperate with the Holy Spirit.

When a believer is filled with the Holy Spirit and experiences this overflowing of the Spirit in his or her life, we use the term the *baptism with the Holy Spirit* to describe it. We are going to take the next three chapters to deal with this important topic, and we begin in this chapter by discussing the reason for the use of the term itself.

The "Baptism with the Holy Spirit": the term

It is important that we learn what the Bible reveals about the terminology that we use. As Christians we can become so familiar with biblical phrases and terms that we begin to lose sight of the richness of their meaning. So where did the term "baptism with the Holy Spirit" come from?

1. Jesus used this terminology

It is a biblical term that He asserted Himself.

> *"For John truly baptized with water, but you shall be baptized with the Holy Spirit not many days from now."* (Acts 1:5)

The terminology is not as important as the experience. The Bible uses at least six other terms to describe this same event throughout the remainder of the book of Acts. Therefore we would make a mistake in being dogmatic about the use of this term as the only one which properly describes the infilling of the Holy Spirit, but we would be equally mistaken if we supposed that this term was merely a religious "label", invented to describe a certain event. "Baptism with the Holy Spirit" is the over-arching term that Jesus used and encompasses all of the other biblical descriptions of the same event.

2. John the Baptist introduced the term when he introduced Jesus

John the Baptist's ministry was to herald the Messiah. His task was to announce that the Messiah had come and in identifying Him, he made dual and discerning observations:

▶ In John 1:29 he declares the *saving* work of Messiah, to redeem: *"John saw Jesus coming toward him and said, 'Behold! The Lamb of God who **takes away the sin of the world.'***"

▶ In John 1:33 he declares the *empowering* work of Messiah, to enable: *"I saw the Spirit descending from heaven like a dove, and He remained upon Him. I did not know Him, but He who sent me to baptize with water said to me, 'Upon whom you see the Spirit descending, and remaining on Him, this is He who **baptizes with the Holy Spirit**.' And I have seen and testified that this is the Son of God"* (John 1:32–34).

Jesus' dual role as Savior-Messiah

Jesus had two distinct roles to fill as the prophesied Messiah. He came as the *Redeemer* and as the *Restorer*.

Man's most fundamental need relates to his lostness without God brought about by his sin. Man needs forgiveness, redemption, cleansing, and a way back to God. Man's sin severed him from the intimate relationship he enjoyed with God before the fall, therefore he needs a *Redeemer* to settle the debt of his sin and reinstate the relationship.

However, Man's sin not only severed His relationship with God, but also his position of rulership in life. Man, bereft of the power to live life the way it is supposed to be lived, is in desperate need of a *Restorer*.

Man lost the power to live purely in relationship with God, and to live effectively in ruling over the matters of life. He needed a *Redeemer* to take care of his sin problem, and a *Restorer* to bring him back into rulership. Jesus comes as the Lamb of God who will "take away the sin of the world," but is also introduced to us as the one who *"baptizes with the Holy Spirit."* Hereby, we meet the Savior, Who will save us through His Cross, transferring His righteousness to us. But He is also the *Baptizer*, Who will restore us through sharing His anointing, transmitting His power for ministry to us. Jesus comes to pour out the same Spirit upon us that anointed Him and made Him the Messiah and King, so that the power of that kingdom life will be upon us also and enable us to rule in life.

The baptism with the Holy Spirit then, is an intrinsic part of the *restoring* aspect of Jesus' dual role. It is something He desires to do in us after redemption has taken place, that will *equip* us with all the fullness of His life. Jesus gives us forgiveness unto life, and then imparts fullness to us for the transmission of that life. The point of being baptized with the Spirit is that it affects everything we do as we "overflow". What God has put within us of the life of His Son, now may begin to be "lived out" in power, in real and tangible ways – touching the world with His love.

Walking toward the Day of Pentecost

We've taken a little time to establish that a part of Jesus' ministry was to administer the baptism of the Holy Spirit and that Jesus is called the "Baptizer with the Holy Spirit", because these terms hold great significance. As we have seen John the Baptist used this terminology, but Jesus also used the same words. Jesus said to His disciples,

> *"You shall be baptized with the Holy Spirit not many days from now."*   (Acts 1:5)

These words of Jesus point us toward a definition of the baptism with the Holy Spirit. As Luke records the words of Jesus in Acts, he quotes Him as saying that this event will take place *"not many days from now."* These words are carefully chosen. Luke is a very precise historian and never uses words recklessly. If we advance to verse 1:15 we read, *"And in those days..."*. The writer maintains the flow of his narrative, anticipating the reader's expectation of an "event" sometime in the immediately approaching days, as Jesus said. But these were "those" days, not *"the"* day – days of prayer and preparation were in process, and Luke's report continues through chapter 1.

Then we come to Acts 2, and read that "the" day has arrived. We read *"When the Day of Pentecost had fully come...,"* and Luke begins to describe the day Jesus referred to. The "not many days from now" have arrived and "the Day of Pentecost was fully come." This historian knows from hindsight, that this day was pivotal, and so he carefully processes bringing us to it, and among the benefits we gain from his careful record is that we are not left to wonder what the baptism with the Holy Spirit is. Jesus said it would come in "not many days"; the Holy Spirit through Luke meticulously catalogs the process to "the day;" and upon its arrival, we can read of all that transpired as the Holy Spirit came and 120 of the first believers were *"baptized with the Holy Spirit."*

I've taken time to make this clear so that we should know what to expect when the baptism of the Holy Spirit happens. What happened on this day was exactly that which had been predicted long ago by the prophet Joel, *"And it shall come to pass in the last days, says God, that I will pour out of My Spirit on all flesh"* (Acts 2:17).

The meaning of "baptized"

This "pouring out" or overflowing is one of the six terms used to describe the experience of baptism with the Spirit, just as Acts 2:4 describes that all the disciples were *"filled with the Holy Spirit."* An examination of the Greek word translated "baptism" gives us further insight into its meaning and the harmony between the other terms used:

▶   *Baptized* – from the Greek verb *bapto* means literally "to dip". It describes a process of complete submersion and is the same word that is used to describe a sunken ship. Not only is the ship in the water, but the water is in the ship! This is not a casual sprinkling. Jesus comes to *immerse* us in the Holy Spirit. Through baptism with the Spirit we have been placed into the working realm of the Holy Spirit, but we have also been *filled* with the Holy Spirit as the sunken ship image implies. This "filling" comes about as the Holy Spirit is *poured* out upon us, as the prophet Joel describes, until we are overflowing.

Such an overflow of the Spirit only comes to people who open themselves up to God so as to receive it. People that are spiritually hungry and thirsty enough will experience the flow of God's Spirit. You can't receive the fullness of the Holy Spirit by having a "quick shower" – you need to be willing to get "in the river" and stay there! Six terms are used in Acts: *"baptized"*, *"poured out"*, *"given"*, *"received"*, *"filled"* and *"come upon"*. They combine in the word (1) *"baptize"*. As Jesus baptizes us, the Holy Spirit is (2) *"poured out"* (i.e. lavishly available to any who come), and (3) *"given"* to those who willingly open to Him, to (4) *"receive"* (i.e. in submitted yieldedness allow), His (5) *"filling"* (i.e. complete overflowing) as He (6) *"comes upon"* (i.e. fully embraces) them. Together, these six words richly fulfill Jesus' prophecy in John 8:37–39, as believers experience the *overflow of* "rivers of living water" in order to release an *outflow* of ministry to the world.

"Baptism with the Holy Spirit" – an applicable term today

"Baptism with the Holy Spirit" is the term that continues to be used to describe the experience of being filled or overflowed with the Holy Spirit, and applies to all believers. However, there are other doctrinal views in the breadth of Christian experience. We will study these in more detail later in this chapter. In summary, the varying views state:

1. That the baptism with the Holy Spirit is an event that happens simultaneously with salvation.

2. That salvation and the baptism with the Holy Spirit are two separate and distinct events (although they may occur at the same time).

3. That the baptism with the Holy Spirit happened one time only on the Day of Pentecost in order to "birth" the early Church.

If the baptism with the Holy Spirit was an event that occurred at the point of salvation, then John the Baptist would not have separated the dual aspects of Jesus' ministry as he did: *"This is the Lamb of God who takes away the sin of the world"* – who brings salvation, and *"This is He who baptizes with the Holy Spirit."* – the One who empowers His followers. This is the first of many sections of Scripture which point to a separate and distinct experience. This does not mean that the two events may not be very closely fused in an individual's experience. With some, receiving Christ as Savior and being baptized with the Holy Spirit happens at virtually the same time. For many others, there is a period of time between the two events (perhaps best used for answering Jesus' call to be baptized in water).

Baptism *of*, or Baptism *with...*?

Some people often use imprecise terminology for the "Baptism *with* the Holy Spirit", in calling this experience the "Baptism *of* the Holy Spirit." This may seem a trivial point to some, but I believe it is one that warrants a brief discussion so as to remove any confusion in people's minds as to *who it is who does the baptizing*. We should try wherever possible to use clear expressions that accurately describe what the Bible teaches, and this in no way detracts from or belittles those who may use the terms incorrectly.

Using the term "baptism *of* the Holy Spirit" implies that it is the Holy Spirit who is doing the work of baptizing, but John said this is Jesus' work – He is the one who does the baptizing when we are "Baptized *in* or *with* the Holy Spirit."

When we fix in our hearts on the fact that *Jesus* is the One who baptizes us with the Holy Spirit, it gives a richer dimension and a greater depth to our perspective on the experience. It moves it from "something that happens to me," to "Someone Who ministers to me" – and that someone is Jesus Himself. When we focus completely on Jesus we realize that this experience,

1. Is not a mystical experience. (It is a Person-to-person encounter with our Loving Lord.)

2. Is not an experience to fear. (Satan will use fear to keep us from anything God wants to work in our lives through grace and love. Fear will always accompany anything that occasions growth in our lives.)

3. Is a clearly focused experience. (We come to Jesus, trusting Him and simply asking Him to baptize us with the Holy Spirit.)

When we begin to think in these terms we will no longer see being baptized with the Spirit as an "experience" at all, but just a natural part of "coming to Jesus" and receiving all the fullness that He intends for our lives. We can lay aside all anxiety about when and how it might take place and just let Jesus be in control.

What manifestations occurred at Pentecost?

Jesus told His disciples that the baptism He promised would be in just a few days. When "the day" came and the power of the Lord fell upon them and filled them, a whole battery of things began to happen in their lives.

1. They spoke with other tongues. This is the first thing that happened to the disciples. But that "they began" does not only apply to "speaking in tongues. Make no mistake, this is only one thing that "began" at Pentecost.

2. Preaching with revelatory insight into God's Word began, and multitudes came to Christ.

3. The love of God became manifest in their lives and began a whole community, formed in the love of God and caring for one another in His love.

4. Miracles which began, continued to attend their lives, and a constant stream of people kept coming to Christ – day by day. They moved in a spirit of prayer, praise, love and appreciation for the Word of God that only the Holy Spirit could have brought about.

These just begin the "beginnings" among those who were the first to have been baptized with the Holy Spirit. It deepens and broadens the dimensions of these things in their life. The element of speaking with other tongues will be covered in detail in Chapter 14, but for now it is sufficient to note that while this was clearly an important element in the mix of the days of "beginning", there were many things that "began" – things very much like those that Jesus wants His Church to experience today as well, just as in the Book of Acts.

The Baptism with the Holy Spirit: the timing

We have seen that the term "baptism with the Holy Spirit" was introduced by John the Baptist and applied by Jesus Himself. Now we come to discuss the *timing* of the baptism with the Holy Spirit.

1. In terms of timing, the baptism with the Holy Spirit is a distinct experience in the life of a believer in Jesus Christ. John 20:22 is a

critical verse in understanding this and says, *"And when He had said this, He breathed on them, and said to them, 'Receive the Holy Spirit.'"* Jesus spoke these words to His disciples late at night on the day of His resurrection. The disciples were secretly gathered together, fearing what might happen to them now Jesus was gone. Jesus appeared to them and commissioned them to carry on His work on the earth, saying *"Receive the Holy Spirit."* The words of Jesus were joined with an *action* on Jesus' part. He *breathed* on them. This was a highly significant act.

2. When God created Man it says that He *"formed man of the dust of the ground and **breathed** into his nostrils the breath of life; and man became a living being'"* (Genesis 2:7). God breathed His life into Man. When Man sinned and "died" spiritually, the breath of God (the Holy Spirit) departed from him and all that remained was the breath of "his nostrils".

    Isaiah alludes to this in a passage where he is warning against dependency on human resources. This is the way the prophet puts it poetically, *"Cease from man whose breath is in his nostrils"* (Isaiah 2:22).

3. When Jesus rose from the dead it signified that now, redemption had been completely provided. The transition from the Old Covenant to the New Covenant had been made. Just as the old creative order began with the breath of God, so now the new creative order Jesus was establishing began with the breath of God the Son. *"For as in Adam all die, even so in Christ all shall be made alive"* (I Corinthians 15:22). [4] So on this night, as soon as the full provision of redemption was completed, Jesus visits His small band of believers and breathes the life of new creation into them – the Holy Spirit. Some have interpreted the actions of Jesus as being merely symbolic, alluding to the Day of Pentecost, but the Greek denotes the immediacy of this action. Jesus is saying, "Receive the Holy Spirit *right now.*"

Even though Jesus breathed the Holy Spirit into the disciples at that time, He still told them that they must wait in Jerusalem before beginning their mission, because the *baptism with the Holy Spirit would happen to them later*. It was a distinct and future experience. He said: *"Behold, I send the Promise of My Father upon you; but tarry in the city of Jerusalem until you are endued* [clothed with] *with power from on high"* (Luke 24:49).

The Holy Spirit *dwells* within and *overflows* believers

As is clearly seen from these scriptures, the Bible makes a distinction between the Holy Spirit dwelling within a believer and the Holy Spirit baptizing and "overflowing" a believer. We can further verify this from Scripture by examining two clear facets of the Holy Spirit's character and work.

1. **The Fountain.** Note the singular, as the first feature of the Holy Spirit is *within* – to satisfy the thirst in our life. This happens as we are saved. In John 4, Jesus, speaking to the Samaritan woman at the well, says, *"Whoever drinks of this water will thirst again, but whoever drinks the water that I shall give him will never thirst. But the water that I shall give him will become in him a fountain* [or well] *of water springing up into everlasting life"* (John 4:13–14). This figure describes the Holy Spirit's indwelling, like an inner fountain at which we drink to find the answer to our own personal need, in Christ by the presence of the Spirit.

2. **The Rivers.** Note the plural, as the second feature of the Holy Spirit flows *outward* – to serve the need of others as the overflow our lives makes us *tributaries* of Christ's life to satisfy other people's thirst. *" 'If anyone thirsts, let him come to Me and drink. He who believes in Me, as the Scripture has said, out of his heart will flow rivers of living water.' But this He spoke concerning the Spirit, whom those believing in Him would receive; for the Holy Spirit was not yet given, for Jesus was not yet glorified' "* (John 7:37–38). This figure describes the Holy Spirit's empowering the believer to reach, to serve, to witness, to love, to give – flowing life to others.

    This second aspect of the Holy Spirit's nature and work is not something which is intended merely to satisfy our thirst for God. It is intended to flow out of us like a river that will touch other people.

What is "proof" of the baptism with the Holy Spirit?

How do you know when you have been filled and baptized with the power of the Holy Spirit? The traditional Pentecostal response to this question would be, "Have you spoken in tongues? If you have then you've been baptized with the Holy Spirit." We will discuss that topic in detail in Chapter 14, but it is enough for now to say that laboring to make an iron-clad case for "tongues as the evidence for the baptism with the Holy Spirit" may be achieved, but it tends to become a very counter-productive pursuit. The objective of the resource we are offered in "speaking with tongues", is clearly not to *prove* with, but to *praise and pray with, to worship and war with,* as this "sign" (Mark 16:15–17) is so preciously given. Let us not bog down in doctrinal debate, but open to the dynamic resources that "spiritual language" provides.

But honest souls will still ask, "How will I know I have been Baptized with the Holy Spirit. What shall I look for?"

1. First, don't be hesitant to expect the benefit of "tongues." It is biblical, it is practical, it is beneficial – all matters we will discuss later. But in any case, expect this that was so freely given from the hand of God, and from the very inception of the Church's existence.

2. Second, expect something so clear in your experience of the power of God coming into you and overflowing your life, that you will *know it.* This is not a matter of having a "good feeling" or an "inner-warmth". You may have such physical feelings or you may not, but you will *know* in your spirit that something has happened.

3. There may be other "miraculous" signs i.e. the Holy Spirit comes to release the miracle life of Jesus through us. You may experience a sudden "setting free" from something that has bound you for a long time; you may experience a healing, or freedom from a character trait that previously you were powerless to change such as anger or fear.

A neglected experience

Many people – not only today, but also in the early Church – would receive Jesus Christ as their Savior and *not* be baptized with the Holy Spirit (Acts 8:4–14). This matter concerned the early Church leaders as it should concern us now.

1. Acts 8:5 tells us that Philip had been preaching Christ to the people of the city of Samaria and that "multitudes" (v. 6) were saved (v. 13), including a principal leader in the things of the

occult – Simon the sorcerer. These people were baptized in water, but did not receive the "outpouring" of the Holy Spirit straight away. The Bible tells us,

> "... *when the apostles who were at Jerusalem heard that Samaria had received the word of God, they sent Peter and John to them, who ... prayed for them that they might receive the Holy Spirit. For as yet He had fallen upon none of them. They had only been baptized in the name of the Lord Jesus. Then they laid hands on them, and they received the Holy Spirit.*" (Acts 8:14–17)

These "multitudes" of people were unquestionably "saved". When a person receives Jesus Christ as Savior, the Holy Spirit has already done a tremendous work in them. These new believers were baptized and by implication made a genuine confession to the Lordship of Christ in their lives. I Corinthians 12:3 says that, *"no one can say that Jesus is Lord except by the Holy Spirit."* They were saved and had received the Holy Spirit to dwell in them. What had *not* yet happened to these Samaritans was the overflowing of the Holy Spirit in all His fullness.

2. Similarly, when the Apostle Paul came across a group of believers in Ephesus he asked them, *"Did you receive the Holy Spirit when you believed?"* Why? Because he detected that something was missing from their lives. He immediately taught, prayed with, and ministered to them, and "the Holy Spirit came upon them."

    We know that Luke, the writer of the Book of Acts, was with Paul in his travels and would have been present when this happened. His careful recording of this event, along with the similar kind of thing happening in Acts 8, not only makes clear the Holy Spirit wanted this in the Bible record, it is evident that the Apostles cared very much about believers not only coming to know the certainty of Christ *in* their lives, but they wanted to assure the multiplying ministry of Christ *through* their lives.

In a very real sense the concept of receiving the baptism with the Holy Spirit is like saying to God, "I not only want the *person* of Jesus made real in my life by You Holy Spirit, but I also want the *power* of Jesus to happen through my life by You." The concern for receiving this power of the Holy Spirit that equips Christ's Church should also concern us to the same degree. The good news is that Jesus is the Baptizer with the Holy Spirit, and He says He wants this to happen to every one of His own.

If you, dear reader, have not earlier received the fullness of the Holy Spirit, let me urge you to come to Jesus now ... to bow before Him, our precious Savior, and invite Him to baptize you with the Holy Spirit. To assist you I offer this guideline for prayer. Your own words will do – but perhaps this will help.

Dear Lord Jesus,
    I thank You and praise You for Your great love and faithfulness to me.
    My heart is filled with joy whenever I think of the great gift of salvation You have so freely given to me,
    And I humbly glorify You, Lord Jesus,
        for You have forgiven me all my sins and brought me to the Father.
    Now I come in obedience to Your call.
    I want to receive the fullness of the Holy Spirit.
    I do not come because I am worthy myself, but because You have invited me to come.
    Because you have washed me from my sins,
        I thank You that You have made the vessel of my life a worthy one to be filled with the Holy Spirit of God.
    I want to be overflowed with Your life,
        Your love and Your power, Lord Jesus.
    I want to show forth Your grace,
        Your Words,
          Your goodness, and
            Your gifts
        to everyone I can.
    And so with simple, childlike faith, I ask You Lord,
        fill me with the Holy Spirit.
    I open all of myself to You,
        to receive all of Yourself in me.
    I love You, Lord, and I lift my voice in praise to You.
    I welcome Your might and Your miracles
        To be manifested in me
          for Your glory
          and unto Your praise.

"And we are His witnesses to these things,
and so also is the Holy Spirit
whom God has given to those who obey Him."

(Acts 5:32)

15

THE BAPTISM
WITH THE HOLY SPIRIT:
THE TERMS

THEME TEXT

"And as I began to speak, the Holy Spirit fell upon them,
as upon us at the beginning."
(Acts 11:15)

We continue our study of the baptism with the Holy Spirit by examining the *terms* – i.e. the basic requirements of heart-prepared-ness which give place to Jesus pouring out the Holy Spirit upon a person. The Lord is ready to baptize in the Spirit all who meet His terms, and those terms are rooted in grace, and abundantly attainable. They are not terms in the sense of *works* to which we attain, but rather are terms defining an *attitude* – a stance of the heart more than a status of achievement. The whole chapter of Acts 10 is the background for our study because it illustrates so wonderfully how willing God is to pour out His Holy Spirit upon those who meet His terms.

Acts 10 describes the story of Cornelius, a centurion of a regiment of the Roman army called the "Italian regiment". He is described as a "devout man who feared God with all his household". He cared for the poor, and always prayed to God. Cornelius receives a vision in which an angel of God tells him to send for the Apostle Peter. The next day, while members of Cornelius' house are on their way to find Peter, Peter is also given a vision from God.

It was about midday and Peter was due to have the main meal of the day, so he was hungry. In the vision the Lord offers Peter animals to kill and eat for food. Peter refuses because the animals are those that Jews are forbidden to eat and are called "unclean" or "common". The Lord says to him: *"What God has cleansed you must not call common."* (Acts 10:15). Peter puzzles over the meaning of the vision as Cornelius' men approach the house where he is staying, then being persuaded by the Holy Spirit, he goes with them to visit Cornelius' house.

As a Gentile, Cornelius was hungry to know God. He was a tough, trained soldier, but an honest soul who dealt honestly with people. Serving as a Roman in that area of Judea[5] he was exposed to the people that God had historically raised up, to be a testimony to the one true and living God. Cornelius obviously wanted to look more deeply into these spiritual matters.

Cornelius was not ignorant of the fundamentals that had to do with Jesus (v. 36). He had heard the message about Jesus Christ preached, but he had never had confirmed to him all the truth pertaining to Jesus (v. 37). Peter assured Cornelius that what he had heard about Jesus was indeed true and made the message of salvation very clear to him. Peter related a thorough report of the Gospel of Christ to Cornelius, and Cornelius responded positively. Then an astounding thing happens! The Holy Spirit is spontaneously poured out on these Gentiles.

As Acts 11 opens we find Peter returning to the church at Jerusalem to explain what has happened. For the first time, Gentiles have received the same work of the Holy Spirit that the disciples had at Pentecost. Reporting back Peter says,

> *"And as I began to speak, the Holy Spirit fell upon them, as upon us at the beginning. Then I remembered the word of the Lord, how He said, 'John indeed baptized with water, but you shall be baptized with the Holy Spirit.' If therefore God gave them the same gift as He gave us when we believed on the Lord Jesus Christ, who was I that I could withstand God?' And when they heard these things they became silent; and they glorified God, saying, 'Then God has also granted to the Gentiles repentance to life.'"* (Acts 11:15–18)

This is the initial occasion of a Gentile receiving the pure testimony of Jesus, and as they opened their hearts to the message of the Savior-Messiah, suddenly the Holy Spirit came upon them, and they were baptized with the Holy Spirit. Later, believers at Jerusalem will express their bewilderment, that someone was filled with the Holy Spirit without observing the rituals of the OT Law. This momentous event marked a major transition in the life of the Church. It was the beginning of the Church opening up, with some difficulty, to the idea of a global vision. God was beginning to break down walls – first, in Peter's heart by the vision he received (Acts 10:9–16), and subsequently in the minds of the other Jewish believers. (The event later led to the convening of the Council in Jerusalem some years later to settle once and for all the issue of the observance of Mosaic Law in the Church – Acts 15:6–29.)

The disciples would begin from this time to understand more of the full implications of Jesus' words to them when He said, *"You shall be witnesses to Me in Jerusalem, and in all Judea and Samaria, and to the end of the earth"* (Acts 1:8). Before that day in Caesarea, they more than likely thought the "ends of the earth" in Jesus' commission was limited to the *Diaspora* – those Jews scattered around the world, not Gentile people of the nations of the world.

The Baptism with the Holy Spirit: the terms

This occasion of Cornelius and his small household being baptized with the Holy Spirit reveals the *terms* or qualities of soul that are important if a person is going to receive a real fullness of the baptism with the Holy Spirit. Before listing these terms, it bears repeating that *everything* we receive from God we receive by *grace*. Such grace flows upon those who come before the Lord with certain attitudes or postures – primarily with an attitude of utter dependency. There are four terms that can be drawn from this passage:

1. Obedience – *Wanting God's will* (Acts 10:2)

Cornelius was a devout man who feared God. We must notice the difference between a man who is trying to earn something *from* God, and a man who simply has a heart *for* God. Cornelius had a heart for God. Devout means "wholehearted". Cornelius had a simple, genuine passion for God. To fear God means to *reverence* Him – to have an awesome respect for Him.

Cornelius did not yet have a relationship with God as we would think of it. He had not yet been born again, but his heart was open to God. He feared God and he wanted to be obedient toward God. While we must guard against an erroneous attitude that thinks mankind is seeking the same God only by different pathways (Universalism), we must surely avoid the small-minded attitude of supposing God pays no attention to the heartcry or the need of people who don't know anything about Jesus. God is merciful and responsive to the heartcry of His creatures and He will do things to show Himself to them. Cornelius is an example of that. The Apostle

Paul speaks of such God-fearing people in Romans 2:14 – people who have little or no knowledge of God's Law, but who live by principles that reflect God's Law.

This does not mean that a person's sincerity can be a substitute for believing in Jesus Christ, the Bible is quite clear that the only way to salvation is through Him: *"... there is no other name under heaven given among men by which we must be saved."* (Acts 4:12)

Subtle Universalism can often creep into segments of the Church, characterized by a kind of "generosity of attitude" – an attitude that says, "We're all seeking the same God, we just do it in many different ways." But the Bible tells us there is only *one way* to God – through Jesus Christ. It is not that we are taking a loveless or small-minded view, it is simply that salvation does not work in a way which encompasses many different routes to God. So in our biblical example, Cornelius has to have the "gaps" in his theology filled in by Peter so that he understands exactly what Christ did for him and how he must come to Him in obedience.

> *"And we are His witnesses to these things, and so also is the Holy Spirit whom God has given to those who obey Him."* (Acts 5:32)

2. Humility – *Wanting God's way*

As Cornelius receives Peter into his home, he gathers the members of his household together and says, *"I sent to you immediately, and you have done well to come. Now therefore, we are all present before God, to hear all the things commanded you by God"* (Acts 10:33).

This statement is loaded with childlikeness! This centurion had every reason to assert his status as a representative of Imperial Rome, yet he acts in the most humble manner. First, he says, "... you have done well to come." This does not mean, "It's a good thing you came when I sent for you, after all I am a centurion!" Rather it reflects a deferential demeanor: "You have done a good thing to me by graciously coming to my house ... you have done me a kindness." He could have postured himself on the grounds of his more powerful social status, but instead he humbly and gratefully receives Peter.

Further, Cornelius says, "Here we are at your disposal to hear what God will say through you." This childlike approach characterizes a depth of humility that simply wants *God's way*. Such humility tends to *honestly inquire* of the things of God. It is a humility that wants to find out God's way so that His way can be followed in obedience.

People who receive the baptism with the Holy Spirit are those who come with an honest, humble heart, open before the Lord and wanting Him.

3. Purity – Wanting God's nature

In Leviticus 11:45 the Lord says, *"You shall therefore be holy, for I am holy."* The book of Leviticus was written when the people of God had been out of Egypt for only a matter of months. In all probability it was written while they were still at Mount Sinai, and a great portion of it was likely written in the forty-day period during which Moses was up on the mountain in God's presence receiving revelation from Him. One of the most notable aspects of Leviticus is the repetition of God's words, *"For I am the Lord"* – a statement which occurs many times throughout that book. Why did God keep reminding His people of this fact? Because they needed to learn that He was *different* from all the "other gods" that pervaded the Egyptian culture in which they had been raised, and from which they were now delivered and called to live apart from.

God is saying, "I am different. My nature is different; My character is different. I am the Lord." He is emphasizing His *holiness*, and by that, His completeness and distinctness from all the false gods of the world. He calls us to that kind of holiness also, that will make us complete and distinct from those living under the world system.

A desire for God

The testimony of Cornelius' lifestyle and heart attitude, even before Peter's visit and Cornelius' coming to Christ, is that he was *"a devout man and one who feared God . . . who gave alms generously . . . and prayed to God always"* (Acts 10:2). It evidences the desire for God – to know Him, to want to be like Him. Similarly, the heart that approaches the Lord, wanting to be baptized with the Holy Spirit, will be one saying, "Lord, I want to be immersed in Your nature" – the *Holy* Spirit. We have seen that the word translated "baptism" means "to be completely immersed". God desires that we come to a place of complete immersion in His Holy Spirit, and that we remain there, "under" the overflowing river of His Spirit.

The Holy Spirit comes to give us power and authority and to bring a purity, a character, and a refinement of Jesus' life and His love. John the Baptist said of Jesus that,

> *"He will baptize you with the Holy Spirit and fire."*
>
> (Matthew 3:11)

On the day that the Holy Spirit was poured out, the disciples actually did have flames that looked like fire over their heads, symbolic of the purifying work of the Spirit (Acts 2:3). Similarly Malachi, prophesying the time when God would "suddenly come" to His holy temple, saying, *"...He is like a refiner's fire"* (Malachi 3:2). On the Day of Pentecost, God "suddenly" came to occupy His temple – the Body of Christ, His Church. On the day the Church was born this "temple" was filled with the fire of God. The disciples received both *power* and *purity*, which was manifest in a *passion* to live in a way that reflected God's nature.

We must be wary today of paying too much attention to ministries that emphasize the power and authority that believers possess, to the neglect of the purity that we are called to. It is not that these things are not true, because they are, but unless such power and authority flows through a character that has been purged by the fire of God and exhibits a righteous humility, it can appear harsh and loveless. Authority and humility are mutually dependent. We must also be wary of falling in the trap of "examining" the purity of others, rather than examining ourselves, for Acts 10:15 says, *"What God has cleansed* [what God has declared clean] *you must not call common."*

The baptism with the Holy Spirit comes to those who want God's nature, who are open to the cleansing work of the Lord in their life, but it is vital that we understand that this does not mean that the baptism with the Spirit *only* comes to those who have *attained* perfection in purity.

God has made a declaration about our worthiness to receive His Spirit: we are justified by faith in Him and declared holy in Christ. On these grounds alone a person has been made worthy to receive the fullness of the Holy Spirit. When we minister to a person who wants to receive the fullness of the Holy Spirit, the only requirement in terms of purity is that they have received Jesus as Savior.

Purity of motive

Acts 8 reminds us that purity of motive is important when we seek the fullness of the Spirit. Simon the sorcerer provides a case study of someone who had been saved and baptized in water, but who still displayed an impure motive regarding the power of the Holy Spirit. He thought he could "buy" the gift of God and was rebuked by Peter (Acts 8:20). Simon was still influenced by his past bondages – a "spirit of control" that characterized his past in the darkness of the occult. Peter told him, *"your heart is not right in the sight of God. Repent ... perhaps the thought of your heart may be forgiven you"* (Acts 8:21–22).

Receiving – *Wanting God's fullness*

The final qualifier for receiving the baptism with the Holy Spirit has to do with a willingness to receive. The word *receive* occurs in Acts 10:47 as Peter describes what has happened to Cornelius and his household.

One of the most interesting aspects of the events that took place in Cornelius' house is that they were baptized with the Holy Spirit *before* they were baptized in water. Why was this the case, given that we have already identified water baptism as a key sign of obedience leading to receiving the fullness of the Spirit?

I believe that God in His grace decided to do things in that order because Peter was still unsure whether these Gentiles could really be saved without keeping the ordinances of the Jewish Law. The Lord poured out the Holy Spirit on them *prior* to their water baptism as evidence of His grace being lavished on all mankind. This was not the usual order of things, and is the only example of this sequence in the entire Bible. Even here, the believers are immediately baptized in water.

It may be that people today have also been baptized with the Holy Spirit before they have been baptized in water. This is quite possible. Who are we to put limitations on the way in which God can work? However, even if this is so, it does not take away the need to be baptized in water. Water baptism is the command of Jesus.

For a person to *receive* presupposes an attitude of openness and one that welcomes what God seeks to do in us. Jesus described the essence of such an attitude when He said,

> "Blessed are those who **hunger and thirst for righteousness**, for they shall be **filled**." (Matthew 5:6)

How do people receive the Holy Spirit?

If you were to ask, "What is the *normal* way in which a person receives the baptism with the Holy Spirit?", the evidence of Scripture, and current practice in the Church today, would suggest it is through the ministry of another person praying with them and laying hands on them. Peter and John laid hands on the Samaritan believers to receive the baptism with the Holy Spirit. Paul laid hands on a small group of believers in Ephesus and prayed for them to receive the baptism (Acts 19:6). People who are receptive to God are usually willing to receive prayer and ministry, and in this way millions of people around the world have received the baptism with the Holy Spirit.

However, the laying on of hands is not a legal requirement demanded by God. The book of Acts speaks of two incidents where no human contact was involved. No one laid hands on the disciples when they were baptized with the Holy Spirit, because there was no one to minister the baptism to them (Acts 2:4). Neither did Peter, having some trepidation about the situation in which he found himself, lay hands on the household of Cornelius. These baptisms with the Spirit both happened spontaneously. While neither of these events could be described as being "normal" – the former signifying the birth of the Church, and the latter signifying the outpouring of God's grace upon the Gentiles – nevertheless, there are many people who receive the fullness of the Holy Spirit without anyone praying for them. The laying on of hands is not compulsory.

So these are the terms by which a person can receive the fullness of the Holy Spirit: obedience, humility, purity, and receiving: *wanting God's will, wanting God's way, wanting God's nature,* and *wanting God's fullness.*

O Holy Spirit come upon me,
Let Your grace and your glory flow around
As I bow at Jesus' feet now,
May the fire of heaven flood this holy ground.
As I worship here in full surrender,
Fill my life and my lips with highest praise
Come fill me now!
Come fill me now!
O Holy Spirit come upon me,
'Til my Jesus – my Lord and Savior Jesus –
Fill all my ways with His praise,
All my days.
(JWH)

ᘓᕬ *16* ᘓᕬ

The Baptism
with the Holy Spirit:
The Tongues

Theme Text

"While Peter was still speaking these words,
the Holy Spirit fell upon them who heard the Word.
And those . . . who believed were astonished . . .
because the gift of the Holy Spirit had been
poured out on the Gentiles also.
For they heard them speak with tongues and magnify God."

(Acts 10:44–46)

Our discussion of the subject of speaking in tongues begins where the earlier chapter left off, in the last few verses of Acts 10. The power of God had spontaneously fallen upon Cornelius and the members of his household and they were baptized with the Holy Spirit. Up until that time the body of the early Church was entirely populated by Jewish believers. This was the first real impact that was made upon the Gentile community[6] and it was a stunning upheaval for the leaders of the church in Jerusalem. It was of course also a significant breakthrough in the fulfillment of the words of Jesus – that His gospel would be taken to all the world as a witness to the nations.

Our theme text describes the response of the Jewish believers who accompanied Peter to the house of Cornelius', amazed, not only that God was pouring out His Spirit on these Gentiles – *"... those of the circumcision who believed were astonished, as many as came with Peter, because the gift of the Holy Spirit had been poured out on the Gentiles also"* (Acts 10:45), but also because of the specific things that were happening to them as they were filled with the Spirit: *"For they heard them speak with tongues and magnify God"* (Acts 10:46).

Peter immediately responded by saying, *"Can anyone forbid water, that these should not be baptized who have received the Holy Spirit just as we have? And he commanded them to be baptized in the name of the Lord"* (Acts 10:47–48).

In the latter half of this chapter we will go on to discuss more of the nature and purpose of speaking in tongues, but before we do, we will discuss tongues in relation to the baptism with the Holy Spirit.

How "Tongues" relates to the Baptism with the Holy Spirit

Fewer and fewer sectors of the Church debate any longer about whether God still performs miracles today, but still there are several who debate or demean the issue as to whether believers today should desire or practice speaking in tongues. Some still debate the issue of "tongues as the evidence of the baptism with the Holy Spirit", but we have discussed that already. Within the writer's own ministry, we find that evenhanded teaching and sensitive ministry of the Word and in the power of the Spirit leads people to an encounter with Jesus, the Baptizer with the Holy Spirit, and that the blessing of spiritual language – speaking with tongues – attends virtually all who receive "the fullness".

Still, we refuse to debate this as "the evidence", but neither will deny the likelihood of this truth. The point is, as earlier remarked in Chapter 14, tongues were not intended as a *proof*, but as a resource for *praise, prayer, worship and spiritual warfare (intercession)*. Throughout the Bible the experience of speaking with tongues as people are baptized with the Holy Spirit is so common that there is no way you can honestly dissociate the two events. But how they are related is not a priority in this work – but rather, that "speaking with tongues" is valid, valuable and vital where rightly discerned in truth, welcomed in experience and applied to life.

Tongues is important to God for His Church

Jesus said, *"And these signs will follow those who believe..."* (Mark 16:17), and gave a list of indications by which people could identify that someone was a believer in Christ. They included:

1. Casting out demons.

2. Speaking with new tongues.

3. Handling serpents without being hurt. [7]

4. Drinking deadly substances without being hurt. [8]

5. Laying hands on the sick and seeing them healed.

▶ *Speaking with "other tongues" is included in Jesus' list* along with other supernatural signs that testify to His presence in a believer's life. It is important to note that it was Jesus therefore, who first introduced the concept of speaking in tongues, long before Pentecost.

▶ *On the Day of Pentecost everyone spoke in tongues.* The fact that every single disciple spoke in tongues, and that Jesus counted it important enough to cite as a sign of a believer in Him, must give us an insight into its importance. Although many prefer not to place any emphasis on speaking in tongues for a variety of reasons, we simply cannot honestly minimize the importance of tongues in God's divine order. Tongues was the *birthmark* of the early Church! It is beyond our domain to preempt the right of Almighty God to have anything He wants as part of the life of the Church His Son died to redeem. And tongues is still a *birthright* of each believer, as timelessly a part of what God wants in the Church as ever it has been. I Corinthians 12 makes this clear:

> *"And **God has appointed** these in the church: first apostles, second prophets, third teachers, after that miracles, then gifts of healings, helps, administrations, **varieties of tongues.**"*
>
> (I Corinthians 12:28)

▶ *Tongues is an **indication** that the baptism with the Holy Spirit has taken place, but we will not make it a **qualification** for being acknowledged as "Spirit-filled".*

Returning to our study of Acts 10, we need to make an important note regarding the Jewish believer's reaction to God pouring out His Spirit on the Gentiles. The text says that they were astonished because the gift of the Holy Spirit had been poured out on the Gentiles (v. 45), *but* because the Gentiles had spoken in tongues. It was a powerful indicator for them because they knew that they too had spoken with other tongues at the moment they were baptized with the Holy Spirit.

On the grounds of this kind of text it is understandable why such a large segment of the Church adheres strongly to the opinion that speaking in tongues is the initial physical evidence that the baptism with the Holy Spirit has taken place in a person's life. That phrase, "the initial physical evidence" is a classic Pentecostal doctrinal statement, though not all streams of Pentecostal Christianity include it in their statements of belief.

I personally believe that you cannot disprove that contention, but at the same time I don't believe that you can conclusively prove it either. You cannot conclusively make tongues a *qualification* for having received the baptism with the Holy Spirit. If you take an iron-clad doctrinal stance that tongues *is* initial physical evidence, and that statement means to others that if they haven't spoken with tongues they haven't been baptized with the Spirit, then you have made it a *qualification*.

People ask, "What about believers who manifest expressions of the life and power of the Spirit, yet have never spoken in tongues? Do you think they are baptized in the Holy Spirit?" I answer: First, if a fellow Christian tells me they have been baptized with the Holy Spirit, I *don't* believe it is my call to deny this "tongues" or not. I resist the dogmatism that separates believers over this issue. However, and *second*, I do believe it is my call to minister to people "receiving the Holy Spirit" in such a way as to engender faith for and entry into the full dimensions of a biblical experience in the baptism with the Holy Spirit. I believe this includes the potential benefit and miracle grace of the worship-praise-and-prayer language "speaking with tongues" as enabled by the Spirit. I lead this way after the biblical model of the Apostle Paul in Acts 19:1–6. But if a believer claims to have truly been baptized with the Holy Spirit, I believe the same humility that brought them to that fullness will, in the light of God's Word, manifest in an equal openness to the beneficial resources of the worship-praise-and-prayer language the Holy Spirit brings with Him.

If we honestly review the scriptures where tongues is mentioned, we see that there is clearly a direct link between tongues and the baptism with the Holy Spirit. It is not a qualification, but it most certainly is an indication. Wherever we see people being baptized with the Holy Spirit in the NT we find them also praising God with other tongues. Other passages from which one can draw this conclusion are:

- Acts 8 where Simon the sorcerer saw a sign that something was happening, and he wanted the power. He probably saw them speaking with tongues, although we can't prove that.

- Acts 2, at Pentecost, where it is clear there is a close relationship between tongues and the baptism with the Holy Spirit.

- Acts 19 when Paul prays for believers in Ephesus and they speak in other languages when they receive the baptism with the Holy Spirit.

Even so, one cannot make an airtight case for speaking in tongues being the evidence of baptism with the Holy Spirit – but you can't conclusively say that it is not either. The healthiest posture is to take the attitude that:

1. It was Jesus who first spoke about the subject.

2. It was a birthmark when the Church was born.

3. The Apostle Paul did not say anything bad about it.

Paul said, *"I wish you all spoke with tongues . . . "* (I Corinthians 14:5), and *"I thank my God I speak with tongues more than you all"* (I Corinthians 14:18). Paul advised his readers that speaking in tongues was something that was open to every believer and was very desirable. He said it in such a way as to not make any person who didn't speak in tongues feel guilty, but commended those who did speak in tongues. Note too, that the acknowledged master-theologian and spiritual intellect of the NT was a self-proclaimed "speaker in tongues," with no apology; with gratitude for the value in his experience, and insistent that no one "forbid" believers to speak in tongues.

Characteristics of the spiritual language

There are several qualities of the spiritual language of tongues that I want to draw attention to that will help us gain a better understanding of this precious gift of God. They are:

1. Majesty

There is a majesty to the spiritual language. Acts 10:46 says, *" . . . they heard them speak with tongues and magnify God."* Acts 2:11 says, *" . . . we hear them speaking in our own tongues the wonderful works of God."* In both these cases people are praising and worshipping God and speaking of His greatness. It is the first biblical clue to the use of the gift of speaking in tongues. There is nothing unworthy or common about this spiritual language. If speaking in tongues does nothing more than enhance your personal expression of praise and worship to God, then receive it gladly on that basis.

2. Miracle

The miracle is that a person filled with the Holy Spirit should have the ability to speak in another language, or a heavenly language. In Acts 15:7–9 Peter is discussing the issue of the Gentiles having received the baptism with the Holy Spirit. "The same miracle that happened to us disciples," says Peter, "has happened to some Gentiles" (v. 8). It seems to me that one of the key reasons why God chose to manifest the gift of tongues at Pentecost was that He wanted to literally put a *miracle* on their tongues – something that transcended their natural abilities and flowed from the fountainhead of God. They spoke with other tongues *"as the Spirit gave them utterance"* (Acts 2:4).

The miracle of speaking in tongues is a case of cooperation between humanity and deity. We speak in spiritual languages because we choose to allow the Holy Spirit to express Himself through us in that way. The Holy Spirit is the source – we cooperate. This does not mean that we lose control of our abilities and the Holy Spirit takes over. God never works like that. He gives us the gift and we have to choose to exercise it. God doesn't do anything without our involvement and partnership with Him. On the contrary, every time we speak with tongues we are exercising our faith and are cooperating with the Holy Spirit.

There is a solid body of truth in Scripture that supports the baptism with the Holy Spirit, including the matter of the liberation of the believer into the use of spiritual languages. At the birth of the Church the gift of tongues was on the believer's lips and today the gift is widely used as a resource for personal edification, praise, worship and intercession.

"... *Building yourselves up on your most holy faith,*
praying in the Holy Spirit ..."
"... *Praying always with all prayer and supplication in the Spirit* ..."
(Jude 20; Ephesians 6:18)[9]

✌ PART 8 ✌

The Second Coming of Christ: Our Blessed Hope

❦ *17* ❦

WHAT WILL HAPPEN
WHEN JESUS COMES? (PART 1)

THEME TEXT

*"Behold, I tell you a mystery: We shall not all sleep, but we shall all be
changed – in a moment, in the twinkling of an eye, at the last trumpet.
For the trumpet will sound, and the dead will be raised incorruptible,
and we shall be changed."*

(I Corinthians 15:51–52)

The Second Coming of Christ is referred to a vast number of times
throughout the NT. If you counted all the references to this event
and then compared them to the number of chapters in the entire NT,
you would find that it is mentioned on average, once for every
chapter. We are therefore dealing with a truth of staggering enormity
and importance.

Over the next two chapters I want to differentiate between the
substance of the Bible's message regarding Christ's second coming,
and what might appropriately be described as the "superficial". I
almost hesitate to use the word "superficial", because some of the
things that we will discuss as falling into that category are perfectly
biblical. What I am seeking to counteract is the attitude of some
believers with regard to their interpretation of figurative or cryptic
passages of Scripture – especially those to do with the timing of
events in the "end times" which are highly speculative.

I believe that such speculation has given rise to an attitude in the
Church of Jesus Christ where much more attention is given to
speculating over *uncertainties* than edifying believers with the *certainties* concerning His coming. Throughout this chapter and the next we
will be dealing with the *certainties* regarding Christ's coming – things
that are very clear and are at the heart of the truth about Jesus
coming again.

The issues of biblical revelation providing the basis for biblical teaching which deals with "last things" – the events surrounding the return of Christ – is called *eschatology*. And we find three primary certainties in this field of study, which are:

1. The Coming of Christ

2. The Resurrection of the dead

3. The Eternal State – heaven and hell

These clear, biblical certitudes tend to be displaced in the thinking of some believers whenever "last things" are discussed and replaced by such interpretive enigmas as "the Antichrist", "the mark of the beast", "the two witnesses of Revelation", "the 144,000 witnesses", "the rebuilding of the temple", "the Tribulation" etc. It is not that the latter subjects are not discussed in the Bible, but their meaning is subject to broad interpretation. Neither am I totally against discussing them, because I've done that myself. But as valid as it is to study these things that the Bible speaks about, they are speculative in terms of their timing *and* in the manner of their interpretation. Essentially, I believe the actual fulfillment of these will never be recognized until they have already taken place – which tends to be the way with all prophetic Scripture.

Jesus Himself said that the reason prophecies are given are not so that people can discuss or guess how they might be fulfilled, but in order that people will recognize, when they are fulfilled, that it wasn't an accident of history, but part of God's divine design (John 13:19; 14:29). He said He prophesied certain events so that when they came to pass people would realize that He was Who He said He was.

In sharp contrast to the uncertainties about the end times, none of the three certainties mentioned above are without crystal clear definition. We will examine the biblical clarity with which the happenings at Jesus' Coming are described.

Three major happenings

1. The heavenly announcement.

2. The dead in Christ rise.

3. The living saints are translated.

The starting point for answering our question, "What Will Happen When Jesus Comes?", is in I Thessalonians 4:16: *"The Lord Himself will descend from heaven with a shout, with the voice of an archangel, and with the trumpet of God.''* We will look momentarily at the three-part heavenly announcement – a shout, a voice and a trumpet – when *"the dead in Christ will rise first"* (v. 16), but first we need to understand the context of the larger passage.

It is precisely true – the dead in Christ will rise first. But those who are in Christ and still living when He returns, will rise so closely and with such proximity to them, that it will appear to be simultaneous. Why then does Paul bother to differentiate between the two?

The Apostle Paul founded the church in Thessalonica in a very short space of time. Normally he would spend months, if not two or three years, establishing a church. This time he had but a few weeks to do so. The Thessalonian believers had heard his teaching regarding Christ's Second Coming, but they had not fully grasped his meaning during this brief period. Some members of the congregation had died and the Thessalonian believers were grieved because they thought these people had "missed" Christ's return and the glory of the "rapture". This tells us something about the heart of the Thessalonian church, and indeed the life and thought of the early Church as a whole. They keenly anticipated the imminent return of the Lord.

So the Apostle responds, *"I do want you to be ignorant ... concerning those who have fallen asleep"* (I Thessalonians 4:13), and then goes on to explain that those who have died in Christ will be raised first and will participate in the rapture *along with* all the living believers.

Notice too, this passage reveals that all living believers in Christ will be *instantly translated*. Verse 17 says: *"Then we who are alive and remain shall be caught up together with them in the clouds to meet the Lord in the air. And thus we shall always be with the Lord."*

What does "translated" mean? The dead in Christ are resurrected, but those who are living are instantly *changed* or *transformed*. Both these groups of people will be suddenly raptured to meet Jesus. ("Rapture" is from the Greek, *harpadzo*, meaning "to be caught away suddenly," as when a bird of prey descends from the sky and snatches a creature upward in its talons.)

1. The heavenly announcement

I Thessalonians 4:16 says *"...the Lord **Himself** will descend from heaven with a shout, with the voice of an archangel, and with the trumpet of God."* The use of the word "Himself" emphasizes the fact that it is the *person* of Jesus that is appearing. It is a real and literal event.

The verse makes note of a shout, a voice, and a trumpet. These events are paralleled in the book of Revelation and explained there in more detail than in Paul's passing reference.

▶ *The shout*

This is the shout of the Lord Jesus. If you pause to think about the fact that Jesus is shouting as He comes to gather His own, it is deeply moving – that the Son of God feels so strongly toward His Church. The implication is of Jesus declaring His ultimate triumph. He who cried, "It is finished!" with reference to redemption as He hung on the cross, will shout out this declaration with reference to the consummation of all things. Jesus is longing to return to claim the fruit of that which He died for with anticipation and excitement – to claim all that belongs to Him, bought with His own Blood on the Cross.

Psalm 47:1 says, *"Shout to God with the voice of triumph!"* This is how I picture Jesus shouting as He returns to claim His people.

▶ *The voice of the archangel*

Some interpret Revelation 11:12 as this call – the cry for the redeemed to rise into the presence of the Living God. This verse suggests that the archangel is issuing a summons to those who are saved to "come" to the Lord, following His shout of victory. This call begins the rapture of God's redeemed.

Before we proceed I want to take a moment to explain this word *rapture* because it is not found anywhere in the Bible, and yet is commonly used to describe the moment when all believers are "caught up" in the air to be with Christ. The word "rapture" in English is usually used to describes the emotion, joy and ecstasy of a wonderful moment. It is literally being completely "caught up" in a state of bliss. The word rapture has come into use as a result of the Latin translation of the Bible where the phrase in I Thessalonians 4:17 reads, *simul* **rapiemur** *cum illis.* But the Greek word translated into the phrase "caught up" in verse 17 has "violent" connotations; not in the sense of doing harm, but of the violent suddenness of the moment. It is the same Greek verb that Jesus used to describe the advance of His kingdom on earth.

> *"From the days of John the Baptist until now the kingdom of heaven suffers violence, and the violent take it by force."*
>
> (Matthew 11:12)

It is also the same Greek verb that is used in Acts 8 to describe Philip being suddenly transported by the Lord from the side of the Ethiopian eunuch and appearing in another community.

> *"The Spirit of the Lord caught Philip away, so that the eunuch saw him no more."* (Acts 8:39)

▶ *The trumpet call*

The shout of the Lord Jesus and the voice of the archangel summoning the redeemed in Christ to be with Him will be a moment that transcends anything we can possibly imagine, and yet it is followed by the ushering in of a moment of abject horror. This is the *trumpet call* or "the last trumpet" and is referred to in Revelation 11:15 and I Corinthians 15:52. It denotes the outpouring of God's wrath upon the earth that will ultimately cleanse the earth of evil.

The final trumpet call takes place during a period of time that is mentioned in Revelation 10:7. This period is referred to as "the days of the voice of the last angel". It is literally saying that he is sounding a trumpet. It is the sounding forth of a call that lasts over a period of time, and it is God's wrath that is being extended. This is not to be confused with the later event known as the Tribulation.

It is important that we see this event in context. I Thessalonians 5:9 says: *"God did not appoint us to wrath, but to obtain salvation through our Lord Jesus Christ."* This is a critical verse for us to understand, and gives us a balanced perspective of the end time events. It distinguishes the fact that whatever may happen of trouble, tribulation, difficulty or trial in this world, the redeemed will never experience the outpouring of God's wrath.

Dealing with the issue of God's wrath is difficult because many seem to be of the disposition that God is looking for any opportunity to vent His anger on mankind. That of course is not true because God loves all of mankind. Why then does He pour out wrath on mankind during the end times? Because it will only be by the means of this cataclysmic, catastrophic judgment that God will be able to cleanse the world of what Man has done to it, and cause us to enter into a new era of His ordained design.

In a sense, the wrath of God is the Almighty turning Man over to the ultimate result of following his own will and way. It is simply God extrapolating to its logical conclusion that which Man has already set in motion by his own willfulness.

2. *The dead in Christ rise*

The Bible says that those who have died in Christ will be resurrected (I Thessalonians 4:16b). Verse 15 refers to these believers as being "asleep in Jesus" at this time. It is important that we understand what this term means because it has been confused by some people. There are three references to these "sleeping believers" throughout verses 13–17 and it is clear that these are believers in Christ who have died.

The use of this word "sleep" has introduced for some people the notion that when we die we enter into an interim state of oblivion that occurs between death and resurrection, and are "unconscious" just as we are when we sleep naturally. Proponents of this belief propose, then, that all those who have died experience a kind of undreaming sleep until the Lord comes again. We do not accept this teaching, generally known as "soul sleep" – an idea that derives its basis from one or two OT poetic references, prior to the fuller revelation of the NT. What appears in the OT is not contradicted, but complemented by the NT, and thus given needed light to be seen clearly.

Some have asked, If these believers are not asleep, then why doesn't the Bible just say they are dead? First, it becomes very clear throughout NT Scriptures what Jesus, by His death and resurrection, has done to "death" itself. For all those who believe in Him death has been *robbed* of its fear and its power. It has become so deprived of its capacity to control Man, that it has in most respects, become a lost word to believers who understand what Christ has done. Thus, it seems as though the writers of the NT could not tolerate the word "dead" for people who had gone to be with the Lord, because it was not an honest description of them. They are alive in Jesus Christ! If they are with the Source of all life, then how can we call them dead? The word "dead" does need to be used for their bodies however, because their bodies *are* dead. Their bodies have run out of the capacity to sustain themselves, but the true substance of their personality is with the Lord. Since these believers would also eventually return and receive new, glorified bodies, the word "sleep" became used for their *physical* circumstance, but not the reality of their being present with Christ now.

This concept is the antithesis of the world system and mindset which focuses all its interest purely upon the "touch, see, feel, taste" dimension of our world. The humanist mindset insists that Man is no more than a cluster of chemicals and that his mind is simply a network of synapses in the brain making certain connections. The logical conclusion of this view is that when a person's body ceases to function as it should, that person totally ceases to exist – there is nothing that follows.

The Bible teaches the exact opposite. In fact the least substantial part of Man is his body. The body will not last, but the essence of Man – the personality – transcends that and is retained. And for those who believe in Christ the future holds the promise of an eternal body that will never deteriorate as earthly bodies do. The bodies that God gave to Adam and Eve in the garden would have lasted forever because they were made perfect by Him. It was only through the entrance of sin that their bodies began to deteriorate and through the transmission of that sin to us, that our bodies also deteriorate and die.

Jesus also used the term "asleep" for believers who had died. In John 11 Jesus is asked by the sisters of his friend Lazarus to come at once, because Lazarus is ill. Jesus however, remains where He is for two more days. After that He says to His disciples,

> " 'Our friend Lazarus sleeps, but I go that I may wake him up.' Then His disciples said, 'Lord, if he sleeps he will get well.' However, Jesus spoke of his death, but they thought that He was speaking about taking rest in sleep. Then Jesus said to them plainly, 'Lazarus is dead.' " (John 11:11–14)

Jesus made clear in coining this term that its use does not mean an individual is without consciousness, but, though their body has died, they are in a state so transcending death, as Man normally views it, that the term "dead" is inappropriate. Philippians 1:21–24 and II Corinthians 5:6–8 clearly indicate that a believer's death means they are immediately present with the Lord Jesus, otherwise, these words make no sense at all.

▶ *What form are the dead in Christ in now?*

The fact that the human soul has a form not unlike the body is established in the Word of God. Paul's revelatory experience reported in II Corinthians 12:4 indicates that *"whether in or out of the body"* could not be discerned by reason of a different perspective on the physical attributes of his being. The soul in heaven, between death and resurrection, is not an ethereal, ectoplasmic, ghost-like blob of nondescript, fluctuating dimensions. A dead believer is identifiable (I Corinthians 13:12) and present with Christ in living fellowship until the appointed time for the resurrection of the dead. Time does not exist for that person because they have stepped into eternity.

▶ *How will the resurrection take place?*

In I Corinthians 15 the Apostle Paul teaches that the decayed body will be restored – the *corrupt* will put on *incorruption.*

> *"There is one glory of the sun, another glory of the moon, and another glory of the stars; for one star differs from another star in glory. So also is the resurrection of the dead. The body is sown in corruption, it is raised in incorruption. It is sown in dishonor, it is raised in glory. It is sown in weakness, it is raised in power. It is sown a natural body, it is raised a spiritual body."* (I Corinthians 15:41–44)

And Paul also describes the "snatching away" of God's own at Christ's coming:

> *"We shall not all sleep* [die physically], *but we shall all be changed – in a moment, in the twinkling of an eye, at the last trumpet. For the trumpet will sound, and the dead will be raised incorruptible, and we shall be changed."* (I Corinthians 15:51–52)

Some ask, *"How can God resurrect the body of a person who has been dead for years?"* Psalm 139:13–16 says that God has a book of "blueprints" for all our physical bodies. Science says that even one human cell contains in its DNA spiral all the specifics of that physical being. In other words, if one cell remains – and that is inevitably true of every creature – there is enough information in the natural realm to reconstruct a facsimile. If this is true naturally, how much more readily can we see that God is able to perform this by the glorious power of His eternal, supernatural resources!

> *"Oh, that my words were written! O, that they were inscribed in a book! That they were engraved on a rock with an iron pen and lead, forever! For I know that my Redeemer lives, and He shall stand at last on the earth; And after my skin is destroyed, this I know, that in my flesh I shall see God, Whom I shall see for myself, and my eyes shall behold, and not another."*
> (Job 19:23–27 –
> the most ancient biblical declaration regarding the Resurrection)

✑ 18 ✑

WHAT WILL HAPPEN
WHEN JESUS COMES? (PART 2)

THEME TEXT

*"Then we who are alive and remain shall be caught up together with them
in the clouds to meet the Lord in the air. And thus we shall always be with
the Lord. Therefore comfort one another with these words."*

(I Thessalonians 4:17, 18)

We continue our study of "last things" – the biblical doctrine of eschatology. Our quest here is to examine what happens to those believers who are living when the Lord Jesus Christ returns to rapture His Church and take His own to be with Him. We also will deal with the major doctrinal question of what *"with Him"* means. Paul says that *"to be absent from the body is to be with the Lord"* (II Corinthians 5:8), and speaks elsewhere of his desire to be with the Lord (Philippians 1:23). But where is "with the Lord"?

Paul's statement in Philippians would be meaningless if he were only referring to a state of suspended animation or "soul sleep". These two verses make clear that when a believer's body dies he passes immediately into the presence of the Lord. There is no hiatus between life here on earth and being in the presence of Jesus.

The dead believer's residence in this realm, however, is only a temporary arrangement while they await the return of Christ to the earth and are resurrected into a new and eternal body. Man is not the only being who is occupying a temporary "mid-point" state while he awaits the finale of God's dealings. There are also angelic beings who have not kept their original estate and calling, and who have been confined in a particular location until the appointed time of their judgment before God. I Corinthians explains that believers will be seated with Christ during that judgment and participate in it (I Corinthians 6:3). After that the angels who rebelled against God and those who have rejected Christ will be committed to their ultimate destination which the Bible calls the "lake of fire".

What kind of body?

Regarding the actual issue of our physical bodies, the rapture and the resurrection, the Bible says:

> *"Flesh and blood cannot inherit the kingdom of God; nor does corruption inherit incorruption. Behold, I tell you a mystery: We shall not all sleep, but we shall all be changed – in a moment, in the twinkling of an eye, at the last trumpet. For the trumpet will sound, and the dead will be raised incorruptible, and we shall be changed. For this corruptible must put on incorruption, and this mortal must put on immortality. So when this corruptible has put on incorruption, and this mortal has put on immortality, then shall be brought to pass the saying that is written: Death is swallowed up in victory. O Death, where is your sting? O Hades, where is your victory?"*
>
> (I Corinthians 15:50–55)

This passage opens with the acknowledgment that the ultimate realization of the kingdom – the rule of God in a universal and eternal sense – shall never be the portion of those living in the limited resources of flesh and blood. This does not mean that the "incorruptible" body will not be flesh, but it will be glorified flesh; that is, a truly physical body in a "glory" state that prepares it for eternal durability. Thus, God gives the redeemed a new and eternal body – one that represents God's original intentions for Man's form. It is Man as he was always meant to be! – just as in the garden of Eden, as long as Man walked in relationship with God, he would never die.

The Bible says that this glorious change in Man's body is brought about when Jesus returns at what is called the "first resurrection" (Revelation 20:4–6) – that is, the rapture of the Church, preceding the millennial rule of Christ. The "second resurrection" occurs when those, who by their rejection of Jesus Christ as Savior have already purchased for themselves eternal damnation, are resurrected in order to come before the Great White Throne judgment of Almighty God (Revelation 20:11–15).

So God's Word reveals that there will be a translation of our bodies to a new and incorruptible state and that this is the beginning of our inheritance of God's kingdom. We will be flesh and bone, just as Jesus was when He was seen by His disciples on various occasions after His resurrection (Luke 24; John 21; Matthew 28; Mark 16), but our new bodies will not be reliant upon blood to sustain them.

The Apostle Paul's glimpse of Heaven

When Paul says in I Corinthians 15:50 "behold, I show you a mystery", he is telling us that what he is about to say has been revealed to him supernaturally by the Holy Spirit. He has had a revelation from God and is faithfully recording what the Lord has told him. He is also saying that this truth is something that, until the present time, had been kept secret, but now God has decided to reveal it. Paul says more about the nature of this revelation in II Corinthians when he writes about the experience he can only describe as being *"caught up to the third heaven"* (II Corinthians 12:2).

This experience was so phenomenal that Paul was not sure whether he was there in his physical body or his spiritual body. That statement reveals something to us of the nature of the spiritual body – the form that a person takes when they pass from earthly life to eternity to await the resurrection.

The Apostle tells us that there were things shown to him that he could not allow himself to talk about, but he does disclose some details of this revelation. First, in I Corinthians 15, he asserts that not everyone will die; that those who are in Christ and still living at the time of His return will be instantly transformed into their resurrected bodies. This event will happen suddenly and dramatically *"in the twinkling of an eye"*. (We know from our studies in I Thessalonians and Revelation that this event marks the beginning of the climax of this age.)

Second, the Apostle says that at the sound of the last trumpet the dead will be raised without decay, and then those believers still living will be instantly changed. This is almost precisely the same wording as I Thessalonians 4:16–17, and joins to the truth that *"this corruptible must put on incorruption"* (I Corinthians 15:53). This means that the body that has been buried and subject to decay must take on an incorruptible form. This incorruptible form is eternal and not subject to any kind of decay. When we are in heaven in these "new" bodies we will know more of the true physical reality of our beings than we ever did while we were in this world. No longer will we need to be preoccupied with our body being kept healthy or sufficiently nourished, or be imbalanced regarding physical appetites that sometime deter us now. The realm of glory that we are promised to enter into will so transcend earthly concerns that they will seem trivial and inconsequential by comparison.

When the transformation of the bodies of those still alive in Christ has taken place, the saying, "O Death, where is your sting..." will have been fulfilled. People often quote this verse as though it had already been fulfilled, but Paul is quite specific in saying that the full significance of this statement will become true when we put on our "immortal bodies" (v. 54), when death will no longer have any potency. It is true that in the sense of spiritual victory, death no longer needs to hold any fear for the believer, but until the Lord's return all our bodies will continue dying. At the time of Christ's return we will experience the full physical dimension of redemption, just as we are now experiencing something of its spiritual dimension.

Paul concludes his thoughts by encouraging his readers to be filled with hope because they are not laboring for the Lord in vain, but with the certain promise of hope for the future – eternity with the Lord. If we really grasp the truth of this verse – that after the fleeting expanse of a man's life with all its trials and troubles, we will spend eternity in glory in the presence of Jesus – then earthly difficulties will no longer hold the same trepidation for us. I am not denying the present realities of life with all its inherent stresses, but when your perspective is set upon eternity, then the temporal nature of earthly life pales by comparison.

What happened in the invisible realm with the death of Christ?

If we examine this issue of the "afterlife" further, we see that some transitions have taken place in the realm of the dead since the death and resurrection of Jesus. The situation of the righteous and unrighteous dead prior to Jesus' death was different from the way it is now.

In Luke 16 Jesus tells the story of a rich man and a poor man. The rich man is not identified, but the poor man's name was Lazarus and he was a beggar. Both men died and Jesus tells us what subsequently happened to them. When Lazarus died he was carried by angels to a place that Jesus refers to as "Abraham's bosom". The rich man went to Hades or hell. [10] He was not in Hades because he was wealthy, but because he was godless; he loved and worshipped his resources more than he did God. Neither does this story imply that poor people automatically gain entry to "heaven" because they have experienced "hell on earth". Lazarus was taken to paradise (sheol) because he was obviously a God-fearing man.

While Lazarus was in "Abraham's bosom" and the rich man in Hades, Jesus says that the rich man could see into this heavenly place across a great chasm that separated the two. Abraham's bosom is a term that suggested, especially to Jews, an "honored place". The word "bosom" represents the act of being embraced and received. It is a poetic term describing a literal place where the righteous dead were residing. Lazarus was *welcomed* into heaven and stood beside Abraham, the father of all believers. Hades is the dwelling place of the unrighteous dead and it is clear from the Scriptures that the rich man was experiencing torment and punishment:

> *"Father Abraham, have mercy on me, and send Lazarus that he may dip the tip of his finger in water and cool my tongue; for I am tormented in this flame."* (Luke 16:24)

When Jesus died on the Cross there was a radical upheaval in this invisible realm, and there are several verses that establish what took place in this "underworld". Upon Jesus' death, the Bible says He descended into the "lower parts of the earth".

This event is mentioned in Ephesians 4:9–10:

> *"Now this, 'He ascended,' what does it mean but that He also first descended into the lower parts of the earth? He who descended is also the One who ascended far above all the heavens, that He might fill all things."*

Paul's use of the term "the lower parts of the earth" is a reference to hell, and one that Peter also alludes to in the same regard:

> *"For Christ also suffered once for sins, the just for the unjust, that He might bring us to God, being put to death in the flesh but made alive by the Spirit, by whom also He went and preached to the spirits in prison who formerly were disobedient, when once the Divine long-suffering waited in the days of Noah, while the ark was being prepared, in which a few, that is, eight souls, were saved through water."* (I Peter 3:18–20)

Peter's account says that Jesus was "preaching" to the spirits in prison, and from Paul's comment we know that this was taking place in hell. *Who was Jesus preaching to?* We should understand that Jesus did not go to hell in order to win any converts. He went to proclaim what had been finished at the Cross. His mission was to proclaim that the salvation that had been long awaited by the righteous dead had now been purchased and completed on the Cross.

That day Jesus ushered the righteous dead from Abraham's bosom into the presence of the Father – a place the Bible calls "paradise". Paradise is the place of eternal peace and rest with the Lord, and it is where the Lord is now. It is not the ultimate New Jerusalem that the Bible describes, but it is the place where the Lord says He will receive us to Himself, and it is where believers go to be with Him when they die.

Jesus emptied that portion of the underworld of those who had eagerly anticipated the coming Savior and who awaited the completion of His salvation. This tells us something about the quality of the covenant God had made with His people, which was still in force until Jesus brought in the New Covenant. The Old Covenant held the promise of the ultimate Savior who would come, removing the need for the ongoing blood of sacrificial animals. The dead "Old Covenant believers" looked forward to the One who would fully and finally purchase salvation for them.

We also see a remarkable statement made in Matthew's account of the death and resurrection of Jesus. Matthew 27:51–53 says,

> *"Then, behold, the veil of the temple was torn in two from top to bottom; and the earth quaked, and the rocks were split, and the graves were opened; and many bodies of the saints who had fallen asleep were raised; and coming out of the graves after His resurrection, they went into the holy city and appeared to many."*

We can only speculate on why this incredible event took place, but I believe God allowed it to happen to establish, in the visible arena of Man, a testimony to the people of Jerusalem of the massive and glorious upheaval that had just taken place in the spiritual realm.

We can scarcely imagine the glory and wonder of the day when Christ stormed the underworld to gather the righteous dead to the Father. The heroes of faith from centuries before would have been assembled there awaiting His arrival – Abraham, David, Moses, Elijah, Elisha, and so on. The Lamb who was slain, with the fresh marks of His death upon Him, but in the glory and might of His unquenchable life, comes into their midst and proclaims, "Now redemption is complete!" That day the righteous dead were transferred from Abraham's bosom to paradise, and among them was the thief who had been dying beside Jesus on the Cross!

3. The living saints are translated

Those who are still living when Christ comes again will be privileged to experience the ultimate and cataclysmic upheaval of the spiritual and natural realm. At that time we will be "transformed" into resurrected bodies. The entire fabric of our beings will be changed so radically that we cannot conceive it. For these believers there will be no interim period of dwelling in a soul/spirit kind of body awaiting resurrection, but an instantaneous metamorphosis. It will be as explosive and glorious a moment as has ever been known in the universe – when the full redemptive purpose of God is manifest for Man, His creature, for whom He sent His Son to die.

That all of this is true is established in two ways:

- **By Jesus' own words**: *"I will come again and receive you ... If it were not so I would have told you"* (John 14:1–3).

- **By Jesus' own resurrection**: *"Because I live, you too shall live!"* (John 14:19).

Christ is risen, He's risen indeed!
Conquered death – its prisoners freed!
Risen now, the Eternal Seed,
Sown to die,
Now alive,
With life overflowing!

(JWH)

❧ PART 9 ❧

*Heaven: The Ultimate Reward
of God's Grace;
Hell: The Ultimate Cost
of Rejecting God*

The Glory of Heaven and the Horror of Hell

Theme Text

*"And this is eternal life, that they may know You, the only true God,
and Jesus Christ whom You have sent.
For God did not send His Son into the world to condemn the world,
but that the world through Him might be saved.
And this is the condemnation, that the light has come into the world,
and men loved darkness rather than light..."*

(John 17:3; 3:17, 18)

This chapter concludes our discussion regarding the Second Coming of Christ. We began our study by bringing into focus three facets of prophetic truth that we can discuss with confident certainty, rather than setting out to speculate on questions for which there is no conclusive answer at this point in history. These three areas of certainty concern:

1.   The fact that Jesus is coming again.

2.   The truth of the resurrection of the dead.

3.   The truth of the eternal state – the reality of heaven and hell.

In this chapter we discuss the reality of heaven and hell. There are few subjects I can think of that are more difficult to deal with than this! The glory of heaven is not difficult to write about, but the horror of hell is, which is why it is important that we take time to examine the biblical truth about it.

Hell is a difficult subject because of the fact that it has been sadly caricatured, and because people have been "burned out" by un-gracious teaching regarding it. The stereotypical Bible-thumping preacher yelling condemnation and preaching fire and brimstone is only too vivid for some. Yet these words, though handled in a uncompassionate way, represent biblical realities.

The Bible has much to say about both heaven and hell, and yet is not a book about them. The Bible is a book about God's way, His will, and His plan for mankind. His love is woven through all the issues the Bible raises. Yet whenever the subject of hell is brought up there inevitably follows a string of petty and unjustified attacks on God. It is a commentary on the pathetic, small-mindedness of Man.

God did not design hell to begin with. Hell was brought about by necessity, and later had to be enlarged to accommodate those who chose to relentlessly defy and deny the will of the One who made them (Isaiah 5:14). Hell became the necessary option for those who willed to set themselves against the Creator of the universe. God refused to simply "resign" from His creation, because it belonged to Him and He was committed to it. Consequently, God had to develop a "place" to confine and deal with that which defiled His creation – if it refused to come into line with His established creative order and goodness.

The verses of the first half of Matthew 18 relate to a time when Jesus was teaching His disciples, and He makes mention of both heaven and hell. Firstly Jesus mentions heaven saying,

> *"Unless you are converted and become as little children, you will by no means enter the kingdom of heaven."* (Matthew 18:3)

Jesus refers to heaven as "the kingdom of heaven". Jesus generally used this term in referring to both the active rule of God happening in a person's life now, *and* the literal place of heaven – the place where believers will be in God's presence forever. He said that if we become like children – full of simple faith, trusting and transparent – then we will enter into the dimensions of kingdom living now, and look forward to a time when we will go to enjoy God's presence in eternity.

A matter of will

It is amazing to me how many people believe in an afterlife, and yet it is an afterlife of their own definition based upon their own choices, with their own will predominating. God does not allow for that. God is ruling a Kingdom not a democracy! *He is the Lord.* But, at the same time, God is not simply a puppeteer, dictating the lives of hapless marionettes. He has created creatures with an awesome capacity for self-destiny and self-will. Consider this proposition: *According to the nature of God's having created Man, the human will is as strong as His.*

Do not be deterred from the truth of this statement by failing to qualify its limits. It is true as spoken, but does not extend human "strength" or "power" to any unbiblical dimensions. For example, our power is nothing by comparison with His. Our knowledge is not even close to His. Our capacities are infinitely less in virtually every way; in fact, our strength of purpose is not comparable to God's. However, while our *will*-power may often seem weak, the *choices* of our will are *almighty* in terms of our choices on eternity's greatest issue: who will we acknowledge as God! Whose *will* will govern my life?

The reason for the awesomeness of the power of the human will is not even within the power of our humanity itself – it is in the power of divine decree which has determined, *the human will shall be a free will, and its eternal choices shall be irrevocable.*

This is what our Creator has ordained in His making us in His image. We have been given a sovereign will and an endless existence. From the time of the beginning of our finite lives, Man can be said to be "God's equal" in this respect alone: we will eternally have the eternity we choose, and God Himself will not overrule that choice because He will not deny Himself.

An astonishing trait of the human mind is, if set against Him, Man will argue his own rightness against God's when Man wants his own way. Yet if this self-will and insistence irresponsibly turns from or against God, Man will argue that God is unjust for granting him the just deserts of his choice; he will cry out against God – demanding He do something to override his human irresponsibility. The human argument against hell is Man's quest to "do whatever I please," yet do so with impunity if the action carries penalty or punishment. But we cannot have it both ways – the human will must decide for God's will and way, His Son and salvation, or for self's will and way, with its loss now and eternally.

When we choose to align ourselves with something other than God's will, we bear the consequences of that responsible choice. But it is not a matter of God *wanting* people to go to hell for disobeying Him, as Jesus clearly stated, *"It is not the will of your Father who is in heaven that one of these little ones should perish."* (Matthew 18:14)

The "little ones" that Jesus spoke of were illustrated by the children He had gathered around Him as He taught His disciples. The application of Jesus' teaching certainly included the children themselves, but extends to each one of us too. We are all called to the teachableness and simplicity of a child, but too often there is found in us something of human arrogance which disallows that.

Self-sufficient and proud, buoyed up by human wisdom, the mind may presume any ideas it chooses – but finally, God's decreed laws prevail. Our wisest course is to cease argument with our Creator, come to Him, and confess our dire need of a Savior.

That's why Jesus said, *"The Son of Man has come to save that which was lost"* (Matthew 18:11). He stated His mission was to rescue us – to bring us from inevitable "lostness" and our total inability to extract ourselves from sin's bondage and destiny – the ultimate of the human predicament.

Answering to God's Word

Jesus Himself taught pointedly regarding the sobering and frightening truth of a place He calls "hell". Described as "the everlasting fire" and as "hell fire" (Matthew 18:8–9) respectively. Jesus' comments have such gravity, it is impossible to casually regard or skip over these verses as if they weren't there. We cannot attribute to Jesus all the wonderful things He said, such as "Come to me all you who are heavy laden and I will give you rest", and then irresponsibly bypass the "difficult" things He says, such as: *"If your hand or your foot causes you to sin, cut it off and cast it from you. It is better for you to enter into life lame or maimed, rather than having two hands or two feet, to be cast into the everlasting fire. And if your eye causes you to sin, pluck it out and cast it from you. It is better for you to enter into life with one eye, rather than having two eyes, to be cast into hell fire"* (Matthew 18:8–9).

Jesus sets before us the challenge of negating our own willfulness, of casting away from ourselves the things that hinder us coming to God and humbling ourselves before Him in submission to His will. Man is endlessly wrapped up in the distraction of fulfilling his own creative capacity (Man's hands), and constantly deviates from the path of God's will (Man's feet). Man is consumed with his thirst for knowledge and increasing his intelligence, and with fulfilling all his earthly desires and goals (Man's eyes). But our greatest capacities will never be discovered if we set ourselves out of a humbly ordered relationship with God.

This is what Jesus longs for us to grasp, and while He leaves us in no doubt about the consequences of not doing so, He leaves no doubt concerning His merciful love and longing for the lost to be saved. So great is His compassionate concern for the human race that He not only warns us of hell, using dire terms, but seems in the next verses (Matthew 18:11–18) to literally "spill out" the heart of God toward humankind. *He* is the Great Shepherd – and *He* is the one

Who came to gather lost ones with such passion, He cannot rest apart from seeking *even one* lost sheep.

Man's persistent argument against hell down the years has usually been, "Who can believe a God of love would make a place like Hell." Let us counter with the question, "Who can believe an intelligent human being would reject a God of such great love." Instead of questioning God, let every person regard the ultimate expression of love He has demonstrated in sacrificing His own Son to redeem us. Let every heart receive His offer of the free gift of salvation. And let every human will choose to turn to the Savior, and turn from the most horrible fact in the universe – a reality called "hell," a fact of such eternal significance every soul is wise to think clearly about it.

The most demanding question any human being can ever answer is, "Where will you spend eternity?" This question has been well-used by preachers, even caricatured. It conjures up pictures of bearded prophets with sandwich boards walking the streets of New York's financial district. Somehow society, because of the scorn with which it has treated such a figure, has also disqualified the question in its mind. Yet each and every person will be faced with the result of the choices they made in this life and will endure an eternity of either blessing and glory or regret and punishment. Every human being will be resurrected after death with an eternal body that will never perish and "living forever" will spend eternity either in heaven or in hell.

The reality of Hell

The word "hell" is used in a number of ways in the Bible. The reality and nature of hell is described in Mark 9. This passage is Mark's account of the words of Jesus we have been reading in Matthew's gospel, but with the addition of a quotation Jesus' makes from the prophetic writings of Isaiah: [11]

> *"It is better for you to enter the kingdom of God with one eye, rather than having two eyes, to be cast into hell fire – where 'Their worm does not die, and the fire is not quenched.'"* (Mark 9:47–48)

▶ *Jesus emphasizes the endlessness of eternity.*

The word *worm* that Jesus uses is the same word for "maggot" and stresses the decaying quality of a life set apart from God. Some commentators have suggested that this has to do with a "plaguing" effect – that a person will turn the events of their life over and over, bitterly regretting the fact that they refused the opportunity to turn to God – that it will be as if a maggot were continually "eating away" at them. Others see a figurative expression, meaning that a person, having given themselves over to their own sin and disobedience, has subjected themselves to such decay that they can be likened to a dead body, ridden with maggots.

▶ *Jesus refers to hell as outer darkness* (Matthew 8:12; 22:13; 25:30).

"Outer darkness" signifies a total dissociation with everyone and everything. It is a place of total aloneness and separation. One of the saddest comments you are ever likely to hear is a person rejecting the Gospel of Jesus with the words, "Well, if I go to hell, at least all my friends will be there." Even if said in jest, some still do think there is truth in it; that they will just be "in the same boat" as friends, acquaintances, etc. Such ideas underscore human blindness and Man's ignorance toward his ultimate destiny. The Word shows, instead, that once a person is totally severed from God due to their own free will choice, that choice will extrapolate to its full implications – ever increasingly distanced from God, and from all other expressions of life of any kind.

▶ *These are horrendous and unimaginable thoughts.*

That anyone would endure such total and utter eternal damnation are horrendous and unimaginable thoughts, but they are gloriously contrasted by the fact that God, knowing the awful consequence of Man's disobedience, has provided a way to save Man from this horrible fate – and He did it by paying the price Himself!

As we noted earlier, God did not plan hell: *"Then He* [the Lord Jesus] *will also say to those on the left hand, 'Depart from Me, you cursed, into the everlasting fire prepared for the **devil and his angels** . . . '"* (Matthew 25:41). Only those will go there who choose to turn from the grace that says, "Let your will turn to Me. Put your trust in My Son." The choice is ours, as C.S. Lewis said: "There are only two kinds of people in all the universe: those who say to God, 'Thy will be done', and those to whom God ultimately says, 'Thy will be done.'"

The reality of Heaven

Heaven is not a starry-eyed dream or a Disneyesque castle-in-the-sky. It is the eternal home of the redeemed, about which very clear statements are given us by Father God in His Word.

▶ *Heaven is a prepared place.*

It has been planned from eternity. It is not a come-lately idea, but a designed place for a desired people – the Father's Redeemed, the Son's Bride. Revelation 19:1–7 describes a mighty crescendo of praise in the Throne Room of heaven, as angelic hosts laud the Living God for His faithfulness and justness. As He concludes judgment upon the evil of Great Babylon – the symbol opposite Zion, the City of our God – the convening of the host to celebrate the marriage of the Lamb takes place. This celebration is in heaven, and the redeemed are rejoiced over as they gather.

▶ *Heaven is a personal place.*

As Jesus sought to counsel and comfort His disciples the night before His crucifixion, He spoke words filled with tenderness: *"Let not your heart be troubled, you believe in God, believe also in Me. In My father's house are many mansions; if it were not so, I would have told you. I go to prepare a place for you"* (John 14:1–2). The distinct designation "for you" moves heaven from simply being a grand and glorious location, to being a warm, personal and inviting place of encounter. Jesus adds: *"And if I go and prepare a place for you, I will come again and receive you to Myself, that where I am there you may be also"* (John 14:3). It is not sentiment that suggests our being personally welcomed in heaven, it is the Savior!

▶ *Heaven is a purposeful place.*

In stark contrast to the horror and awful necessity of hell, where purposelessness and darkness, separation and anguish abide, God not only planned heaven, He has plans for meaning-filled activity and service there for the Redeemed. Jesus says to the righteous who have acknowledged Him as Lord: *"Come, you blessed of My Father, inherit the kingdom prepared for you from the foundation of the world . . . "* (Matthew 25:34). The words "inherit the kingdom" convey responsible participation in some not-yet designated role of companionship in the King of kings rule and administration. Some see it solely referencing a millennial rule with Him, on the earth. This is certainly in the Word (Revelation 5:10), but there is profound evidence for some eternal purpose even beyond this world. Ephesians 2:7 speaks of an unfolding of divine purpose that will show us "the exceeding riches of His grace" into the *ages to come*. One wonders if this references something of what the entire cosmos is awaiting, as noted by the Apostle Paul in Romans 8:18–22, when the redeemed family of God ultimately "comes into our own."

▶ *Heaven is a peaceful place.*

It will be the reward faith receives and which grace lavishes forever. Everything that is the fruit of Satan's rebellion, Man's sin, Earth's sorrow or Hell's hatred, will be removed from any influence or touch upon the beauty of God's designed home for us. Revelation 21:1–2, 6 describe the beauty of Heaven and these wonderful verses speak eloquently of the promised place prepared for the redeemed.

> *"Now I saw a new heaven and a new earth, for the first heaven and the first earth had passed away. Also there was no more sea. Then I, John, saw the holy city, New Jerusalem, coming down out of heaven from God, prepared as a bride adorned for her husband. And I heard a loud voice from heaven saying, 'Behold, the tabernacle of God is with men, and He will dwell with them, and they shall be His people.'"*

> *"God Himself will be with them and be their God. And God will wipe away every tear from their eyes; there shall be no more death, nor sorrow, nor crying. There shall be no more pain, for the former things have passed away ... And He said to me, 'It is done! I am the Alpha and the Omega, the Beginning and the End. I will give of the fountain of the water of life freely to him who thirsts ...'"*

▶ *Heaven is a permanent state.*

The verses immediately following the above, go on to describe the wonder and glory of this "new heaven" – its beauty and perfection; how the light of God lights the city, superceding the need for either sun or moon. Then, in the companion passage in Revelation 22, the Bible says of all the servants of God and of the Lamb, *"And they shall reign forever and ever ... These words are faithful and true ..."* (vs. 5, 6). There is nothing of transiency, though there will be nothing of boredom. There will be God's eternal presence, directing the Redeemer's eternal purpose, and the ages will bring unending discoveries of the greatness of our God and the wonders of His plans for us all. But *once we arrive in heaven, its blessings are forever!* Listen to the words of the beloved hymn writer, Esther Kerr Rusthoi:

> It will be worth it all, when we see Jesus
> Life's trials will seem so small, when we see Christ.
> One glimpse of His dear face, all sorrow will erase,
> So bravely run the race, 'til we see Christ.

What of the Lost?

Can a person have a second chance?

When the awfulness of hell and the wonders of heaven are addressed in the light of God's Word, inevitably the question is raised, "Can someone have a second chance once they have been condemned to hell?" Everything in our human way of thinking ponders the possibilities that some dimension of later-to-be-discovered-mercy will be found beyond this life. But there is no evidence of this in Scripture. Honesty with the Word of God forces us to note these facts:

1. God did not intend hell or eternal judgment for anyone (II Peter 3:9). That is why He sent His Son, so that none need perish (John 3:16).

2. The gift of free will carries with it the consequences of choices made. The Judge of the earth will always "do right" (Genesis 18:25), but even His administration of "what seems right" cannot reverse the choice of any human's will.

3. Since God is the final arbiter of these issues, it is never your or my duty to consign anyone to eternal torment. If that is their final destination, self-invoked by reason of human will, we are wise to leave it to God to handle and not feel we need to tell anyone that a given person is "in hell," or is certain to go there.

It is because there is no indication of there being a second offer of salvation beyond this life that Scripture continually underscores the importance of making responsible choices in this life. Scripture infers that the god-like authority of the human will is exercised with such definitive finality in this life, that after you have gone beyond this life, you won't want to change your mind.

One author concluded that if a person was given a second chance to make a plea before God after their death, that they would simply argue their case using the same viewpoint as they always held, using the same arguments that they used continually while they were alive on earth. The revelation of God's Word is that we are each shaping eternal values in our hearts. We have no idea what will solidify of the heart's attitude and choice, either for or against God, once this life is over.

For that reason, the living, loving God who made us cries out, "*I have set before you life and death, blessing and cursing; therefore* **choose**

life, *that both you and your descendants may live"* (Deuteronomy 30:19).

And God laid before us the ultimate choice, provided at immense cost.

"For God so loved the world, that He gave His only begotten Son
that whoever believes in Him should not perish,
but have everlasting life."

(John 3:16)

❧ PART 10 ❧

Tithes and Offerings:
The Cycle of Abundance

CHRIST'S NEW COVENANT ON GIVING

THEME TEXT

"Give, and it will be given to you:
good measure, pressed down, shaken together,
and running over will be put into your bosom.
For with the same measure that you use,
it will be measured back to you."

(Luke 6:38)

Our motivation to include this section of teaching on stewarding our finances is neither rooted in a materialistic pursuit nor by the sometime-popularized emphasis common in certain circles of the believing community today. But sound doctrine involves preparing people to *live*, and there is nothing more fundamental to our daily life than the issue of how we manage our money.

Stewardship is that term which describes the management of *everything* in our lives, including everything we are and do, have and hold, and influence by our skills, presence, words or investment of time, talents or funds. To learn to manage money is to lay the groundwork for learning to manage the rest of life. Mismanagement of any part of live manifests in the mismanagement of our funds – whether large or small. The reverse is true as well.

Thus, sound teaching on biblical grounds, establishing scriptural understanding and principles in the members of Christ's Body, can achieve immeasurable good.

1. God becomes glorified in the arena of human experience where Mammon seeks to rule.

2. Believers embrace the *spirit* of giving because they understand the *truth* of doing so.

3. Joy abounds by reason of the spiritual fruitfulness of applied wisdom at life's most pragmatic dimension.

4. Resources abound for the purpose of ministry, personal suffi-
    ciency and practical need.

It is no wonder that a surprisingly large portion of Jesus' teaching
centers on *stewardship* – the management of life and resources –
essentially money. He was not hesitant to do so, and no one
questioned His motives – then or now. So it is, because of His clear
emphasis on these matters, that we seek to do the same.

The divinely ordered law of reciprocity

Our theme text presents the key to the proper stewardship of our
money, here in the founding principle Jesus gave us concerning
giving:

> *"Give, and it will be given to you: good measure, pressed down,
> shaken together, and running over will be put into your bosom. For
> with the same measure that you use, it will be measured back to
> you."* (Luke 6:38)

Jesus, without apology, explains that there is a reciprocal law of
giving. It means simply that when you give, something comes back.
Whenever a statement like that is made there is usually an uprising
among sections of the Christian community who would contend
that we should not give in order to get. Well, let me answer that: *I
don't think we should either!* However, that is not the point (though we
must face up to the fact that *God* is the one who has established this
initiative in reciprocation!).

But the point, most clearly, is that Jesus was not trying to convince
His disciples to give with an incentive program that they would get
something back if they gave. Instead, He was focusing on the issue of
"life-release" – wanting us to understand that an actual, divinely
ordered spiritual dynamic is set in motion when we give.

We are dealing with a reality God Himself has written into the
universal order of things. The divinely ordered arrangement *of* life, is
that the fullest dimensions *in* life are only released through the
action of *giving*. The inverse of this reality is equally true: *all* life is
stifled, shrunken, withered when giving is not exercised.

There are people who don't have any friends because they do not
give themselves in friendship; people who can't cultivate relationships
because they don't make themselves available to others; people whose
money doesn't work for them because they never give any of it away.

Human worry over "Having enough"

In Matthew 6:25–32, our Lord inserts extensive guidance for His disciples, confronting the issue of human preoccupation about material adequacy:

> *"Therefore I say to you, do not worry about your life, what you will eat or what you will drink; nor about your body, what you will put on. Is not life more than food and the body more than clothing? ... Therefore do not worry, saying 'What shall we eat?' or 'What shall we drink?' or 'What shall we wear?' ... For your heavenly Father knows that you need all these things. But seek first the kingdom of God and His righteousness, and all these things shall be added to you."*

Four times during this discourse in Matthew 6, Jesus says, "Don't worry." He is not making casual comment about human concerns, as though He were so spiritual that material need was of no interest to Him. But He said it to stress the fact that "the Father knows what you need."

Jesus describes the faithfulness of our Creator to taking care of all He has created, and He gives examples: "Look at the birds. Look at the glory of the flowers in the fields. If God bothers to make flowers as beautiful as they are, even though they will wilt tomorrow, don't you think He cares about you?"

As we seek to understand Jesus' command to not be preoccupied with worry over money, there are two things that are significant:

1. Jesus' command is based on Father God's commitment to be a faithful steward of everything that is under His charge. *We* are required to manage the resources that God gives us well, but the Father seeks to remind us that we are all under *His* charge, and He will faithfully take care of us. He manages the events of our lives to ensure that we can manage ours.

2. To fail to acknowledge God's faithful stewardship and respond appropriately by being good stewards ourselves, can cause us to fall into a trap of idolatry. Idolatry is the word describing all tendencies to focus upon *self*, not only the idolatry of worshipping money. When I am preoccupied with "self" I will manage to have what I want, in order to do what I want to do, and become concerned when I don't have what I want or think I need. If this is the case I am obviously stuck in the "I"! The initial letter of the word says it all: I-dolatry! When we worry

over the affairs of our lives and become preoccupied with those concerns, we begin to violate the principles of giving that God has put in place.

One of the greatest traps for all Christians is thinking that we cannot afford to give. We say to ourselves, "I really want to give, but I've got to manage things first..." But what we are really saying is, "I can manage my affairs better than God", and that is idolatry. Of course, no one is foolish enough to face God and say those words, but that is often what we end up doing. That's why the Lord warned us not to get caught in the trap of worry. It cultivates a "self-preservation", survival mentality. But God says, "Your survival is up to Me. I can take care of you and I will."

Giving is not to be for "show"

In Matthew 6:1–4, Jesus spoke discipling directives concerning the impropriety of people born into His Kingdom to concede to the human practice of displaying one's giving. Jesus said in regard to the act of giving, *"Take heed that you do not do your charitable deeds before men, to be seen by them. Otherwise you have no reward from your Father in heaven"* (vs. 1).

This first comment of Jesus precedes a number of statements He makes concerning the believer's conduct. He says that when we pray we should not emulate the hypocrites who pray on street corners so that everyone sees how spiritual they are; that when we fast we should not go around looking sad and disfigured like the hypocrites do. Similarly Jesus says that when we give we should not make a boastful show of our "generosity".

Jesus drew His disciples attention to this one day as they sat in the temple and observed people putting offerings into the nearby treasury. Many people came and went, including several wealthy people who gave large sums of money. The treasury was situated in the Court of Women and offerings were placed into thirteen chests fashioned in the shape of trumpets. The wealthy tended to call attention to the fact that they were giving large sums of money by making their deposit ostentatiously, but a widow caught Jesus' attention as she deposited two mites in a coffer and went on her way unnoticed. [12]

Jesus said to His disciples:

> *"Assuredly, I say to you that this poor widow has put in more than all those who have given to the treasury; for they all put in out of their*

*abundance, but she out of her poverty put in all that she had, her
whole livelihood."* (Mark 12:43–44)

Jesus wanted His disciples to understand that this lady had given
far more than anyone else, not only in the spirit of her giving, but in
the percentage of her resources. The widow did not make a show
about the fact that she was giving all her money away, and Jesus
teaches us to behave in like manner. Jesus also put it this way:
*"...when you do a charitable deed, do not let your left hand know what
your right hand is doing"* (Matthew 6:3).

Again He makes the point that *we should not give with pomp and
ceremony*, and also that we should not seek recognition from others
by our giving. But Jesus also cautioned us against giving in this way
for another reason. Sometimes people will give in order to seek to
retain control of a situation. They will manipulate a person or a
circumstance by *investing* into it. But a gift, by definition, is not a gift
if it obligates the person who receives it.

An example of this is the person who gives a gift to charitable
organization or perhaps a church building program and then wants
to have significant input into how the money is spent – especially if
the gift is substantial. Such an attitude is outside the parameters of
biblical giving. People who really understanding God's principles
of giving never expect to own any special rights, no matter what
amount they give, great or small.

Misunderstandings about "not parading giving"

To be clear about observing the guidelines which Jesus gave us, we
also need to understand what "parading our giving" *isn't*. Some
sensitive and very sincere people have become confused regarding
"not letting the left hand know what the right hand is doing." For
example, I have found sincere yet real misunderstanding in this
regard when people think they are "parading" if they appropriately
deduct charitable contributions from their income tax as anyone else
would.

This is a mistaken application of this principle. The private
"declaration" of one's charitable giving in this way is not a violation
of Jesus' command. On the contrary, such good record keeping and
accounting practice is totally consistent with God's principles of
good stewardship, moreover, the tax benefit realized not only
evidences wise handling of funds, but allows you to give more!

Another practical example is raised in this regard when someone may
ask: "Is it against Scripture to receive a gift-response from a ministry

because you gave to it?" A case in point is when (as in many Christian radio and TV offers) a ministry sends a book, tape or other gift to those making donations. To answer this question, the first issue is for each one giving to examine his or her own motive when giving. My own feeling is that Jesus' teaching is not violated if one gift is made *to minister to someone* when they have made a gift *to enable ministry to others*. Many "response-gifts" are designed to contribute to the growth of the person who has given to a ministry – in other cases, so that someone else may be served or touched with ministry through the one who has given. When a ministry can say, "If you feel we have served you in any way, then let us partner with you further by allowing us to help your life to become all it can become in Christ," the spirit of Jesus is not jeopardized.

It is *not* right if a ministry sends items that foster superstition or nonsense – such as vials of tears of someone who has been praying for you; small sacks of sand from the Holy land where Jesus walked, etc. These examples are not an exaggeration! And even more viciously ridiculous means have been known to be used. These are a travesty on the Gospel, and unworthy enterprises, completely out of line, not only violating the disciplines Jesus taught, but violating the people who are exploited by such ruses.

The standard of giving

The essence of what Jesus had to say about the "standard" of giving is wonderfully captured in one verse of Matthew 23:23:

> *"Woe to you, scribes and Pharisees, hypocrites! For you pay tithes of mint and anise and cummin, and have neglected the weightier matters of the law: justice, mercy and faith. These you ought to have done, without leaving the others undone."*

Take time to examine all that our Savior is saying here. First, Jesus mentions three small herbs – mint, anise and cummin, then underscores three immense principles of God – justice, mercy and faith. What a comparison! Jesus condemns the scribes and Pharisees for taking great care over such minute details while neglecting the whole point of the Law! The scribes and Pharisees were hyper-religious purists who were so caught up in their religious system that they had lost sight of the love of God.

Jesus observed that the scribes and Pharisees were so "religious" that when they picked some mint to season a meal, they would rigorously separate a tenth of it in order to take it to the temple as a tithe. Jesus was not condemning this as a bad deed, but He saw that they were taken up with the minutia of spiritual life while neglecting the really important issues.

Biblical giving is no substitute for obedience in other matters

When Jesus pinpoints these three areas He is speaking of *real life* situations, not philosophical ideals. The scribes and Pharisees were tithing spices, but forgetting to apply justice, mercy and faith in their day-to-day living. The word faith here refers to being *faithful* so as to be trustworthy. They weren't just, merciful, or trustworthy. Various accounts in the gospel bear this out.

▶ *They lacked* **justice**.

These men that Jesus was talking to were the same men that conspired to arrange liars and false witnesses in order to ensure that He was put on the Cross. Their unjust conspiracy led to His death.

▶ *They were* **merciless**.

The case of the woman caught in adultery reveals these "religious leaders" aching to stone her and put her to death for her sin. They would have murdered her on the grounds of judicial impunity had not Jesus saved her by reminding the Pharisees that there was such a thing as mercy.

▶ *Their* **faithlessness** *was manifest in the way they exploited their wives*.

They were indifferent to their relationships and looked for ways in which they could discard one wife in order to take another. They did not prize or value the deepest human relationship of all.

There are those who, like the Pharisees, believe that paying their tithe "earns" them exemption from God working to further purify their lives. In other words allowing God to teach you how to love your wife and kids, and to show mercy to people who may not seem worthy to you. But payment of tithes does not give us license to be indifferent to God's ways.

Tithing is not invalidated by Jesus' remarks, but re-validated

While Jesus shows that biblical giving is no substitute for obedience in matters of justice, mercy and faith, He points out that tithing remains important and necessary. Jesus concludes His reprimand of the Pharisees by saying: *"These you ought to have done, without leaving the others undone."*

Biblical giving includes the principle of tithing. Jesus affirms the righteousness of exercising mercy, justice, and faith, and reaffirms the righteousness of tithing – of *not* leaving it undone. Jesus does not dismiss tithing. Rather, with these words, He brings this foundational principle of giving into the New Covenant principle of tithing. Tithing *preceded the Law* (see Abraham's and Jacob's worship with the tithe) and here, Jesus brings it *beyond the Law*, while at the same time upholding the Law in the setting He addressed at that moment. His capacity to embrace and exceed all that historic tradition observed, and take it to a new level, is another case of His divine wisdom at work.

The multiplying power of the tithe

Tithe literally means "tenth". It is not a fluctuating figure. Why is the tithe ten percent? No one can answer that question but God. Perhaps it represents the smallest amount you can give and still set in motion the principle of dynamic multiplication. The law of giving is a reciprocal law that God has built into the law of life as surely as the law of gravity is built into the law of nature, and the payment of the tithe sets in motion a *multiplied response.*

There is a certain gratification achieved whenever you decide to give, and I believe that alone testifies to the wisdom of giving. But in addition to that, God desires us to be obedient in giving our resources away so that He can bestow an even greater blessing upon us.

> *" 'Bring all the tithes into the storehouse, that there may be food in My house, and try Me now in this,' says the* LORD *of hosts, 'If I will not open for you the windows of heaven and pour out for you such blessing that there will not be room enough to receive it.' "*
> (Malachi 3:10)

Our learning to give constitutes God's way to bring us into line with the possibilities of heaven's breakthrough into our world – with blessing, revival, saving grace and abounding adequacy for human need. So we are reminded, *giving is not so we may get something back, but that it releases a God-given principle that unleashes His life and mighty grace into our world.* This *multiplication* of life has to do with everything – it is not just a matter of money, but of fulfillment, purpose and destiny.

As we learn the workings of God's economy we are loosed from the cycle of self-preservation and preoccupation with needing to be in control.

When thinking of giving, the picture that springs to my mind is that of a water wheel at an old-fashioned mill. Water comes rushing down from a river or creek into a small channel where the wheel is housed, and the troughs on the wheel collect the water as the wheel spins around. Very little water is gathered in the troughs, compared to the amount rushing through the channel, and yet this small amount is enough to power the wheel and run the machinery inside the mill. This machinery grinds the grain into flour that will make bread and ultimately feed people.

The whole principle of tithing is that God allows resources to flow toward all of us, and in order to set in motion what will multiply and bless, a certain amount of these resources must be given away. It doesn't take a huge amount – just about ten percent! The only difference between our analogy and real tithing is that the resources do not automatically go into the trough. *We have to make a choice to put them there.* We administrate the giving, upholding God's principles of good stewardship as He models them to us through His care and provision of our needs.

Jesus said, *"Give, and it will be given to you: good measure, pressed down, shaken together, and running over."* My prayer is that every believer will grasp the importance of this principle, put it into action, and therefore enjoy the blessing of God's very best for their own life.

> *"But this I say: He who sows sparingly will also reap sparingly,*
> *and he who sows bountifully will also reap bountifully.*
> *So let each one give as he purposes in his heart,*
> *not grudgingly or of necessity; for God loves a cheerful giver.*
> *And God is able to make all grace abound toward you,*
> *that you, always having all sufficiency in all things,*
> *may have an abundance for every good work."*

(II Corinthians 9:6–8)

∽ 21 ∽

MONEY AND THE CHILDREN OF LIGHT (PART 1)

THEME TEXT

"So the master commended the unjust steward because he had dealt shrewdly. For the sons of this world are more shrewd in their generation than the sons of light."

(Luke 16:8)

The parable of the shrewd steward

The words of our theme text seem to stand, upon first reading, as among the most bewildering words in the Bible. By all appearances, Jesus is commending a self-serving, conniving manipulator, consumed with nothing more than his own well being, and willing to utilize any dishonest scheme to achieve his self-protecting goal. But to the contrary, we are captivated by Jesus' picture-lesson, as we realize He has not used this fictitious crook as an example for us to follow, but as a comparative study in the operative practices of the people of two different kingdoms – the kingdom of this world, and the Kingdom of God. As citizens of the latter, let us open our hearts to hear the instruction of our Savior, King and Chief Rabbi in this Kingdom – Jesus Himself.

Opening His subject, Jesus uses the figure of a steward who worked for a rich master. "Steward" is a term that means "manager" – one who had the executive management role in his master's household. He owned nothing himself, but was in charge of all his master's resources.

In Jesus' story, the rich man had heard that his steward was mishandling funds, so he called him to come and give account of his stewardship, telling him that he might lose his job. The steward was rightly worried about losing his livelihood. He knew that he had no skills as a laborer and was accustomed to his "white-collar" job.

What was he to do? He decided to take a course of action that would "make him some friends" in the event of him being turned out on the street. He hoped that these people would then *"receive ...* [him] *into their houses"* as a result of his kindness. The Greek word translated "houses" does not simply mean their homes, but encompasses the realm of "business" as well – a house may be a dwelling place, but also a place of work or a business.

So the steward contacted all of his master's debtors and asked each one how much they owed him. He then systematically "reduced" each person's debts to gain favor with them. He was banking on the fact that one of these people would give him a job when he was fired because he had "bought" their obligation. He made every effort to ensure that some business would have a spot for him.

Surprisingly, when the master discovered what had been going on he commended the steward for his shrewd actions, saying that he had dealt wisely. He was not condoning the man's dishonesty by this statement, but was saying that in the context of the world system, based as it is on seeking to establish your own security at the expense of others, *the steward had acted wisely.* The world system says, "secure your future at any cost" – even if that cost means the violation of integrity and conscience. Because the steward recognized how the system worked and exploited it to his full advantage, his master called him "wise".

Then in verse 8, Jesus, having concluded the parable, begins the application – giving His teaching principles and commenting on the outcome by saying, *"For the sons of this world are more shrewd in their generation than the sons of light"* (Luke 16:8).

On the surface, it seems conflictive with our view of what we would expect Jesus to say: is He saying, "People of the world are smarter than the people of God"? Obviously, He is not commending the dishonest behavior of the steward, but His statement sounds as though it is working against His own principles and purposes.

The world's children – wiser than God's?

The crux of Jesus' point, however, is that the children of this world are, *in their generation,* wiser than the children of light (v. 8). By "their generation" Jesus means "the realm in which they live" and He is observing how worldlings – in their dark, blinded kingdom of life and living – are more faithful to live consistently with the world-spirit that than believers – as children of the Kingdom of Light – to live consistently within their own realm. In short, our Lord is saying: "The world works its system for all it's worth, but the children of God aren't that smart – they fail to maximize the dynamics of the new realm into which they have been ushered!" How is this true?

The fact is, the habit of the redeemed to "sometimes live in the light and sometimes live in the dark" is no more evident that when it comes to money – the subject of Jesus' lesson. The fact that there are two distinct realms is clearly established, but each individual has to decide which realm they will function in. When it comes to certain issues, Christians can tend to "blur" the edges.

The fact that Christians don't always live in the light when it comes to money can be traced back through the history of the Church and finds its roots in two streams of thought known as Gnosticism [13] and Monasticism [14] – which, without expanding the terms in detail here, have developed the line of thinking that true spirituality shuns everything material and physical. These beliefs have filtered down through Church history to the extent that many Christians, without devoting themselves to monastic disciplines, are left with the notion that money is distasteful or that God is somehow against it.

What is "unrighteous mammon"?

The Bible never refers to money as "dirty", but it does have things to say about the spirit that dominates it. The Bible draws a line between "money" and "mammon." Money itself is amoral, and how it is handled will determine its relative "purity." Jesus, in naming "mammon" identifies the spirit that controls the lust for financial power and the covetousness for money that dominates so much of society. That's why He calls it *"unrighteous mammon"*. But Jesus also points out that the children of light can, by the power of the Spirit within them, move into the realm of finance and refuse to be dominated by that spirit of darkness, *as long as we bring our money management practices into the light.* This, of course, can only happen as we each make a personal decision to put our resources in God's hands and so bring our money into the light.

In other words, we are being faced with the need to function consistently according to the financial principles of God's kingdom. But, unfortunately, there is a frightening mixture of realms practiced among believers – employing the world system of "self-security" (as with the steward), while living by God's Word in other matters. The real question this text poses is, "Which realm will you live in when it comes to finance?" Jesus' next words help us decide wisely, though His comment has sometimes been misinterpreted. "And I say unto you, make to yourselves friends of the mammon of unrighteousness; that, when you fail, they may receive you into everlasting habitations" (Luke 16:9 KJV).

As we noted, Jesus is not commending the *actions* of the corrupt steward, but his *consistency* in functioning within the world system he represents. In saying "make friends" with unrighteous mammon, He isn't advising us to "buy relationships" as the steward in the story did. He is saying, "Get to know money" – that is, establish a *right relationship* with it. How does one do that? The answer is in His words: it will require us to relate to money as *children of light*, not as children of the world; and Jesus' instruction points to the foundational issue to flavor all our thinking about money – it will ultimately fail, prove inadequate, and be insufficient to answer all we need!

The literal reading of the text indicates that *money* will fail. It shouldn't surprise us, for in time everyone learns, seeking to build a life that is secured on the vacillating unpredictability of the world's financial systems, is certain to bring worry, disappointment and, too often and too sadly, loss and despair. Because money will ultimately fail us. There will always be a shortage of money; there will always be people who lose their jobs; there will always be changes in the world economy; there will always be drastic shocks to the stock market. And since the impact of any of these things will affect us all – either directly or indirectly, Jesus gives very practical (and spiritual) advice: your security is to relate positively to money (i.e., "make friends with"), but learning to relate to it on the terms of God's *lasting* Kingdom, not the world's "failing" one.

Relating to money as children of light

"Children of light" describes us who have been "translated" from the kingdom of darkness into the kingdom of light (Colossians 1:13; I Peter 2:9). Living "in the light" describes the process of drawing ever close to Jesus, experiencing more of His glory in your life, and becoming ever further away from the perimeter of the kingdom of darkness. When we live as children of light we submit to Christ's rule and depend on His life and power.

So then, the proper handling of money has to do with learning to live in the midst of a material realm where becoming "more spiritual" does not mean forsaking material things, but ruling over them in the life and power of the Lord Jesus Christ – not allowing ourselves to be ruled by them.

This is not merely "prosperity" teaching. While there is much truth at the core of those scriptures often used to help believers break the yoke of poverty and understand God's desire for their prosperity, serious confusion is also possible. Errors traveling under the name of "Prosperity" are sadly common in circles where self-centered quests for financial well-being motivate supposed "faith giving", or wherever financial success becomes the definition of one's having become spiritually mature. Jesus never said that, and the Bible nowhere teaches it. To the contrary, God's Word is realistic about the troubles and trials of life that happen to believers as well as unbelievers. Clearly there are Christians who are very needy, but are no less walking in faith than those who possess wealth.

However, Jesus did teach here that if you have been faithful with the resources God has given you, when hard times come you will be able to go them – through a recession; through a loss of work; through a time when you don't know how you will make ends meet – because you will have learned how to relate in the material realm on God's terms rather than the world's terms. And having made Him and His ways your security, you will have a point of reference and refuge beyond this world – a place of retreat into the promised provision of the Living God, *because You have related to money within His system, not the world's.*

▶ **The way of children of the world is**: "What am I going to do to set myself up for the future?" It has a "Get whatever you can" mindset.

▶ **The way of the children of light is**: "Give yourself away and function under the abundance of the Father." It has a "Give whatever you can" mindset.

"Isn't it right, and good common-sense to secure ourselves financially?" someone asks. The answer is, that it all depends on what motivates you. It's one thing to exhibit wisdom in the proper planning of your future, and another matter entirely to cling on to resources because of fear for the future and a lack of trust in the Father's provision. When you make God your source and depend on His care you become unshakeable. Let's follow on, as Jesus says, *"He who is faithful in what is least is faithful also in much; and he who is unjust in what is least is unjust also in much"* (Luke 16:10).

Jesus has already given us a case study of this idea. He contrasted the earlier dishonesty of the steward with the later, after he was confronted by his master. The steward had already been unjust (corrupt) with smaller matters concerning his master's money, so when greater pressure came, he was even more unjust. Jesus teaches us that this equation will have an inverse effect in spiritual dynamic when applied to the children of light. If we apply *God's principles of good stewardship* – being faithful with what we have been given by Him – then He will entrust even more resources to us, *knowing we will manage that by His Spirit of giving and faithfulness, not controlled by the world's spirit of self-centeredness and acquisitiveness.*

Fear of managing finances "God's way"

Every believer wrestles with the issue of *trust* in their lives; of resting in the knowledge God has our best interests at heart, will care for us and lead to what is best for us. This is perhaps truer in the area of our finances than in any other area of our lives. Children of light are too often afraid to operate their finances under the Father's eternal principles. They have a lot of faith as long as they are talking about "spiritual' things", but not much faith when it comes to cooperating with the Lord in the handling of their finances.

It is a warning against our not being "faith-full" about handling money in this world, that occasions Jesus' further pressing His point, saying, *"If you have not been faithful in the unrighteous mammon, who will commit to your trust the true riches?"* (Luke 16:11). In short, He makes it clear that we cannot expect to experience true spiritual power and authority (*"the true riches"*) when we cannot apply God's simple principles of good stewardship in the material realm.

There can be only two reasons why we fail to relate *faith* and *finance* together:

1. Because we hold the view that material things are carnal and unspiritual and will contaminate us. But the Bible *never* proposes this. Rather, *God's Word calls us to penetrate the material realm with the power of the Spirit.*

2. Because of our own fear and selfishness. Although there has been much abuse in teaching about money in the Church, and we should be rightfully concerned for the balanced biblical truth to be heard, *we cannot escape the fact that Adam's race is shot through with fear and selfishness, and prefers not to be told how to handle its possessions.* This selfishness does not necessarily manifest itself in greed, but in the fear of *not having*. The fear of *want* is what hamstrings faith.

Work with money on God's terms

Jesus concludes His message by saying, *"No servant can serve two masters; for either he will hate the one and love the other, or else he will be loyal to the one and despise the other. You cannot serve God and mammon"* (Luke 16:13). In other words, you cannot operate in both kingdoms, but if you learn how to function in one realm, then it will release you to function in the other.

In all, Jesus is exhorting us – the children of light – to become acquainted with money on God's terms so that when the world's system of cash fails (v. 9), we can live in the circle of the confidence of His provision, walking in faith God's way financially.

Whose steward are you and who do you work for? If your only perspective is that you work for the person or company whose name is on your pay-check, then you have been functioning in the kingdom of darkness with regard to your finances. Of course we have responsibility and accountability in our jobs, but ultimately we are the Lord's stewards and our task is to faithfully manage the resources He gives us.

The world's system says *"Get –* and secure yourself." But God's way says, *"Give –* and I will secure you." Our Master's parabolic teaching makes it crystal clear – we cannot serve God and mammon simultaneously! We will either "work the world's system" by protecting ourselves in our money management, or "function in God's system" and trust and operate by His giving principles in our finances. To function on the world's terms is to be *without* when the system fails. To function on God's terms is to always be *within* – within His promise, grace and provision, whatever takes place in our world!

Let us continue, studying what God's Word says about becoming "wise" in *His* system of money management.

✒ 22 ✒

MONEY AND THE CHILDREN OF LIGHT (PART 2)

THEME TEXT

"'Bring all the tithes into the storehouse, that there may be food in My house, and prove Me now in this,' says the Lord of hosts, 'If I will not open for you the windows of heaven and pour out for you such blessing that there will not be room enough to receive it.'"

(Malachi 3:10)

We have seen from Jesus' teaching in Luke 6 that there is a strong contrast between the way the world system relates to money and the way believers should handle money – according to God's principles of good stewardship. It is the difference between living in the dark and living in the light. These two ways of handling money can be summarized as follows:

▶ **World's system**: "Get everything you can in order to secure yourself." People in the world are totally consistent to its system regarding their finances.

▶ **Principles of the Kingdom of God**: "Give and let God secure you." People in the Kingdom of God can tend to mix up their principles. Sometimes they give and sometimes they worry about securing themselves.

Problems occur for believers when they try to "work" the world system in their lives. Jesus said that you cannot serve both God and "mammon" – the controlling spirit behind the world's finances. When a believer seeks to live by the world's principles concerning money, not only does it mean that they are keeping this area of their life "in the dark" by not surrendering it to God, they are also robbing themselves of God's abundant blessing. God's system is one of *overflowing* resources.

God's system of abundance

The Word of God calls us to learn God's principles of money management, and they begin with His promise. Knowing our human tendency to fear, Jesus confronts the fear with a promise:

> *"Give, and it shall be given unto you: good measure, pressed down, shaken together, and running over will be put into your bosom. For with the same measure that you use, it will be measured back to you."* (Luke 6:38)

We have studied this earlier and have seen this is no cheap, human incentive program, but it is a statement of the principle of reciprocity: "As you measure ... so it is measured."

This brings us to the issue of what *amount* of giving we practice, while noting the *response* of giving we might expect. Prior to this principle, we have been told how the Father is committed to making you secure and taking care of you. Now, His Son is calling you to give and trust in the fact that He *can* and *will* provide for you. The economics of the kingdom require a distinct faith in God's nature and character. The believer has reason to trust God in regard to his money, for:

▶ God will always faithfully keep His Word to us.

▶ God has unlimited resources at His disposal.

Of course we can rely totally upon the nature and character of God. He never breaks His word and He never lets us down. The Lord commits Himself to be bound by the principles He imposes. Not only that, but in order to prove His faithfulness in the area of giving, God decides to return a blessing that goes beyond a fair share. He promises a blessing that is *"pressed down ... shaken together ... running over."*

Jesus did not stop at "Give and it will be given unto you." His description of God's economy was, first and foremost, an accurate representation, and secondly given to help us understand what kind of Father we have – abundant, generous, extravagant, willing to pour out multiplied blessing.

Jesus wants us to understand God's nature by illustrating the amount that God seeks to return to us, and He wants to show us the avenue through which God will respond to us. And notice the practicality of the expectation Jesus teaches in the world: men shall give into *"your bosom"* (Luke 6:38 KJV). The text shows that God's blessing will manifest in favor and open doors around us – His distribution in response to us isn't promised like manna from the sky. God uses other people, circumstances and situations to return blessings upon us. Salary increases, unpaid loans recovered, surprise benefits, etc. – these are only samples of things God can bring about by His special blessing and favor.

To begin building our faith and establishing our obedience in managing our money on God's terms, we will look in detail at the timeless, foundational principle of the tithe. There are additional practices of giving, but all growth stems from this beginning point. It is nowhere more clear, hope-filled or dramatic in its explanation than in Malachi 3:8–12.

Tithing opens to blessing in finances

To realize the possibilities of God's economy means to become a channel through which God blesses others. You can become an avenue of ministry through your giving. The Lord directly relates the practice of *tithing* to the blessing of the believer in finances. God has set a minimum amount of ten percent which we are to give away in order to set in motion His cycle of blessing. God says that if you function according to this principle there are special benefits to you. If you don't, then they are not there. It is not because God *withholds* these benefits that we fail to receive them, but because we *choose* not to enter into the covenant promise that releases them.

1. The tithe is non-negotiable

> *"You have robbed Me ... in tithes and offerings."*   (Malachi 3:8)

The Lord makes a strong statement in Malachi 3, saying that to omit to tithe is actually "robbing" Him. So God says, "Do it!" He even invites you to "try Him" or prove His word in the matter by obeying Him and then observing as He releases *"such blessing that there will not be room enough to receive it"* (Malachi 3:10).

Note these points about the practice of tithing:

▶ **It is a practice of New Testament believers** (Matthew 23:23). Although Jesus rebuked the "religious" practices of the Pharisees, He did not negate the practice of tithing. Instead Jesus affirmed it and accepted it as something His disciples should do. He endorsed it as a godly principle.

▶ **The tithe is *the Lord's*, not ours** (Leviticus 27:30). The tithe is that portion of our resources that actually *belongs* to God. When we tithe we are not giving an offering to God but *paying* back to Him that which is already His. The Lord lays claim to the first ten percent of our resources and this is "non-negotiable". Because the tithe is "the Lord's" and not ours, it is His responsibility, and therefore we have no right to hold on to it.

▶ **The word "tithe" means "tenth"** – i.e. ten percent. Less than ten percent is not a tithe and anything over and above ten percent is an offering. The tithe is a *set amount*, or a fixed percentage that does not fluctuate.

2. All the tithes are to be brought into the storehouse

God's mandate on tithing includes the instruction that our tithe should be brought into "the storehouse" (Malachi 3:10). The store-house is essentially the place where you do your spiritual *feeding*, which generally means the place where you fellowship, or your home church. It is your spiritual base.

I feel it is important to state here that everyone should have a "home" church – a place where they belong and are committed to. The practice of "spiritual wandering" from church to church as the mood takes you will yield very little long-term benefit. Instead of being built up into a mature follower of Christ you will remain a spiritual "juvenile delinquent".

Having no home church or base means that, not only are you under-nourished in your spiritual life, but you are probably not tithing either and therefore not entering into the covenant of blessing that God has ordained. Neither can you argue "Well, I tithe wherever I am." That is not investing into a storehouse. It is like a farmer driving all over the country, randomly dumping the grain he has harvested! No person would engage in such madness. The farmer safely gathers his harvest in and stores it in one place on his own land.

Why should the tithe go to the church where you fellowship? Tithes are meant to come into your storehouse so that everything necessary for ministry can be released by that avenue and admin-istrated in a responsible fashion. The leadership of the early Church was entrusted with the resources of the believers and they used those resources wherever the greatest need was (Acts 4–6). Your tithe should be given in to your home base where you are fed and cared for, and beyond that, if you are aware of specific needs, or ministries that you want to support, then you can give gifts to them which are your *offerings*.

3. The Lord promises an abundant return

"See if I won't open for you the windows of heaven and pour out for you such blessing that there will not be enough room to receive it."
(Malachi 3:10)

The tithe is an instrument which God uses in order to release blessing to you. Not only that, but God wants to *pour* blessings upon you. Jesus draws our attention to a critical factor in the equation at the end of Luke 6:38: *"For with the same measure that you use, it will be measured back to you."*

In other words, you decide where to draw the line. If you are tight-spirited about your giving then do not expect abundant returns. But if you are generous in your giving, don't be surprised as time progresses to see how God increases resources so that you can continue being generous – it become a virtuous circle. But this can only happen when you decide to operate within God's economics and His principles – *completely*.

Having said all of this, we must be clear about the fact that God does not love you any more or any less because of your giving. He simply invites you to move in the dimensions of the possibilities of His Kingdom, because He wants to bestow His blessings upon you. If you never gave anything at all God would still love you and it would not affect your salvation in any way. You could give *nothing* and God would not think any more or any less of you. The only restriction you would have placed over your head is the limiting effect you have chosen, by restricting the release of God's law of reciprocity. God's love is still disposed toward you, His mercies are still new every morning – *even His promise to care for your need is still in place.* However, what *is* limited – by the choice of either our fear, disobedience or neglect – is His high hope of making you an avenue of His abundance in the practical issues of your material life and service to others.

4. The Lord promises divine protection

"I will rebuke the devourer for your sakes, so that he will not destroy the fruit of your ground." (Malachi 3:11)

God promises you divine protection as part of His covenant regarding your tithe. If you are faithful to pay your tithe, God will drive back anything that would hinder your fruitfulness or erode your resources in any way.

"Offerings" – Learning to be a "giver"

I want to learn to be a giver, because according to the measure I give, it is measured back to me. I never miss a chance to give an offering. If I have something to give, even small change, and the opportunity for an offering arises, I give ... for my own sake.

Offerings should not be made solely in response to emotional appeals or as a result of being moved for the moment, but as a regular part of your budget. The Apostle Paul recommended a planned approach to offerings and instructed the churches under his care to "budget" their giving (see I Corinthians 16:1–3). Neither should we give grudgingly, the Bible advises us, because God loves a cheerful giver (II Corinthians 9:7). This word translated *cheerful* is the Greek word *hilaros* from which we derive the word *hilarious*. It describes an exuberant, joyful generosity without restraint.

When you have learned God's principles of giving you have gained not only *God's covering for your life financially*, but you have gained *the Lord's tremendous blessing* which heaps all kinds of "life" on you. Not just cash, but LIFE! *The multiplication of HIS ABOUNDING LIFE AND GRACE is always and ultimately the high design of any teaching on giving. We teach faith IN finances, not faith FOR them. And wherever living faith is applied it advances God's will in our lives.*

This addendum may be studied for personal use or congregational use as individuals or groups may wish. Its best use is following several teaching sessions on biblical giving.

A personal inventory concerning financial stewardship

I have included here a personal giving inventory that is intended to help a person assess his or her own stewardship. I have used this in distribution to my own congregation, not in any way to cause any to feel under condemnation as a result of answering these questions. Rather, it was offered as a part of teaching; helping enable people bring their management of God-given resources into perspective, and to urge them to live "in the light" in this area of life. My prayer in doing so has been that each may understand through our teaching, and apply through careful self-analysis via such a tool as given here, the principles that will release the momentous blessings that God seeks to pour on them. Many have done so, and have either chosen, or been expanded in, God's covenant of giving.

1. I believe that my tithe is one instrument by which the blessing of God is released in distinct areas of my life. Yes_____ No_____

2. I agree that the tithe is non-negotiable:
    (a) As a practice by the New Testament believer. Yes_____ No_____
    (b) As a practice disallowing any percentage of fluctuation. Yes_____ No_____

3. My opinion as to my liberty in the distribution of my tithe:
    (a) May be distributed to any ministry I wish. Yes_____ No_____
    (b) May be given in part or all to help the needy. Yes_____ No_____
    (c) Is to be given through the fellowship I attend. Yes_____ No_____

4. Concerning my practices regarding my *tithes* and *offerings*.
    Tithes:
    (a) I always tithe on all I receive. Yes_____ No_____
    (b) I tithe most of the time. Yes_____ No_____
    (c) When I don't tithe I "redeem" [15] it later. Yes_____ No_____
    (d) I tithe, plus I give the "firstfruits" [16] of all increases. Yes_____ No_____

    Offerings:
    (a) I give beyond my tithe by a specific plan every month. Yes_____ No_____
    (b) I give to special projects when I am moved. Yes_____ No_____
    (c) I never miss a chance to give *something* in an offering. Yes_____ No_____
    (d) I support world ministries in some way as a regular part of my budget. Yes_____ No_____

PART 11

Divine Healing:
A Covenant for Life and Strength

❧ 23 ❧

The Covenant of Healing

THEME TEXT
*"If you diligently heed the voice of the LORD your God
and do what is right in His sight,
give ear to His commandments
and keep all His statutes,
I will put none of the diseases on you
which I have brought on the Egyptians.
For I am the LORD who heals you."*

(Exodus 15:26)

As an infant, barely one-year-old, I was healed from a severe muscular condition that would have eventually taken my life. At the age of three, having contracted polio, I again experienced the awesome healing power of God. Both these cases were attended by physicians – who in both cases, acknowledged the healing was unrelated to anything of medical attention, for each case exceeded their capacities. And both were cases where believers sought God for my healing (the first, prior to my parents knowing Christ, the second after they had begun with Him) – and I was healed! With this a host of additional life-experience testimonies are within the scope of my own home, family and ministry. It is more than theory when I discuss this theme. On the authority of God's Word which promises the possibilities, and in the light of times we have known the grace and privilege of such mercies, I can personally attest to the fact that we serve a God who gives gifts of healing and Who keeps a covenant of healing.

I believe that God desires to usher into the life of the Church a greater outpouring of His healing power than we have ever known before. God is calling us to understand the healing life and power that is available through His Son Jesus Christ, covenanted to us by God Himself. God desires to reveal His power and glory to us in ways that we have not even comprehended.

In our theme text from Exodus 15:26, God pledges a wonderful promise to His people regarding healing. This statement occurs after a poetic passage known as the "Song of Moses". This was a song of triumph sung by the people of Israel just after they had come through the Red Sea and had experienced God's miraculous double deliverance. They had escaped from the bondage of slavery, and they had seen God destroy their enemies in the waters of the Red Sea. Now, in a setting immediately following God's display of His mighty *hand*, at the challenging moment of their need for water, with only bitter water available, God opens His *heart* to His people. The situation occasions His establishing a covenant with them – one we call, God's covenant of healing.

We earlier studied how God reveals Himself to us by using different names – each one revealing a different facet of His character and attributes. This time God reveals Himself as the One who heals – *Jehovah Rapha*. God was revealing that He, who had delivered them from slavery, would be the answer to their every need as well. Whenever they were sick God would heal them.

Distinguishing the "covenant" and the "gift"

There is a distinction between God's covenant of healing, and individual gifts of healing that God gives to us. A gift of healing is an unexpected revelation of God's love toward us. From time to time God will unexpectedly heal someone as a demonstration of His divine grace and mercy. The person concerned has not done anything to earn this free gift. The healing ministry of the Lord Jesus continues today by the power of the Holy Spirit and spontaneous healings still occur in the Church.

A "covenant of healing love" is also a gift in a sense, but there are *terms* which each party must fulfill. Before going any further, it is important to understand that God's healing covenant is as applicable to us today as it was to the people of Israel then. Some argue that the covenant of healing was a dispensational covenant that ceased along with the Mosaic Law when Jesus instituted the New Covenant. But this healing covenant was established by God *before* the Law that was given to Moses at Sinai. God has made a timeless covenant with His children and voluntarily put Himself under obligation to them.

A gift is something that is given to you at a certain point in time. Gifts are often very precious to you and are usually gratefully received. A covenant however, is an ongoing agreement that you can *live in*, the benefits of which are continually being received. God says to you, "I am committing Myself to you on these terms."

In developing this theme, let me be very, very clear. We wish to avoid exaggerated or legalistic efforts to apply this great covenant of *love* and turn it into a covenant of *law*. Unwise approaches sometimes suggest, for example, that God needs to be continually "reminded" of His promises – as it were, confronted with His obligations to (by law) do what He has already voluntarily (in love) said He would do. It amounts to shaking verses of Scripture at God to goad Him into action; to remind Him that He should be busy doing the things He has promised to do! It is a painful point of misunderstanding that occurs because people don't realize that the promises of God flow towards us out of a heart of love. We don't need to come to God insistently, stamping our feet to get His attention and saying, "Lord, You said . . ." God is already fully aware of His commitments to us.

There are some devout and sincerely intended souls who take this approach, but this only serves to bring people into areas of legalism, and becomes a point of bondage for the believer. If a person achieves the result they want by lobbying the Lord in this way, then they will often tell you, "You need to do this . . . and this, like I did, then you'll get what you want." That is sheer legalism and shows a flagrant disregard for the loving character of God and His ways.

The Living God, who has covenanted with us, has not called us to be a people who accept and live by a *law* of healing, but who accept His *love* in healing made available to us.

God's covenant of healing is provided by His *grace*

God's healing covenant was established before the Mosaic Law, provided for in grace, and is personified in Jesus. The Father said, "I am the Lord who heals you," and in Jesus Christ we see the fullness of the Godhead. In the person of Jesus we can see how this covenant works. His covenant is a provision of healing being made available, but through *grace* alone. His covenants should not be treated as legal documents, but as evidences of God's loving commitment – written, attested-by-His-unfailing-Word, evidences of His care for us. In this case, regarding the covenant of healing, He shows His practical and powerful availability to answer one of life's most practical needs.

In our text, God wanted His people Israel to understand that they were entering a new phase of living having crossed the Red Sea – a new way of walking with Him. They had just been liberated from Egypt having suffered four hundred years of slavery. No one could remember what it was like to live in freedom. The Lord says to them that He will *"put none of the diseases on you which I have brought on the Egyptians."*

This references more than the plagues that the Lord sent upon Egypt. Elsewhere the OT records that other diseases blighted them (Deuteronomy 7:15). And yet, ancient Egypt was not a primitive culture, but was as medically and scientifically advanced as any civilization of its day. Rather than dismissing the medical expertise of that culture, God is saying to His people Israel, "I have resources available for you that far transcends what Man can do."

Today God is saying the same thing to us, living in our highly sophisticated culture. For all our immense accomplishments in the field of medical technology, God has a resource that goes way beyond that which we can do for ourselves. This statement is absolutely true, but again we must be careful not to become confused about its practical outworkings. Such misunderstandings can led to erroneous, unscriptural beliefs.

One such seriously mistaken belief is the supposition, "If I am really trusting God, I must not draw on the resources of natural medicine." This is a biblically ignorant and spiritually ill-informed application of Scripture, and one which Satan, whose goal is to mislead and distract believers, will use to spread further confusion. Be wise to know, that anything that works for the physical well-being of humanity is a God-given resource. Satan isn't conjuring up helpful devices for human comfort. By virtue of His broad, general grace, God has given us the resources of medical technology to be of benefit to us. I recognize the fact that medicine, in the hands of fallen Man even at his present best, is an imperfect science, often with unwanted side-effects and difficulties. Nonetheless, what is beneficial should be seen as a part of God's general provision and care for His creation, and those serving in health and medicine as agents of that goodness. Don't make the mistake of thinking that the use of these things is opposed to, or outside, the will of God.

Conversely, don't make the mistake of thinking that the provision of medicine is the sum expression of all God *can* do or is readily present *to* do! The covenant of healing far surpasses what Man can do. The Lord is *not* disqualifying the things that have already been provided, but He *is* transcending those things to declare Himself our Healer.

God's covenant is an abiding one

Those who come to understand and begin to appropriate the healing covenant of God's love, come to realize that it is a *way of health* – not just *getting healed*. The way of health is connecting with the flowing life of the Healer. Through the Lord Jesus Christ all that the Father covenanted has been transmitted to us.

God's statement to us *"I am the LORD who heals you"* reveals more than just the *healing* aspect of His nature. Whenever God uses the term "I Am" He is calling to our attention His timelessness, His self-completeness, and His self-initiating love – everything that flows forth from His being. God says "I Am who I Am" – He never changes and is still the same today as He was when he revealed Himself with those words to Moses (Exodus 3:14). God is still the same today as He was when He pledged His covenant of healing to the Israelites at the waters of Marah. "I am the Lord who heals you" remains a timeless revelation of this facet of His person. He is God our Healer today.

Bitter water in the wilderness

The situation in which God chose to reveal Himself to His people as Healer tells us much about our need for healing. At that time there was no epidemic or plague sweeping through the tribes of Israel. In fact nobody was sick. The only issue troubling the Israelites was that their water supply was bitter and undrinkable.

After three days in the wilderness with no water, you might think that the revelation His people most needed was God as their Provider, rather than their Healer. Although finding drinkable water was a pressing and urgent concern, no one had yet become sick. So why does God say He is their Healer?

It is the reaction of His people Israel in that predicament that provokes God's revelation as Healer. It opens up the issue that is central to understanding about being healed and living in health. The Lord was not dealing with any physical affliction, but with a deeply ingrained thought process which was revealed by their response and their attitude to having no water. They griped, they groaned, they grumbled and they murmured. They started to complain to Moses. Their complaining betrayed the deepest sickness in man, which manifests itself in two ways.

Firstly, human habit tends to respond negatively to anything which tries or tests him, and secondly, we tend to look for help in the wrong direction. People invariably turn and lash out at other people and circumstances, instead of crying out to the Lord. The Scripture says that Moses alone, reacted differently: *"So he* [Moses] *cried out to the Lord..."* (Exodus 15:25). I'd like to think that Moses called on God because he knew better than the others, but I've been a leader long enough to know that it was probably out of desperation!

The "bad attitude" that was manifest among the Israelites is so characteristic of every one of us, and is evident in so many different ways – according to the degree to which we have learned to discipline our behavior in the expression of our attitudes; and the way in which we respond to situations according to our temperament. Some people are very vocal about their negative attitudes and tend to spew out everything they are feeling. Others will internalize such feelings and allow them to fester, causing bitterness. Both are different manifestations of Man's "murmuring", complaining nature.

The further medical science advances along the path of physiological and psychological examination, the more the medical fraternity become convinced that Man's body and his mind cannot be treated in isolation. Man is a single entity that cannot be dissected in terms of his emotional wellbeing and thought processes, and his physical wellbeing. They are totally and entirely interrelated.

So when God comes to say to His people, "I will make a covenant of healing with you", He is encountering them not in a moment of physical pain, but in a moment of attitudinal difficulty – because that is the heart of human sickness. That is where the problem lies. God begins at that point of emotional need to establish His covenant with them. It was God's heart to reveal Himself in healing to His people all along, but in order to do that He had to teach them this lesson. He brought them to a place of bitter water because He wanted them to see that they were a people prone to bitterness. God desired to break their habit of murmuring and becoming bitter, and to replace it with the habit of depending on Him and calling upon His name.

The sign of the tree

Moses cried out to the Lord, and the Lord showed him a tree and told him to throw it into the water. When he did so, the waters became sweet and miraculously they now had a fresh water source. I Corinthians 10:11 asserts that such Old Testament stories are written for us who live in the last times, so that we might see God's plans and purposes throughout Scripture, and so that we might learn the ways of God through the exploits of others. The activities that God engaged His people in often had far greater symbolic ramifications beyond their historical application.

Therefore, when the Lord showed Moses *a tree*, there is no question in my mind that God wanted to show us in this day, that the answer to the afflictions and bitterness of life; the answer to our trying circumstances; the answer to the things that crowd in on us and test our attitudes, that demean us – is a *tree*. And that tree is *the Tree* – the place where the God of covenant established a new covenant, signed in His own blood – the Cross of His Son Jesus, our Savior, our Deliverer, our Healer!

To sweeten the bitter circumstances of life you need to apply the Cross-tree. And if you can learn to do that, then you can learn how God's covenant begins to be released. When we come to our points of hopelessness, God wants us turn to the Cross of Jesus Christ – to die to our own self-righteous standards and our self-serving ways; to die to the attitudes that we feel so justified in holding on to. The Lord wants to show us the tree where the most unjust act in all history took place, and therefore reveal the depth of the love He has for us.

Where you have been mistreated, unkindly dealt with, and where you are hurting and it looks as though there is no way out – God wants to free you, and freedom comes where the Cross is applied.

The condition of the covenant

There is a condition to this covenant which is spelled out in Exodus 15:26:

> *"If you diligently heed the voice of the* Lord *your God and do what is right in His sight, give ear to His commandments and keep all His statutes . . . "*

In order to experience the blessings God promises we need to observe certain requirements. Covenants are a two-way commitment with both parties binding themselves to meet certain details if the covenant is to work properly.

1. Listening to God's voice

People who want to live in the covenant need to learn to pay attention to the "still, small voice" of the Lord. Every person can testify to the fact that they have been aware of, at intervals in their life, a quiet "inner voice" that has told them the course of action they were planning on is wrong. God has built into every human being "inner sensors" intended to guide our actions. In addition to that, God speaks to us with quiet encouragement, direction and correction as necessary. His voice may often be felt through a lack of *peace* if we are about to take a bad decision. Again this is an issue of trust. God says, "Trust in Me and I will guide you. Listen to My voice."

Some people say, "Well I hear things but I don't know whether it is God or not." The answer to this problem is: get on you knees and say to God, "Lord, is that you?" You won't necessarily hear a booming voice from heaven, but if it was God speaking to you then His peace will come into your being and you will simply *know* that it was God speaking to you. If you are still unsure, you should seek the advice of a trusted elder, or mature brother or sister in Christ, and ask their opinion on what you feel God is saying. The critical point is this: do not move forward in confusion. Wait until you are clear about what God has said to you.

2. Keeping God's commandments

God's commandments should not be viewed as *restrictive* but rather *protective*. The Lord asks us to observe and live by the commandments He gives us because they are *life principles* – keeping them will lead to a happy and whole life, and will avoid Man's often self-destructive practices. For example: God does not tell us to avoid fornication because He is against sex. A healthy sexual relationship within the boundaries of marriage was God's idea. But God prohibits fornication because it violates the promise of trustworthy relationships, and further, eventually can bring physical ruin, and inevitably will scar people emotionally. God says "Do not lie", not only because He loves truth, but because He wants to preempt the vicious circle lying produces, keeping one forever running from the last thing lied about. God says "Do not steal", because He knows that crime undermines and erodes society. God's knows these things are harmful for Man, and so He establishes commandments – principles to live by that will ensure freedom from bondage.

Keeping God's commandments therefore is about more than just keeping a righteous position before God, which is of vital importance. Keeping God's commandments is important because neglecting them has seriously detrimental *physical* implications for Man.

3. *Keeping God's statutes*

The books of Leviticus and Deuteronomy contain detailed lists of minor laws of God concerning diet and other health-related practices. Under the Old Covenant, people followed those statutes to show that *they* were the people of God. Under the New Covenant, God no longer requires that we eat a certain way to prove that we belong to Him. Salvation comes by grace through faith in Jesus Christ alone. However, God's laws concerning diet were very practical common sense principles. There are a whole host of ailments that our bodies are subject to today if we continually violate fundamental nutritional laws. Therefore we should be wise in following the wisdom of God's natural, health-giving statutes.

The Lord has basically said that He will *be our health*, but there are conditions we must observe. It has to do with our attitude; with the sensible conduct of our lives according to His safety guidelines, and our commitment to live according to basic principles of health. Your response to these things will not alter your salvation one little bit, but there is a better life of health that can be realized if we cooperate with God's terms.

Let me add, in reference to noting the "natural" wisdom of God's provided way of health, that when we discuss His covenant, we are relating something far more than that. His covenant is not merely naturalistic. Yes, if we think right, do right and eat right, that will certainly save us from a host of sicknesses that we would otherwise suffer from. But there are many points in life when we need more than human hands or the natural order can provide us. We face things that bring affliction that call for a supernatural grace – and for that, we need a Healer. The Lord has said He will be that for us. He puts us in a position to receive a resource we never had before. Above all we should understand that God is not covenanting with us for a quick-fix, instantaneous healing way of life, where we indulge to our heart's content and then appeal to God to help us. God is covenanting with us for an enduring way of health that will lead to a fuller life of service for Him and to others.

So let the living Church open to Him Who is "The same, yesterday and today and forever" (Hebrews 13:8). Let the spirit of praise rise to so great and tenderly loving a Father, Whose gentle grace reaches to us at every dimension of our need – spirit, soul and body! Let a song of praise rise to the Son, our Savior, Whose suffering incorporated a provision of healing for the whole person, as surely as His death has accomplished forgiveness and eternal life! And let a welcome to the Holy Spirit be extended, to move among us as God's people in ways that continue, now and ever, to glorify the present ministry of Christ by manifesting His presence in our midst, and by distributing healing gifts in tribute to His glorious Name!

"Bless the Lord, O my soul; and all that is within me, bless His holy Name.
Bless the Lord, O my soul, and forget not all His benefits:
Who forgives all your iniquities, Who heals all your diseases,
Who redeems your life from destruction . . . !"

(Psalm 103:1–3)

THE MINISTRY OF HEALING

THEME TEXT

"Jesus went about all Galilee, teaching in their synagogues,
preaching the gospel of the kingdom, and healing all kinds of sickness
and all kinds of disease among the people ... and they brought to Him
all sick people who were afflicted with various diseases and torments,
and those who were demon-possessed, epileptics, and paralytics;
and He healed them."

(Matthew 4:23–25)

We have examined God's covenant of healing – that God has voluntarily obligated Himself to a healing relationship with His people. God says, "I am the Lord your Healer." "I am the Lord committed to your health and wholeness." A covenant is an ongoing arrangement where both parties uphold the agreed terms. Now we are looking at God's general gift of healing to mankind. This is distinguished from His covenant with His *own*, and references His loving reach with healing mercies overflowing to all mankind.

This distinction abides then, for sake of our study: Chapter 23 presents *God's covenant of healing* as available to His redeemed, healing attitudinal problems (thus inviting full dimensional health), and assuring an ongoing provision for physical strength, health and wellbeing, as faith appropriates His provision. Chapter 24 presents *God's gift of healing* as the continuing message expecting the same manifestations of healing grace and miracles today as the word of the Gospel is proclaimed, according to Jesus' commission which included, *"They shall lay hands on the sick and they shall recover"* (Mark 16:17).

As with Jesus' ministry, so it was in the early Church. Wherever the Gospel of the kingdom was proclaimed, the Word was confirmed with signs following. The scriptures we study are to review the patterns of Jesus' healing ministry, to open to the same expectation, believing that marvelous works of healing were and are a hallmark of Jesus' ministry. (In referring to God's *general* gift of healing promise and power, we will not be focusing directly upon the "gifts of healing" mentioned in I Corinthians 12, but it should be understood that those manifestations *are* indeed included in the general, broad scale gift of healing that God has lavished upon mankind through the Gospel of Jesus Christ, God's Son – He Himself being the Father's greatest gift to all humanity.) Let us divide our study into five points of focus, on:

1. The relationship of the ministry of healing to the Gospel of the Kingdom.

2. The evidences of healing in Jesus' ministry as He proclaimed that Gospel.

3. The difficulty society has at times in responding to the invasion of healing grace.

4. The basis of the lavishly gracious ministry of healing offered in Jesus' Name.

5. The basic hindrances to Jesus' healing ministry in the Church today.

Jesus' healing ministry

1. *The relationship of the ministry of healing to the Gospel of the Kingdom*

Matthew 4:23 says that Jesus was "teaching and preaching" in the synagogues of Galilee. In other words, the "word of the Gospel" was going forth. What does "word of the Gospel" mean? It amazes me that some people's definition of "Gospel" only extends as far as: "All have sinned" and "the wages of sin is death". These things are true and people need to know them, but this definition falls far short of the "good news" that Jesus came to bring.

In our effort to proclaim biblically sound doctrine we often approach people in a completely different way than Jesus did. The call to repentance that Jesus issued when He said, "Repent and believe the Gospel," *was* a call for people to turn away from their sins, but it was not so much an indictment of them as sinners as it was the offer of an alternative to their present futility and dilemma – He offered truly "good news". The news that Jesus brought was a word of hope, assurance, and healing. (To make this observation is not to demean preaching which calls sinners to repentance, but simply to liberate us from presumptuous notions that the approach of "mercy" ministry as an entrée to calling the lost to repentance is not misguided or unworthy.)

Indiscriminately, without any regard for the worthiness of His hearers, Jesus lavished healing upon those who came to Him as confirmation of the fact that God loved them, cared for them, received them and was forgiving. Jesus said, "Look! God is reaching out to you and touching you!" Jesus was showing that the rule of God was entering right into the midst of where they were. And if there is anything mankind needs, it is the rule of another kingdom! Mankind is ruled by the kingdom of flesh, the kingdom of fear, the kingdom of doubt, and all manner of evil reigning principalities that dominate, torment, manipulate and ruin people's lives.

The "word of the Gospel of the Kingdom" then, is an expansive message of good news to mankind in which Jesus proclaims to us, "You no longer need to live under the tyrannical rule of the devil, or of your own flesh, fears, doubts, weakness and sinning. You can be released from all of that into God's glorious life in all its fullness." As Jesus preached, verification of the fact that the word He brought was dynamic, real, living and active, and would touch all aspects of human life. He began to heal people. Jesus was healing people *physically* so that they could grasp the fact that God wanted to heal them *spiritually*. God's good news was provision for Man's *whole being*. As Jesus spoke the message of hope and healed people, they knew that the kingdom of heaven, full of life, love and power, was indeed in their midst.

The Gospel of the kingdom resulted in a full spectrum of healing. God's gift of healing was manifest first and foremost in the physical realm. Let us take note that Jesus did not say, "The most important thing is the salvation of the human soul." As true as this is, the Savior in mercy met people at their point of pain and need, then moved forward from there. Of course, we *do* affirm that repentance and faith in Christ, unto salvation, is of primary significance in the spread of the Gospel. But the ministry of healing should never be subtly debunked when the kind of statement made above is said as a precursor to either demeaning or denying the need, availability or desirability of the ministry of physical healing.

Sometimes the same thing is done with the gifts and fruit of the Spirit; someone suggesting that the *fruit* of the Spirit is more to be desired that His *gifts*. But God does not pigeonhole spiritual blessings as being preferred one above another as though His works of grace and power were in competition. As far as God is concerned *saving* a person means: forgiving, healing, helping, loving, preparing, embracing – anything and everything that person needs, God is ready to provide through salvation. He embraces the whole of human need, pain failure, sin, disappointment, and frustration.

Humankind desperately needs forgiveness of sins – there is no salvation apart from that which is offered and needs to be received in the name of Jesus Christ, God's Son. But let us not isolate the issue of sin, guilt and loss outside of Christ from a message that embraces every human need. If we do, we are miscalculating the ministry of Jesus. As God's love and power was manifest in His Son's ministry, His presence invaded mankind's circumstance, the full spectrum of human pain was being addressed: neurological disorders, physiological disorders, spiritual disorders, congenital defects, psychological disorders. Jesus dealt not only with physical sickness but with a wide range of demonic activity. This is another bondage that hinders human health which Jesus came to defeat. Matthew 4:24 says:

> *"Then His fame went throughout all Syria; and they brought to Him all sick people who were afflicted with various diseases and torments, and those who were demon-possessed, epileptics, and paralytics; and He healed them."*

Jesus also confronted the idea that a congenital defect or illness was God's will, and must thereby be lived with it for the rest of one's life (see John 9). God's gift of healing is all-encompassing and all-powerful. Jesus healed every kind of disease and every kind of sickness among the people. The healing power of God is poured out through the person of His Son, who is *"the same yesterday, today, and forever"* (Hebrews 13:8).

2. The evidences of healing in Jesus' ministry as He proclaimed the Gospel of the Kingdom

The NT is replete with examples of God's healing power in action through the ministry of the Lord Jesus. Matthew gave us a short summary of the type of healings that took place in Matthew 4, and then describes in detail in later chapters some of the specific events that occurred:

*   **Matthew 8:1–4** describes how Jesus, descending the mountain [17] with a great crowd following Him, after having given the sermon on the mount, immediately heals a leper who approaches Him.

The leper appeals to Jesus saying, *"Lord, if You are willing, You can make me clean"* (v. 2). Jesus, stretching out His hand and touching the leper, replies, *"I am willing; be cleansed"* (v. 3). Instantly the man's leprosy was cleansed.

- **Matthew 8:5–13** tells how Jesus healed the servant of a centurion. The servant was at home lying paralyzed and was suffering great pain. The Bible says that Jesus was greatly moved by the suffering of others and He responds immediately saying, *"I will come and heal him"* (v. 7). As it happened, Jesus did not need to go to the man. The centurion had faith enough to believe that if Jesus just said the word his servant would be healed. Jesus said to the centurion, *" 'Go your way; and as you have believed, so let it be done for you.' And his servant was healed that same hour"* (Matthew 8:13).

- **Matthew 8:14–15** describes how Jesus, having come into Peter's house, discovered that his mother-in-law was lying sick with a fever. Jesus touched her hand and she was instantly healed. The fever left her and she got up and began serving Jesus and His disciples.

- **Matthew 8:16–17** reveals an all-encompassing reference to the general healing ministry of Jesus. It says He cast out demons and healed the sick, linking this to Isaiah 53 – the prophecy of the suffering, dying, redeeming Messiah: *"When evening had come, they brought to Him many who were demon-possessed. And He cast out the spirits with a word, and healed all who were sick, that it might be fulfilled which was spoken by Isaiah the prophet, saying: 'He Himself too our infirmities and bore our sicknesses.' "*

- **Matthew 9:35** is another general reference that describes how Jesus traveled through various cities and villages, teaching in synagogues, preaching the Gospel and *"healing every sickness and every disease among the people."* This verse focuses Jesus being *moved with compassion* – a proven key to having our hearts qualified for the ministry of healing today. He saw the crowds of weary, broken people like sheep without a shepherd. Matthew 14:34 is another case of the same, as Jesus encounters those who were bound by sickness or spiritual oppression: *"And when Jesus went out He saw a great multitude; and He was moved with compassion for them, and healed their sick."*

- **Matthew 14:34** says that when Jesus arrived in Gennesaret and was recognized, the people who lived there brought all those who were sick to Him. They begged Him to be allowed to touch the hem of His garment. All those who did were completely cured.

- **Matthew 15:30** describes another occasion where Jesus is surrounded by a great crowd of people. This time the people laid the sick at His feet and He healed them. Different types of sickness are described: lameness, blindness, muteness, physical deformities and "many other" types that aren't specifically mentioned. As they witnessed all these sicknesses being healed and people restored, the crowd marveled and *"glorified the God of Israel."*

3. Society has difficulty handling the invasion of divine healing (Matthew 8:28–34)

Matthew 8:28–34 describes how Jesus delivered two demon-possessed men. They were so tormented that they had been abandoned to the region's graveyard. The evil spirits afflicting the men immediately identified Jesus as the Son of God and begged to be allowed to go into a herd of pigs nearby. Jesus gave permission and the men were delivered.

So marvelous was the healing that the stunned populous could not handle the miracle that had taken place. When the news had spread, the scripture says that the whole city came out to meet Jesus and pleaded with Him to leave their region.

Society often reveals its inability to handle the invasion of divine health. Man is so accustomed to his afflicted circumstance that he "accommodates" sickness as a fact of life. Therefore, when health and deliverance begin to flow, people think that it is something peculiar. One of the basic problems of the Church is that we too quickly seek to avoid anything that threatens the equilibrium of "normal" life. When the power of the Holy Spirit is being poured out, people are being healed, and demonic forces are being repelled, sometimes a large portion of the Church says, "I'm not sure I want that." It is then that ecclesiastical traditionalism becomes a threat to the healing power of Jesus, and this attitude is not beyond any one of us. We tend to *formularize* the healing power of God. We expect Him to work in certain ways, according to our limited theological understanding and interpretation of Scripture – discarding anything that doesn't fit into our equation.

Jesus just wants to make people *well*. He wants His *wholeness* to touch every part of a person: the mind, the spirit, the emotions, their home, their personal relationships, their business. In fact, God's mandate for healing is so expansive that He even extends it to the healing of whole nations, if His people will covenant with Him in prayer and intercession for their land. God is capable of transcending even the limitations of political complexities if His people will open to His healing power (II Chronicles 7:14).

4. Jesus' healing ministry lavished freely and established fully (today)

The two most significant factors that the gospels highlight about Jesus' healing ministry is that it was *lavished freely*, but the Scriptures also show that it was *established fully* – soundly based in the Messiah's promised ministry *and* His redemption work on the Cross.

Matthew 8:17 says that the many healings that Jesus administered, and the casting out of demons, happened to *fulfill* the words of the prophet Isaiah: *"He Himself took our infirmities and bore our sicknesses."* Matthew quotes from Isaiah 53:4. Until the revelation of the NT Scriptures, Isaiah 53 must have mystified people living under the Old Covenant. Even in much of today's religious Jewish community, the question exists: "How could it be that the Messiah would die?" The people then, and some today, could not conceive of such a thing happening because the Messiah was the Eternal King. How could He come in triumph and suffer in death? But since the Cross and the Resurrection, we understand. The King *did* come in majesty, *gave* Himself unto death and *then rose again* in victory. He now reigns at the right hand of the Father over all powers and principalities.

While Isaiah's words spoke of the *future*, saying in approximately 750 BC, "He shall bear their sicknesses as well as their sins," he was pointing to Messiah's ministry – all in the future. What is thrilling to notice is that *that future began in Jesus' ministry and continues to this moment.* Notice when Jesus was actually ministering, in the *present* tense of the season Matthew 8 reports, the text says those words of Isaiah were being fulfilled right at that time. But when we turn to the Apostle Peter's word (I Peter 2:24, 25), he summarizes the blend of all that Jesus did "in His own body on the tree" and declares that what was achieved in the Cross affords today's believer the hope of a full provision – a salvation of forgiveness, justification, recovery from the scarring destruction of the soul due to past sin, grace for physical need and healing – and abundant salvation! Let us enter to possess the promise; let us declare its truth and hope to others.

The healing ministry of Jesus Christ then, is fully established. We are not dealing with random moments where God "felt sorry" for people and healed them spontaneously. We are not dealing with a sporadic, unpredictable possibility to be casually regarded. We are facing something that is included as a residual benefit of the Cross, where He not only died for your and my sins, but where he also provided for relief from all human suffering.

This blend of the dual features of *forgiveness and healing* are exemplified in the occasion Jesus healed a paralytic. He did so with the words, *"Son, be of good cheer; your sins are forgiven you"* (Matthew 9:2). Two things stand out:

▶ That Jesus used the manifestation of His healing power to authenticate His right to forgive sins.

▶ That Jesus illustrated that deliverance from sin and deliverance from sickness are interrelated and available to all who come to God through Him.

Question: If both sin and sickness were dealt with at *the Cross*, then how could Jesus go around forgiving people and healing them before His crucifixion? *Answer*: because the sinless, wholesome, healing, holy qualities that were present in Jesus when He went to the Cross to bear our sins, were already present in Him then. The King had come to earth, and where the King is, the kingdom is present. The invasion of the power of God's kingdom in forgiveness and healing was already beginning to emanate from Jesus, even though it would yet be months until it would be purchased and secured on the Cross. No human affliction could hinder the work of Jesus because of the holy, healing power that was resident within Him as the King.

The same healing presence that was manifest in Jesus' ministry and the power that flowed from His body, He has invested today in the body of His Church, because He longs to lavish gifts of healing wherever His people go.

Basic hindrances to Jesus' healing ministry today

Though Jesus longs to pour out great healing on all people, there are two basic hindrances that prevent His power being displayed as it should.

1. Formulated faith

What is our reaction when we see a sick person? Do we give them a tape to listen to, or say to them, "Let me pray for you in Jesus' name"? There's nothing wrong with people receiving teaching from a tape, God's healing word can come to people in a multitude of ways. But how much better it is to lay hands on someone and allow the healing power of God flow to them through you.

The healing presence of Christ moves wherever the Gospel of the kingdom goes forth. The need is for people to simply speak it out. So often we trap ourselves into thinking that we must speak the word of healing in a certain way, or else it will be ineffective. God deliver us from such religious notions! We cannot reduce the awesome healing power of God, or any other aspect of His life and power, to a formula that we control. Jesus used numerous methods to heal people and never stuck to some kind of religious formula. Neither does He want us to.

We don't need to use any clever words or receive an amazing revelation about a person in order to pray for their healing. As the Holy Spirit prompts you to do so, ask permission to pray for someone who is sick and simply ask God to touch them with His healing power. Some people might not want you to physically lay hands on them and pray for them there and then, in which case you can tell them that you will pray for them later, on your own. But more often than not, people will be happy for you to pray with them – not only because God's power will be released, but also because you have shown God's love to them.

Very often people sought out Jesus because they heard *someone else say* that He was healing people of all kinds of things. Based on this word they went looking for Jesus, either because they were sick themselves, or had a sick relative or friend. Today God is still looking for people who will *say the word* about Jesus' healing power. The Church must *proclaim* the Gospel of the kingdom – that there is complete *wholeness* for every person.

2. Fear of people not being healed

Fear is a major hindrance to the flow of the healing power of God. We are often afraid that we might pray for someone, raise their hopes, and then they won't be healed. We might also fear that, apart from them not being healed, such an incident might knock their faith in God.

How do we explain cases where people are not healed? We develop all kinds of philosophies and rationales to "explain" why, despite every effort, some people still don't get healed. But there is no more a "system" in the Bible explaining why people *don't* get healed, as there is one explaining why they *do* get healed. *God does not concern*

Himself with explaining to us why some people aren't healed, just as the Bible doesn't spend time explaining why everybody doesn't get saved!

The fact is no one can explain why some people are not healed. I wish I could give an explanation, but God has not called us to do that. It is none of our business who may or may not receiving healing. Our responsibility is solely to proclaim the Word and let God do His sovereign work. We should not be afraid to proclaim God's healing power. We fulfill our duty by proclaiming the word and leave the rest in God's hands, so that the healing ministry of Jesus may be loosed to touch every dimension of human experience.

Surrounded by a world filled with a welter of need, let us go forth again today, as at the beginning –

"And they went out and preached everywhere,
the Lord working with them and
confirming the word through the accompanying signs.
Amen."

(Mark 16:20)

RECEIVING CHRIST
AS LORD AND SAVIOR

It seems possible that some earnest inquirer may have read this book and somehow still never have received Jesus Christ as personal Savior. If that's true of you, that you have never personally welcomed the Lord Jesus into your heart, to be your Savior and to lead you in the matters of your life, I would like to encourage and help you to do that.

There is no need to delay, for an honest heart can approach the loving Father God at any time. So I'd like to invite you to come with me, and let's pray to Him right now.

If it's possible there where you are, bow your head, or even kneel if you can. In either case, let me pray a simple prayer first and then I've added words for you to pray yourself.

My Prayer

Father God, I have the privilege of joining with this child of Yours who is reading this book right now. I want to thank You for the openness of heart being shown toward You and I want to praise You for Your promise, that when we call to You, You will answer.

I know that genuine sincerity is present in this heart, which is ready to speak this prayer, and so we come to You in the Name and through the Cross of Your Son, the Lord Jesus. Thank You for hearing.

(And now, speak your prayer.)

Your Prayer

Dear God, I am doing this because I believe in Your love for me, and I want to ask You to come to me as I come to You. Please help me now.

First, I thank You for sending Your Son Jesus to earth to live and to die for me on the Cross. I thank You for the gift of forgiveness of sin that You offer me now, and I pray for forgiveness.

Do, I pray, forgive me and cleanse my life in Your sight, through the blood of Jesus Christ. I am sorry for anything and everything I have ever done that is unworthy in Your sight. Please take away all guilt and shame as I accept the fact that Jesus died to pay for all my sins, and through Him I am now given forgiveness on this earth and eternal life in heaven.

I ask You, Lord Jesus, please come into my life now. Because You rose from the dead, I know You're alive and I want You to live with me now and forever.

I am turning my life over to You and turning from my way to Yours. I invite Your Holy Spirit to fill me and lead me forward in a life that will please the heavenly Father.

Thank You for hearing me. From this day forward, I commit myself to Jesus Christ the Son of God. In His Name, amen.

NOTES

1. If the reader is desirous of beginning a relationship with God through receiving the gift of His saving grace in His Son Jesus Christ, turn to page 247 for guidance on how to come to Him in prayer, according to His Word.

2. The subject of the Godhead's activities pertaining to redemption is presented in detail in Chapter 5: The Eternal Godhead (Part 4).

3. In the context of Galatians 4:4–5 "the law" that Paul speaks of is the "law of sin and death" under which Man outside of Christ stands condemned, not the Old Testament Law.

4. Jesus is also referred to redemptively as "the Second Adam" (I Corinthians 15:45).

5. Caesarea where Cornelius lived was the Roman capital of Judea in the time of Christ, located approximately 60 miles north-west of Jerusalem.

6. There had been an 'outbreak' of the Holy Spirit in Samaria prior to this when Philip preached the gospel to them (Acts 8:4), but Samarians were 'half-Jewish' and not, strictly speaking, Gentiles.

7. This refers to being able to "cast away" a snake without being harmed (see Acts 28:3–6).

8. No believer should ever consume a deadly substance in order to "prove" God in this respect, for to do so would be an act of disobedience, but the believer can count upon God's protection in matters pertaining to food and drink. Many missionaries have testified to such divine protection when in foreign cultures.

9. Praying "in the Spirit" is the same as praying or speaking in tongues as Paul makes clear in I Corinthians 14.

10. 'Hell' is the English word for the Greek term 'Hades'.

11. Isaiah 66:24 which speaks of the fate of those who are disobedient and have persistently rebelled and sinned against the Lord.

12. A *mite* was the smallest coin in circulation in Palestine and was worth around one eighth of a cent. Mark sets this value in context for any Roman readers by saying it was the equivalent of a *quadrans* – that is one sixty-fourth of a *denarius* which was a laborer's daily wage.

13. *Gnosticism* was a religious movement that attracted followers during the 2nd and 3rd centuries AD. It was a schism from true Christian doctrine that held a number of erroneous beliefs, including that the material universe was wholly evil. Accordingly, money would have been deemed beyond any redeeming application to spiritual life.

14. *Monasticism* is the manner of life practiced by those whose devotion to Christ involves the total abandonment of, and removal from, the world system so as to live in an exclusively Christian community. Vows of celibacy and of poverty usually accompany the strictly monastic life. Accordingly, the influence of this system has, to this day, placed a shadow over the subject of finance, seeming to suggest that a believer could never have much money and be "truly spiritual."

15. *Redeeming* a tithe is the practice of adding one-fifth to your tithe if you defer paying it until a later date, as outlined in Leviticus 27:31.

16. *Firstfruits* offerings are special offerings of thanks for the "first" part of any increase. Historically this related to harvesting crops, but a contemporary example could be a wage increase.

17. The precise location of the mountain is not certain but was probably in the vicinity of Capernaum.

If you have enjoyed this book and would like to help us to send a copy of it and many other titles to needy pastors in the **Third World**, please write for further information
or send your gift to:

**Sovereign World Trust
PO Box 777, Tonbridge
Kent TN11 0ZS
United Kingdom**

or to the **'Sovereign World'** distributor in your country.

Visit our website at **www.sovereign-world.org**
for a full range of Sovereign World books.